From Here to Tierra del Fuego

From Here to Tierra del Fuego

Paul Magee

University of Illinois Press

Urbana and Chicago

An earlier version of chapter 4 appeared as "Famous First Colonist, Lucas Bridges, Finds His Fetish at the Uttermost Part of the Earth" in *Journal for the Psychoanalysis of Culture and Society* 3.2 (Fall 1998): 99–107. © by the Ohio State University Press.

Earlier versions of some of the material in this book appeared as "Changing Channels" in *LIKE* 5 (Summer–Autumn 1997–98): 29–31.

Library of Congress Cataloging-in-Publication Data
Magee, Paul, 1970–
From here to Tierra del Fuego / Paul Magee.
p.   cm. — (Transnational cultural studies)
Includes bibliographical references (p.   ) and index.
ISBN 0-252-02555-5 (cloth : acid-free paper)
1. Tierra del Fuego (Argentina and Chile)—Description and travel.
2. Travelers—Tierra del Fuego (Argentina and Chile)—History.
3. Ethnology—Philosophy.
I. Title. II. Series.
F2986.M34   2000
982'.76—dc21   99-006942

C 5 4 3 2 1

The wrinkles and creases on our faces are the registration of the great passions, vices, insights that called upon us; but we, the masters, were not home.

—Walter Benjamin

Contents

Preface   ix

Acknowledgments   xiii

BOOK 1: WHEN THE SHEEP HAD WINGS

1. When the Sheep Had Wings   3
2. Grounding   19
3. Out-of-Date Theory   32
4. A Time Capsule   45
5. On the Rebound   63
6. To Recapitulate   81
7. Seeing "One's Mirror Image Close Its Eyes"   99

   Appendixes   109

   Map of Tierra del Fuego   111

   Photo of Ushuaia   112

   The Pears' Magic Soap Anecdote   113

BOOK 2: THE SUSPENSION OF DISBELIEF

1. A New Angle   117
2. Whose Imagined Community?   128
3. The Object of This Ridiculous Journey   139
4. And the Postage Stamp?   149
5. A Home away from Home   158

   Bibliography   167

   Index   177

Preface

Tierra del Fuego, the island at the southernmost tip of South America, attracts visitors from all over the world who come to experience the ancient wonders of "The Land of Fire." The island was named by Ferdinand Magellan, its first European visitor, for the Indian campfires he observed on its shores. Today these campfires are all extinguished. In their place rise oil rigs and small cities, foremost among them Punta Arenas (Chile) and Ushuaia (Argentina).

Split between the sovereignties of Chile and Argentina, the island properly belongs to the four Fuegian tribes, the Selk'nam (or Ona), the Yámana (or Yaghan), the Haush, and the Alakaluf, while the Tehuelche inhabit the region of southern Patagonia just north of the island. Following Charles Darwin's famously harsh judgment ("the most abject and miserable creatures I anywhere beheld"), the Indians have often been regarded as the world's most primitive inhabitants.

Now understood to possess an extremely complex social organization, these original Fuegians were literally decimated in the fifty years following the first full-scale white colonization in the 1880s. Fencing indigenous land off into huge *estancias,* the early colonists repopulated the island with sheep and proceeded to make what are to this day some of the largest fortunes in South America. Sheep still massively outnumber the island's small, largely urban population (ca. 150,000), who work in grazing, petroleum, tourism, and some small-scale industry (e.g., television manufacturing in Ushuaia).

The visitor to Tierra del Fuego today, traveling back along the route taken by Magellan, Darwin, and even Bruce Chatwin, should pack plenty of sunscreen. Due to severe ozone depletion, the sub-Antarctic sky now rains down upon the island the fire it was once seen to emanate. From the start of the colonial era to the end of this industrial one, Tierra del Fuego anecdotally figures a Europe that has been turned on its head. It is now a showcase for the world's densest concentration of ozone-blind sheep.

≕ ≕ ≕

Book 1, "When the Sheep Had Wings," is an attempt to catch a traveling subject in flight. Based on fieldwork among Western travelers in Tierra del Fuego, the book seeks to map the movements of a footloose culture whose imperial antecedents are never far away. Why, I ask, do people travel to the End of the World? The fact that my informants are there for no reason other than to laugh at the absurdity of doing so puts my research project (officially, an ethnohistory of the white colonial subject traveling through time to Tierra del Fuego) on shaky ground. How do you cast a nexus of power/knowledge around a subject that does not take itself seriously?

Shedding the truth-seeking subject of Foucauldian theory, I turn to investigate this very offhandedness. I focus upon the bad jokes, the intentional ironies, and the dumb anecdotes with which these travelers ceaselessly punctuate their discourse. From laughing accounts of "backward" Indians who use Coca-Cola bottles as altarpieces through anecdotes of indigenous awe at the "white man's magic" and on to the television factory at the End of the World, I make a rather startling discovery. My informants are not sheep, yet they constantly find blind faith in the all-believing eyes of the "primitive" Other.

I proceed, in chapter 3, to set forth the temporal scaffolding of these throwaway images. Such primitivist jokes are as steeped in the theory of racial recapitulationism (put simply: their present is our past) as any bad nineteenth-century anthropology. My text itself begins to adopt these time-traveling strategies, as I project my researches into Tierra del Fuego's apparently one-dimensional and "barbaric" colonial past. Finding similar humor in the colonial archive, I invoke Karl Marx to comprehend these strange coincidences. Then, as now, anecdotal accounts of a native obsession with the "white man's magic" run hand-in-hand with the traveling advances of sheep-bearing capital.

Marx's theory of commodity fetishism takes on a strange resonance in these End of the World anecdotes. Read through Michael Taussig, Slavoj Zizek, and Sigmund Freud, such findings become all the more uncanny. As I return to the self-distanced and ambivalent present, I find the category of self-reflexive consciousness increasingly incapable of comprehending such self-absence. So I attempt—*on shaky ground*—to bring home some of the power of those ancient elsewheres from which the cynical present runs suspended in disbelief.

≡ ≡ ≡

Written one year later, book 2 starts at home, and attempts to take up a new angle on the same terrain: the ethnohistory of the white colonial subject traveling through time to Tierra del Fuego. Turning from commodity to the imagined community, I read Benedict Anderson's theory of national imagining into the faultline splitting Argentine/Chilean Tierra del Fuego in two. Anderson's syllogistic "unknown soldier" figure is played off against the history of Fuegian stamp collecting, while Bruce Chatwin pops up now and again too.

"The Suspension of Disbelief" reads the book of nations back into the Fuegian landscape and seeks to reveal—revisiting the "uncanny" moments of book 1—just what the traveling subject might have invested in home itself.

Acknowledgments

This book is dedicated to my father, who was always there for me, who had such grace in his presence and yet understood the importance—until the end of the world we shared—of not being there for me too.

▭ ▭ ▭

I want to thank Klaus Neumann and Vera Mackie for the consistent support they have given to the airing of these ideas. In allowing me to call them beyond the call of duty (and even by international reverse charges from Tierra del Fuego in Klaus's case) they have kept my ideas in flight and my feet steady. Their assistance—officially, unofficially, mutually, respectively—has been extraordinary, from the moment I first started work on this project back in 1995 right up to the deadline I now rush to meet. Thanks for helping me to walk tightropes.

No hay ningun fin del mundo, as Moníca Giavotti of Ushuaia knew so well. This thesis would not be without Moní and all the others who befriended me in Tierra del Fuego and Magallanes: Horacio Ticera, Andrea Garone, Alberto Quesada, Oscar Zanola, Alejandro, Guille, Nina, Tatiana Alvarez, Werner, Cecilia, Viviana, Marcos, Mithra, Juan Carlos. I long to see you all again, here or there.

Michael Taussig's writing has—obviously—given wings to mine. Mick's correspondence and company has been a pleasure. Stephen Muecke and John Frow together examined an earlier version of this work when it was still an M.A. thesis; their encouragement to publish was crucial. Mick, Stephen, Nick Thomas at ANU, and, above all, Klaus have directly helped me find my way into journals, seminars, and now the book you hold in your hands. Thanks for opening the doors of publication (as well as perception).

Kate Darian-Smith has seen me through the writing of book 2 and the preparation of the final manuscript. Her patience and academic support have been invaluable. Andrew Sartori's time, care, and criticism have been a constant—for all the distance—throughout this time. Our e-mail debates keep my mind in motion. Kate, Klaus, and Vera have all read over the manuscript for me; for their comments, and those of Pat Coppel, Chris Francis, Andrew Smith, Richard Vabre, and especially Jon Stratton, I am very grateful.

As a teacher, colleague, and friend, my mother, Anne Magee, taught me not merely to love language but to do, with it or without it, whatever I wanted. In this last year I wanted to write an opera. My collaboration with David Chisholm has blown up ideas in all directions. His feel for stagecraft, timing, and texture wrote its way into my libretto, at the same time that the Hegel Reading Group was sharpening my sense of the dialectic. Doubtless these influences can be felt here too.

If Madeline Andrews's name does not appear in this text, it is because she found a way into my words that takes me beyond them . . .

☷ ☷ ☷

To all who have had a hand in this book, I now hand it back to you, with gratitude, and in the hope that you like it.

From Here to Tierra del Fuego

Book 1
When the Sheep Had Wings

Remember the Future

—Orlan

1
When the Sheep Had Wings

You Can See It on the TV

Watching MTV by cable in Ushuaia, the capital of Argentine Tierra del Fuego, is slightly surreal. Watching a Swiss surrealist put an egg on top of the television set is even more so. "Christian," I asked, "What the bloody hell are you doing?" No answer. He was watching the egg, waiting for it to hatch. "*Aqui,*" he finally said, in broken Spanish, "*todo es possible!*"—everything is possible here! Christian was a theater director from Basle. Back home he had written and performed a play about Tierra del Fuego in the time of the Indians and Angels. He translated the title as *Cuando las Ovejas Tenían Alas*—When the Sheep Had Wings. Christian was currently researching the place he had already written about, a time-traveling methodology derived, I suspect, from the idiosyncrasies of that same play. Its author, however, was adamant that such miracles were grounded in the magic at the End of the World itself: "*Aqui,*" he repeated, "*todo es possible!*"

A weekful of Swiss Tierra del Fuego was enough. "I can't understand why a person would want to act like such a *pendejo* [fuckwit]!" Horacio exclaimed. He ran the hostel where Christian and I were both staying and had little patience for fly-by foreigners who wanted Tierra del Fuego to be as weird in person as it was in name.

Such reactions make me realize the fundamental sense to *Het dak van de Walvis,* that crazy mix of anthropological scientism and primitivist fantasy which the Chilean director Raul Ruiz made in Europe and set "On Top of the Whale."[1] Starting in the "Socialist Republic of Holland," a communist bureaucratic state that is the direct inverse of the present-day Netherlands, the film proceeds to follow its cast in their journey to an eerily war-torn and weird Tierra del Fuego. Through such framing, Ruiz grounds this upside-down Fuegian ethnography in a mythical *elsewhere,* the origin of which is none other than the fantasy of civilized Europe. From this European elsewhere arises the *Aqui todo es possible* plotline in which a Dutch communist anthropologist arrives at the conclusion that the Fuegian Indians are telepathic predecessors to the Phillips-Fox television manufacturing company.

One night Horacio, a few friends, and I went to El Disco Dalí, a tacky provincial nightclub for passing tourists. We couldn't afford the admission, so we bought some beer and went to the beach instead. We lit a fire, stared across the Beagle Channel at Chile, and chatted about foreign lands, travel, and being elsewhere. Horacio was planning a trip to the United States. He wanted to work that place out, he said, to see for himself "*¿cómo es la película?*"—literally, "how is the film?"—which is to say, to investigate the ridiculous image those *yanquis* cast across the Continental Divide. So we warmed ourselves on ancient technology and talked about images of elsewhere, there in the place Lucas Bridges (one of the island's first white colonists) termed the "uttermost part of the earth."[2] To a passing ship, we must have looked like Magellan's Indians or Darwin's "most abject and miserable creatures," we refugees from the overpriced Disco Dalí, postcard primitives, crudely visible in the distant firelight.[3]

Would Michel Foucault Go to Tierra Del Fuego Just for the T-Shirt?

Thinking about why the Swiss surrealist seemed such a *pendejo,* I realize that he was the only traveler I met in all of Tierra del Fuego who actually took himself seriously. No one else had any other than a purely ironic reason to be in Ushuaia. All of the foreigners I interviewed said that they were there, quite literally, albeit as a joke, "just to say I've been here." What other reason could there be for tourists to travel thousands of miles through unpeopled pampas, Patagonian deserts, and treeless pastures to end up in a town with little to recommend it beyond its designation as *El Fin del Mundo*—The End of the World? How could a visitor pretend to have any other than an ironic relationship to the mythical dimensions of their travels in that ancient land of upside-down Antipodeans, the site for five centuries of fantastic European projections, the contemporary world capital of ozone-blind sheep? Christian was the only traveler who treated the weirdness of elsewhere as actually adequate to its object, and for that reason he was there to experience it, carrying out that discourse to the letter. By giving Fuegian sheep wings, and according their televisions procreative powers, he truly seemed to articulate what James Clifford has termed the "rhetoric of presence": to believe that he was actually in Tierra del Fuego, just because he was actually in Tierra del Fuego.[4]

The fact that this Swiss surrealist's naïve belief in his own rhetoric made him such a black sheep among the other travelers is rather unsettling for one searching for the discursive groundings of the neo-imperialist travel project as it courses through South America. What does it mean if no one, except a fool, actually believes in the travels he or she enacts?

My project, *an ethnohistory of the white colonial subject traveling through time to Tierra del Fuego,* necessitates taking seriously whatever it is that drives and has driven such movements. The ethical imperative to analyze and thus contest the motivations behind the initial colonization of Tierra del Fuego is obvious. The genocidal process, whereby the Fuegians' ancestral lands were stolen to make way for sheep flown in from elsewhere, must not be repeated. For all the obvious difference between that hundred-year-old atrocity and the seemingly innocuous and frivolous tourism of the present, there is an equal imperative here to comprehend and contest what is not merely one of the largest industries in the world but is also fast becoming one of the economic mainstays of contemporary Chilean and Argentine Tierra del Fuego.

With all the force of persuasion at their disposal, international and local neoliberal elites are now promoting the tourist industry as one of the great "hopes" in the "restructuring" and "rationalizing" of these and other economies in the region. The force of these hopes should not be ignored. Through the inequitable flows of international capital that it channels, the highly gendered division of labor it either solidifies or sets in place, and the internal political repression that it is used to justify, the international tourist industry has become "one of the principal pillars of contemporary world power."[5] Tierra del Fuego is on the absolute periphery of such global concerns and may well seem a trivial object for critical concern too. Yet, far from frivolous, the following study is conceived in the hope that the ideology of a movement that is itself so all-encompassing can be usefully analyzed and critiqued from a peripheral point at which certain otherwise unnoticed characteristics come into focus—like the fact that travelers need have no faith in what they are doing to do it anyway.

The joke played out in Tierra del Fuego makes havoc of the standard paradigms for the study of travel cultures, which focus overwhelmingly on the faith component of these rituals of participatory observation and self-discovery. Victor Turner's theorization of pilgrimage, for instance, has been invoked in various ways to comprehend the constitution of the sacred within contemporary travel landscapes.[6] Julie Marcus has taken from Turner to characterize New Agers' attempts to find, in their travels to Ayers Rock, a contemporary site for the sacred through ecstatic "union" with Aboriginal cultures at the "heart" of the Australian nation.[7] Yet Marcus's borrowing is hardly reverential. The spin she gives to Turner's vocabulary, in analogizing it to the delusions of New Age imperialism, only under-lines the obvious post-structuralist critique of his work. Few today would have much time for his "spontaneous existential communitas," that unifying and lib-erating ejaculation of "anti-structure" through which pilgrims find themselves and their truth.[8] A Foucauldian critique would see such "resistances" as internal to power itself—the very point of Marcus's essay.[9] The fact, however, that she aims her whole attack at this minority of easily ridiculed revivalist believers, begs the question as to how she would address the mass of other pilgrims who, far from seeking "the sacred center of a rapidly developing settler cosmology," visit the Rock for no other reason than the simple secular fact that it is there.[10]

At first glance, Foucault's treatment of the history of sexuality as the self-inscribed truth of the subject would appear to have much more to offer the study of exotic travel than any theory of transcendent spontaneity. The pretextualized practice of subject constitution in such travel representations could be likened to the self-discovery through discourse that for Foucault makes sex "tell us our truth."[11] Further, the "erethism" that characterizes this "incitement to discourse," the will to power through knowledge, could be appropriated to theorize the ex-traordinary growth of contemporary travel and tourism.[12]

Yet for all the incitement to Foucault in the social sciences today, the attempt to track such travels down through discourse theory trips up on the very "truth" it seeks to uproot.[13] Foucault grounds his history of contemporary sexuality-as-truth in the Catholic confessional he sees as its predecessor.[14] This only under-lines the cogency of religious analogy (for him genealogy) in attempting to ana-lyze such modalities of discourse, a word with classical roots in movement and premodern connotations of sermonizing.[15] Indeed, for all the differences, the fundamental tenet shared by these Turneresque and Foucauldian paradigms can be discerned through the theological terms they both invoke: pilgrimage, con-fessional, self-discovery. Both presuppose that the being of the subject is predi-cated upon the search for and discovery of truth. This is particularly the case for Foucault. The truth-seeking subject is integral to his Nietzschean insistence on the preeminent role of the will to knowledge in the constitution of power, as much as the constitution of the positive subject him- or herself.[16]

But how can one use such theories to account for the fact that in Tierra del Fuego, this sincere, fundamentally faithful subject looks like such a *pendejo*? How can one analyze the nexus of power/knowledge in a place where there is no truth to be discovered; indeed, where the search for and discovery of truth is the very sign of stupidity? Just as there is nothing in the ecstatic spontaneity of the pil-grim's communitas, there is nothing in the faith-finding "truth effect" of confessional discourse to explain the dead-letter disbelief that impels someone to go to the End of the World "just to say I've been there."

Why else would you go to the End of the World? A Swiss woman I spoke to in Chilean Puerto Natales was going there, she boasted, "just to buy the T-shirt that says I've been there." Her friend, meanwhile, planned to bypass Ushuaia altogether and fly to Puerto Williams, the Chilean naval installation on the other side of the Beagle Channel. This place, as the *Travel Survival Kit* will tell you, is truly the southernmost inhabited place in the world, despite Ushuaia's claim to be *El Fin del Mundo.*[17] Even though there is nothing to do there, you may as well go anyway: "If you've come as far as Tierra del Fuego, you can hardly turn back now."[18] That such an empty, even unbelievable, formality is so compelling as to be enshrined in the "traveller's bible" points to the impossibility of explaining such a culture in terms of the discursive truth through which its believing subjects constitute themselves as subjects.[19] Nor can such an ironic culture, so geared toward *going through the motions,* simply be passed off as a bad joke—unless one accepts that a bad joke has the power to make Tierra del Fuego one of the preeminent tourist destinations of South America. As a woman in the Punta Arenas Tourist Bureau told me, Tierra del Fuego is now "*de moda*" (in fashion). Not that she or any of the other locals I spoke to seemed to have any faith in the future of the fickle industry currently advertised as their economic salvation. Indeed, they seemed as skeptical about the whole exercise as the travelers. Yet surely one must have faith in one's fashion? Not to mention one's self-fashioning? And surely the pilgrim traveler needs to find more than simply a stupid T-shirt relic in the process?

In Patagonia: The Rhetoric of Absence

To guide us through these questions I want to turn to Bruce Chatwin's *In Patagonia,* one of my favorite books as a child. It was this travelogue which inspired me, now grown-up and in half-hearted imitation, to head to Tierra del Fuego. Hitchhiking down through Patagonia, Chatwin takes a lift with a truck driver, whose dashboard is adorned with "a statuette of the Virgin of Luján, a St. Christopher and a plastic penguin that nodded with the corrugations of the road."[20] Thus the traveler, in motion, nods at the patron saints of travel, observing at a distance the divinity they carry for his Argentine driver.

Chatwin is on the trail of his Great-Uncle Charley, a man who had lived as a colonist in turn-of-the-century Punta Arenas. Charley had once sent Chatwin's grandmother a piece of "dinosaur" skin, which he discovered in the Cueva del

Milodón (Cave of the Milodon), just north of Puerto Natales. To young Bruce, growing up in the late 1940s, this colonial souvenir symbolized all the adventure and romance of an exotic place in a bygone era. Now in the 1970s, this token of Chatwin's childhood, irrevocably lost, becomes the pathetic beacon (a mock version of Jules Verne's lighthouse at the End of the World) inspiring him to travel back through Fuegian texts and landscapes in search of the relics of a past he can no longer own.

So bemused by the beliefs of others, Chatwin would probably have appreciated the irony of the canonical status his book now has among travelers in Patagonia, for whom *In Patagonia* seems as much of a Bible as any guidebook. Yet anyone who searches for a fundamentally believable image of Tierra del Fuego will find this collection of ninety-seven travel fragments decidedly lacking in guidance.[21] Chatwin's authorial voice, far from providing any "I-witness" hard rock of Petrine presence, seems the very matrix of futility at the dead heart of this assemblage of plastic penguins and displaced elsewheres.[22] The only meaning articulated in this profoundly skeptical book is the pointlessness of meaning itself.

Nor does the text's pseudo-conclusion—as Chatwin at last reaches the mythic Cueva del Milodon—offer any resolution. Here the traveler, dazed and momentarily questioning his sanity, finds amid the dirt and darkness some strands of what he decides to take for Milodon hairs, but which are obviously little more than symbols for the circuit of discursive automatism and half-disowned desire impelling the text on to nowhere. So he accomplishes "the object of this ridiculous journey," arriving at the cueva, to arrive at nothing.[23] Chatwin hardly finds his truth in Patagonia.

Nor is there any truth here for Chatwin's readers, for whom the futility of such searching is mimed through the experience of reading itself. Like its author, Chatwin's book seems constantly on the verge of falling apart. Anecdotal fragments and chapter divisions join, jar, and enjamb different stories and experiences. The reader's movement through narrative, connotation, and association is simultaneously articulated and disarticulated to the point that this movement itself becomes an impossible search for the truth of the text, its ever-disappearing author, and perhaps even its reader. In this sense, to follow Chatwin through his text of travels is to end up in the cueva too, which becomes a metaphor for the ceaseless circulation of mimesis and desire within this traveling, searching, reading.

Reading this elusive prose while traveling in Tierra del Fuego alerted me to the similarities and minor key echoes I encountered of its author's self-stylized "insane restlessness."[24] In Puerto Natales I met a British hippie who similarly articulated and failed to answer—though only a fool would try to answer—the rhetorical question which provides the title for one of Chatwin's essay collections and pervades his entire empty body of writing: *What Am I Doing Here* (*sic:* no question mark).[25] The stopover flight from New Zealand had dropped Richard some six hundred kilometers north of Ushuaia. Having very little money, he had not planned to travel in Argentina, which was expensive. Furthermore, Ushuaia was at least two days away, through multiple bus connections or an even more difficult hitch, and everyone said there wasn't actually anything there, apart from the End of the World. "Shit!" this Richard said to me, complaining about the stupidity of a trip he eventually did undertake: "I just know that if I don't go, now that I'm this close, I'll regret it."

An even emptier echo of Chatwin's meaningless meandering, this tale of un-literary annoyance reveals the everyday underside of that same repetitive joke: *I'm here just to say I've been here.*

Bad Nomadology

What was I doing there?—taking down tales like this, looking for a thesis on Fuegian travel discourse, finding nothing? Was I thus, in my travels, realizing the meaninglessness of motion woven through Chatwin's text, that endlessly shift-ing surface of pure form and irony? Should I treat *In Patagonia* as one of Barthes's "scrible" texts, an antitheological scripture through which the critic, "by refusing to assign a 'secret,' an ultimate meaning, to the text (and to the world as text), liberates what may be called an anti-theological activity, an activity that is truly revolutionary since to refuse to fix meaning is, in the end, to refuse God and his hypostases—reason, science, law"?[26] And could I, as traveler-critic, well read on Chatwin and now traveling back through the "world as text" of Tierra del Fue-go, be born again as the scriptor of his ironic and meaningless songlines?

To the extent that Chatwin will admit of a god, one finds him here, in observ-ing the "refusal of meaning" that is movement itself. Long before arriving at the cueva, Chatwin encounters a missionary of the Baha'i faith, and the following dialogue ensues:

> "Which religion have you?" Ali asked. "Christian?"
> "I haven't got any special religion this morning. My God is the God of Walkers. If you walk hard enough, you probably don't need any other God."[27]

This liberating, albeit laconic, hymn to being-in-motion later gives associative power to the pathos of Chatwin's description of the genocide. From the moment the white settlers first arrived in force in the 1880s, the nomadic Fuegians began to die. They appear literally fixed to the stake by "God and his hypostases," as

Chatwin describes them, herded in and butchered by land-grabbing capitalists, imprisoned by God-fearing priests, and reduced to Thomas Bridges's famous *Yámana-English Dictionary*, the monumental text which contains their last remains in language as if it were a tomb.

Now on the porch of Bridges's *estancia* in Tierra del Fuego, Chatwin reads the dictionary and quotes approvingly the definition of the word *wejna*, which means, among other things, "'to swing, move or travel'—or simply 'to exist or be.'"[28] Through ceaselessly articulating such associations, Chatwin begins to appear a nomad himself, restlessly moving through his own text, requiring the reader to find him, by becoming him, by trying to track him down. As Eric Michaels has written of another of Chatwin's "para-ethnographies," through the multiple ellipses, evasive analogies, and other such refusals to set meaning, Chatwin literally becomes "Other" to his reader, going native, slipping off the page, never falling into the trap of being himself.[29] In thus transcending the truth of his own traces, Chatwin could be seen as the patron saint of antitheological activity.

Going through the Motions

What the disciple of such scriptures too easily forgets is that, for all of Chatwin's rhetoric of absence, he does effectively travel, seek, and find *as if* he really did believe in the meaning of the motions he goes through at such self-distance. For Chatwin could be the patron saint of Peter Sloterdijk's *The Critique of Cynical Reason* too.[30] Parodically entitled after Kant's, the critique attempts to supplement the theory of "false consciousness," which comprehends lies, errors, and ideology, to include cynicism, which Sloterdijk describes as "enlightened false consciousness."[31] He argues that the post-1960s zeitgeist is characterized by subjects who bear a "schizoid" relationship to their activities and words. The "falseness" of their discourse is already "reflexively buffered" against critique by their recognition of its falsity.[32] In Slavoj Zizek's paraphrase of this work and parody of the Marxist text through which he then reads it: "They know very well what they are doing, but still, they are doing it."[33] For Sloterdijk, as for Zizek, there is nothing "truly revolutionary" at all about Chatwin's "anti-theological"—i.e., "reflexively buffered"—travels.

The Critique of Cynical Reason would have been a good guidebook to take to the Benetton retail outlet which I visited (just to say I've been there?) in Ushuaia. The cynical advertising campaigns through which this multinational company lures people into playing out the politics of representation under its logo has won it a certain notoriety.[34] The irony of "the United Colors of Benetton" is apparent the moment you turn to Benetton's postmodern politics of production, founded in anti-unionism and decentralized subcontracting. Thus the company unites a factory of female pieceworkers of various colors, each invisible to the other.[35] Benetton represents the fashion, again literally, in neoliberal industry now being so heavily promoted to the populations of the "backward" countries of South America. The company has large property holdings in Patagonia as well as retail outlets in Punta Arenas, Ushuaia, and Rio Gallegos. As with tourism, such neocolonial relations do not necessarily elicit any faith in those who find themselves within them. Indeed, the publication I purchased in its Ushuaian outlet, *Colors: A Magazine about the Rest of the World*, makes no effort to advertise the company's production lines.[36] It concerns itself instead with laughing at those people who, in such a world, are still naïve enough to believe in anything.

One night Horacio, our friend Mónica, and I sat around her house, laughing our way through a few issues of *Colors*. First we turned to issue number 9, *Shopping*, which comes in the form of a mock catalogue of all the nasty and weird things money can buy: South African skin whitening creme (U.S. $5), Italian land mines with photo of young Thai victim (U.S. $41), rubber cast models of feet for mail-order foot fetishists (U.S. $74.95), etc.[37] The foot fetishists stand out here, amid the rather crude Barbara Krügerish consumerism critique, for their representation of the weird elsewhereness that characterizes the humor of this magazine. The fetishes of others are even more integral to the second issue we leafed through, *Religion*. In between critiquing and poking fun at the conservatism of the "vast cultural industrial complex called the Catholic church," this issue focuses on the commodification of religion. The humor derives from the idea of others dumb enough to believe that a disenchanted modernity can be miraculously reenchanted by the glitter of money.[38] An article entitled "Instant God," for instance, opens with the ironic header, "If gods want to be a part of our lives they are going to have to adjust to our schedule." They will need to make use of more time-saving devices, like the Electronic Rosary Counter, which, its manufacturers claim, "helps you pray" (U.S. $32.95).[39]

The staginess of the left/liberal stances which *Colors* consistently assumes, in the midst of such jokes, is grounded in the fact that Benetton is itself, like the Vatican, a "vast cultural industrial complex." How else could these Italian magazines fly so far into the periphery as to turn up in Tierra del Fuego? Yet the irony of Benetton's own vastness, far from constituting an omission in an otherwise critical magazine, openly pervades the whole enterprise. The difference between Benetton and the church is that Benetton is quite open about the fact that it does not believe in its mission. The one actual advertisement for the company within *Shopping* takes up the final two-page spread and features nothing more than a blank roll of toilet paper alongside the phrase "the United Colors of Benetton."

Coming at the end of this mock catalogue of all the things that can be consumed and turned to money, this advertisement ironically reduces the magazine to the very code it critiques, alongside forest-devouring chopsticks, penis enlargers, and Nestlé milk powder for babies.[40] Only an idiot, the logic unfolds, would believe that it is possible to work outside this stinking circuit of capital, consumption, and exploitation.[41]

The ironic, "reflexively buffered" manner in which Benetton represents its own obnoxiousness is matched by the toilet-paper manner in which *Colors* reduces its own discourse to rubbish. This is where postcolonial critics are made to wear their own desire to fix meaning. So Nimmy Akaiba of Phoenix, U.S., found, after submitting the following (eagerly published) letter:

> I quite like your magazine, however, I really, really hate your motto (a magazine about the rest of the world). It comes off as ethnocentric, tinged with some sort of imperialist perspective. Like "us" the important ones, and "them" the rest of the world. Exactly who is the "us" and who the "them"? . . .

> Dear Nimmy: We thought it meant that wherever you read *COLORS,* it's about somewhere else.[42]

A Thesis about the Rest of the World: Capitalizing upon the Other's Naïveté

Rather than falling into the trap of trying to catch *Colors* out seriously misrepresenting itself or others, it strikes me as much more important to attempt to unravel the magazine's offhand humor. The discursive strand uniting all these throwaway images of other people's weirdness is the set of absolute beliefs the magazine postulates not for the self, but rather for the Other. More than anything else, reading *Colors* that night in Ushuaia, we laughed at "them," the people who believe religiously in the commerce and the products that we would otherwise enact or consume so indifferently. Rubber cast feet and electronic rosary counters are only amusing the moment one imagines "them," those naïve people who live elsewhere to "us" and who place faith in such things. Our own ambivalence and self-distance thus enabled us to laugh at the picture of a Coke bottle, full of flowers and lovingly placed on a peasant shrine to a saint who died of thirst. It was uncanny for all of us to realize, on reading the caption, that the photograph was actually taken in Argentina. Having the naïveté of the rest of the world reduced to your own living room at that world's end gives you an awkward inkling of the need the disenchanted have for "somewhere else" to laugh about. Indeed, of the various critiques of Sloterdijk's work, none has noticed the way the subjects he addresses offset their cynicism with ceaseless delineations of the naïveté of others.[43]

This is equally apparent reading *In Patagonia*. The way such naïve scriptures are repeatedly called in to supplement Chatwin's crisis of faith causes me to question the sincerity of his disbelief. If *In Patagonia* is such a perfectly post-structuralist refusal of meaning, why does it derive so much of its movement from the beliefs of others? The long line of deluded Others among whom Chatwin travels leaves him, at the book's end, still laughing laconically at the naïve Other. This time it is the mad poet of Punta Arenas who is left reciting Lorca to his Pet Rocks as Chatwin's boat leaves for England.[44] Why is it so amusing for this fundamentally skeptical and meaningless man to find faith in the fantasies of others? Take Anselmo, "the Pianist" of Welsh Patagonia, who is possessed of "the authentic blinkered passion of the exile."[45] As the naïve accompanist to Chatwin's text, Anselmo plays his part to the letter: "The playing was remarkable. I could not imagine a finer *Pathétique* further South. When he finished he said: 'Now I play Chopin. Yes?' and he replaced the bust of Beethoven with one of Chopin. 'Do you prefer waltzes or mazurkas?'"[46] Chatwin's End of the World is populated with such displaced characters, whose distance and difference causes them to misrecognize the magnitude and the meaning of Europe and its things. Without their (rhetoric of) presence, his text would be not only dead, but lifeless.

As much as Chatwin's meaninglessness speaks to me and my travel experiences, so too does this ironic, self-superior humor. I am reminded of myself, lazing around the hostel in Ushuaia, getting drunk with various other travelers and swapping anecdotal accounts of indigenous naïveté. Carlos, who was now realizing his childhood dream to visit Tierra del Fuego, told us about an Indian who wanted to know whether he had hitchhiked to Bolivia from Spain or taken a bus the whole way. Marcelino, an alcoholic travel writer from Madrid, author of the *Rough Guide,* began to describe an experience of his in Peru: how during a ceremony of some sort or other, he had seen the Indians decorate their cars to look like altars. They laid out offerings on the hoods and even seemed to be praying. I joined in at this point with a Fuegian anecdote, the story of my visit to the Salesian mission near Rio Grande. The priest I had wished to interview about the mission's history was too busy to see me, so I left without learning anything. As I walked through the parking lot I caught sight of him, in a full ceremonial dress, blessing the cars of weary travelers. The mysteries of automobile benediction had us all laughing and sparked off more tales of backwardness and naïveté from whatever other traveling elsewheres people could remember.

Method: Of Garbology

What am I doing here? It would be dishonest not to add that my fieldwork was itself a bit of a joke. That, at least, was what I told people in these hostels, in between other jokes, parties, hangovers, and occasional undirected and unrelated reading in provincial libraries. Why not spend a few months overseas at the End of the World, ha ha ha, to party around and get paid for it? I was watching surrealists watch eggs on top of Fuegian television sets. I was researching Benetton advertisements, giving reader-response surveys to ozone-blind sheep. I was writing an ethnography of sacred shopping and liminal experience at the Ushuaian Surty Sur supermarket, focusing on the Dantesque banner adorning its threshold: "*El Placer de Comprar!*" The Pleasure of Shopping!

I remember occasionally meeting people who, on hearing such rubbish, would look at me quizzically, not playing along, but rather *holding me to my words,* treating me as if I really meant what I was saying. The discomfort that *that* entailed was uncanny, for it forced me to acknowledge that on some level I did mean what I was saying. Such an uncanny feeling only reinforces my resolve to explore precisely this realm of anecdotal, throwaway rubbish. Indeed, the fact that I am throwing myself at these awful travel anecdotes, the throwaway end of anthropology to be sure, suggests to me the seriousness of my endeavor. Things are thrown away with reason. Of the rigidly positivist discipline of economics, Donald McClosky writes that it is in the jokes which economists tell while getting drunk after conferences that one can detect a certain crisis of faith in the methodological postulates to which they perforce subscribe.[47] My intoxication with the trash of anthropology seems set, on the other hand, to uncover a certain displaced faith behind the empty subject of my own undisciplined movements.

The shores of the Beagle Channel, where archaic middens are found alongside rusty beer cans, offer a perfect place for investigating exactly those bad jokes and stupid anecdotes which a rigorously academic method would leave in its wake. To prefigure this technique, I want to steal a gem from an overblown passage in Claude Lévi-Strauss's famous tourist-hating *Tristes Tropiques.*[48] In attacking the vulgarity of modern beach culture, the anthropologist laments for the solitudinous sublimity he can now find only in peopleless mountains and alpine heights. Yet while declaiming against the "villas, hotels and casinos" that clutter our coasts, Lévi-Strauss characterizes, albeit only to denigrate it, the very terrain to which I wish to descend: "Beaches, where once the sea offered us the products of its age old tumult, an astonishing gallery of objects which showed that nature always belonged to the avant-garde, are now trodden by hordes of people and serve only for the arrangement and display of nondescript rubbish."[49] Such modernization is apparent along the increasingly disenchanted shores of the Beagle Channel too. Yet these same shores make Lévi-Strauss's metaphor seem curiously upside-down. For beached rubbish has its own random aesthetic of "arrangement and display" and its own surreal appearance, as anyone knows who stumbles upon a discarded Coke can—*Coca Cola, la bebida de fantasía, hecha en Chile*—outside of Puerto Williams, along the mountain-edged coast once inhabited by the world's "most primitive inhabitants." Forget the "age old" rocks and sentimental sea shells. The notion of the beach as an instantaneous "avant-garde" gallery applies with far greater cogency to the random pop-art deployment of "nondescript rubbish" like "the drink of fantasy, made in Chile."[50]

This is to propose an ironic and even self-defeating notion of *salvage ethnography,* a science that works by scavenging through the rubbish which doesn't usually make it back home in one's cultural baggage.[51] Take the following throwaway line from the Australian anthropologist Sir Baldwin Spencer, the archetypal salvage ethnographer, author of *Wanderings in Wild Australia.*[52] Spencer traveled to Tierra del Fuego in 1928 to search for the ancient origins of European "Man" only to catch, in the corner of his eye, the primitive constitution of the civilized commodity. Writing to his English friend R. R. Marrett from Punta Arenas, where he was waiting for his ship to leave, Spencer described his haphazard digs at the archaic Tehuelche middens, which line the shore.[53] The ethnographer fossicked among these primitive Patagonian kitchens, traveling back in anthropological time, "while the steamer," traveling in the opposite direction, "was loading frozen mutton which you probably buy and appreciate under the designation of 'Best Canterbury.'"[54] Thus the salvage ethnographer witnessed the nature and origins of Europe at the End of the World.

Patterns of "arrangement and display" also structure the trashy travel anecdotes which I related above. Many of these throwaway tales seem to rely, for their display, upon a certain chronological framework: the developmentalist schema through which underdevelopment and primitiveness make sense and allow one to laugh at the backward. This same temporal scaffolding is apparent in many of Chatwin's incongruous juxtapositions. The photograph which accompanies his text, of a 1920s Dodge in contemporary Welsh Patagonia, derives its anecdotal significance from the way it situates the European past in the Patagonian present. Such trashy images may have a twentieth-century avant-garde appearance to them, yet they structure the weirdness and naïveté of the Other through one of the most powerful metanarratives of nineteenth-century cultural science. It requires all the "homogenous empty time" of bad evolutionary science to place their "primitive" present in our past.[55]

I shall write of garbage and the philosophy of history much more within the course of this book. For the moment I want simply to recall the avant-garde tactics of one of the foremost philosophers of either phenomenon. In his *Passagen-Werk*, Walter Benjamin sought to write the history of the nineteenth century not as it was, but rather *as it had been forgotten,* by focusing on what he termed the "trash of history."[56] In what follows I want to present the ethnohistory of Tierra del Fuegian travel—*as it would be forgotten*—as trash.

Notes

1. Ruiz, *Het dak van de Walvis.*

2. E. Lucas Bridges, *Uttermost Part of the Earth.*

3. Darwin, *Voyage of the Beagle,* 149.

4. Clifford, "On Ethnographic Allegory," 112.

5. Enloe, *Bananas, Beaches, and Bases,* 41. These are some of the reasons why the Ecumenical Coalition on Third World Tourism characterized the international tourist industry, back in 1984, as "a violation of human rights." See Crick, "Tourists, Locals, and Anthropologists," 10.

6. Turner, "Pilgrimages as Social Processes," 166–231. For one such application of Turner to travel, see Pearson, "Travellers, Journeys, Tourists," 125–33.

7. Marcus, "The Journey out to the Centre," 254–74.

8. Ibid., 268. See also Michael Taussig's comments on Turner in *Shamanism, Colonialism, and the Wild Man,* 442.

9. "Resistance is never in a position of exteriority in relation to power" (Foucault, *History of Sexuality,* 95).

10. Marcus, "The Journey out to the Centre," 254.

11. Foucault, *History of Sexuality,* 69.

12. Ibid., 32.

13. "The political question . . . is not error, illusion, alienated consciousness, or ideology; it is the truth itself" (Foucault, "Truth and Power," 75).

14. "Western man has become a confessing animal" (Foucault, *History of Sexuality,* 59).

15. The etymology passes from the Latin *discurrere,* "to run about, to run away," through the French *discours,* to the archaic English meaning of "a treatise, a speech, a sermon" (*Chambers Etymological English Dictionary,* 173).

16. Foucault, "Truth and Power," esp. 74–75.

17. Samagalski, *Chile and Easter Island,* 235.

18. Ibid.

19. The "traveller's bible" is the ironic phrase used to describe the *Travel Survival Kit: Israel,* in *Colors 8: Religion,* Sept. 1994, 118.

20. Chatwin, *In Patagonia,* 77. The Virgin of Luján is, as Chatwin explains, the "patron of travellers" (50).

21. There has been a great boom in such travel literature. For an account of a Tierra

del Fuegian trip, instancing, with less skill, many of the features of Chatwin's work, see Iyer, *Falling off the Map*, 35–59. "Not surprisingly," notes Iyer, Ushuaia "looks like a mirror image of Isafjördhur or the other eerily silent Icelandic fishing towns around the arctic circle" (56). Bill Bryson's *Neither Here nor There* derives much of its humor from his pointless "just to say I've been there" trip to this northern town. Poles apart, both Ushuaia and Isafjördhur reveal the potential self-absence of a traveling culture that is scarcely serious about what it might find at the end(s) of the world.

22. On the "I-witness," see Pagden, *European Encounters with the New World*, 51–87.

23. Chatwin, *In Patagonia*, 182.

24. Ibid., 83.

25. Chatwin, *What Am I Doing Here*.

26. Barthes, "The Death of the Author," 147.

27. Chatwin, *In Patagonia*, 35.

28. Ibid., 130. This is a fun game. Compare the entry I found: "*anemaköna* a. Restless in disposition. Restless, not staying still, or at home, given to wandering about from idle curiosity or sinful pleasure. Wanton, dissatisfied, lewd" (Reverend Thomas Bridges, *Yámana-English Dictionary*, 24).

29. Michaels, "Para-ethnography," 174. In this essay Michaels reviews Chatwin's *The Songlines*.

30. Sloterdijk, *Critique of Cynical Reason*.

31. Ibid., 3.

32. Ibid., 82, 5.

33. Zizek, "How Did Marx Invent the Symptom?" 29, referring to Marx, *Capital*, 47: "They do not know that they are doing this, but they are doing it."

34. For one of the better analyses of the controversy, which I regard as a debate without merit, see Giroux, "Consuming Social Change," 5–31. Benetton jumps at the chance to "defend" its work in Sischy, "Advertising Taboos," 68–71. Such "defenses" have their own staginess. Critique does not harm these people. The very controversy over the company's techniques is grist to the mill (or, rather, wool to the sweater). See, if necessary, the book Benetton published to showcase these critics: *What Does AIDS Have to Do with Sweaters?* ed. Toscani.

35. For a short analysis, see Giroux, "Consuming Social Change," 5–20.

36. *Colors 9: Shopping*, Nov.–Dec. 1994.

37. Ibid., 69, 79, 31.

38. *Colors 8: Religion*, 116.

39. Ibid., 30.

40. *Colors 9: Shopping*, 29, 65, 98.

41. The introduction to the shopping issue smears the reader's face with a foretaste of Benettonian irony: "*You are what you buy*. So we went shopping! . . . We found out that everything (and everyone) has its price. Browse our catalogue. All goods are as described. Prices are reasonable. Your satisfaction is guaranteed" (ibid., 16).

42. *Colors 8: Religion,* 120.

43. For a critical appraisal of the work, see Huyssen, "Foreword," x–xix. See also Zizek, "How Did Marx Invent the Symptom?" 29–35.

44. Chatwin, *In Patagonia,* 184.

45. Ibid., 28.

46. Ibid.

47. McClosky, *Rhetoric of Economics,* 30, 76.

48. Lévi-Strauss, *Tristes Tropiques.*

49. Ibid., 443–44.

50. Lévi-Strauss was, mind, no stranger to the pleasure of such incongruities. James Clifford describes him in wartime New York, in company with André Breton, Max Ernst, and other exiled surrealists, as they searched the city's various antique stores for *objet trouvé* "survivals" of primitivist artwork. "New York was perhaps Lévi-Strauss' only true 'field-work,'" Clifford comments, cattily casting a bit of "the rhetoric of presence" back at the legendary pre-post-structuralist (*Predicament of Culture,* 245). The Frenchman himself wrote of a surreal experience he had at this time in the New York Public Library: "Under its neo-classical arches and between walls panelled with old oak, I sat near an Indian in a feather headdress and a bearded buckskin jacket—who was taking notes with a Parker pen" (237).

51. On "salvage ethnography," see Clifford, "On Ethnographic Allegory," 112. For the *locus classicus* of the anthropological salvage mission, see Bastian, "The Waning of Primitive Societies," 215–19.

52. Spencer, *Wanderings in Wild Australia.*

53. Spencer, *Spencer's Last Journey,* 52.

54. Ibid., 52.

55. Walter Benjamin, attacking Ranke's *wie es eigentlich gewesen* conception of history, in the "Theses on the Philosophy of History," in *Illuminations,* 252.

56. Benjamin, "Konvolut N," 5. I am indebted to Klaus Neumann, both for this reference and for an understanding of the ideas within; see his "Finding an Appropriate Beginning," 1–19.

2

Grounding

An Offhand Thesis

"We're just like sheep, aren't we?" I overheard an elderly *yanqui,* a package tourist, sigh whimsically to all the others clumped around her. They were in the Punta Arenas departure lounge during one of those interminable Third World flight delays. Two hours of being dragged back and forth, from office to office in search of their flight, led her to articulate the truth of their package tour to the End of the World. "We're just like sheep, aren't we? We do whatever they say." I laughed, beneath my breath, and saved the story to share with other travelers (yet in a sense my breath depended on that laughter).

Chatwin's endless deferral of meaning in pursuit of his travels, Benetton's self-corroding irony in search of commerce, and my own disbelieving role in this process—in Tierra del Fuego just to say I've been there—may all seem miles from such mass-migratory remarks. The self-superior primitivist jokes with which I ended the last chapter surely reveal the enormous gulf separating travelers from those among whom they travel. Yet my breath depended on that laughter. Their packaged naïveté is integral to our cynicism. Indeed, there is no greater grounding for the being-in-motion of Chatwinesque travelers than the all-believing sheep who believe in the world around them and do whatever they are told.

Disco Dalí

It was Christian, the Swiss surrealist with his *Aqui todo es possible* blind faith, who drove me to investigate these dubious images. I was taken by the laughter and annoyance such a person evokes in fellow travelers by seeming to believe in the space of their disbelief. His *pendejo* status, in the late 1990s, makes for an intriguing contrast with the early status of the surrealist project before it took on the dated, forced, and naïve appearance it has at present. Surrealism may now have the appearance of advertising copy, but in its beginnings, and at least until Dalí, the movement was nothing if not earnest. To focus upon the dating of such earnestness will hopefully reveal some of the mechanisms whereby the naïve Other takes on such a denigrated and yet preeminent role in the eyes of the cynical present.

The signatories of the first "Surrealist Manifesto" aimed, through automatic writing, revolutionary activity, and other such "surrealist researches," at banishing the disabling distinctions between conscious and unconscious, subjective and objective, word and world. Far from cynical, surrealism was to be nothing less than a revolutionary assault on the self-reflexive ego function through which one disbelieves and disenchants the reality of the world of dreams and desires. The manifesto proclaimed the following definition of the movement that sought to break all other definitions: "*Surrealism,* n.m., Pure psychic automatism, by which it is intended to express, verbally, in writing or by other means, the real functioning of thought. The dictation of thought, in the absence of all control exercised by reason, and outside all aesthetic or moral preoccupations."[1] In this manner, André Breton sought to adapt the Freudian clinic to a revolutionary praxis that would aim to liberate, much more than stabilize, unconscious forces.

To this end, Breton carved the identity of the surrealist at the most primitive and supposedly explosive point in Freud's progressivist (but double-edged) historical schema, which linked the rise of civilization with the intensification of repression/sublimation. This evolutionary schema explains the *disagreement* Freud introduced into his *Totem and Taboo: Some Points of Agreement between the Mental Lives of Savages and Neurotics.*[2] Both these groups are, Freud argued, driven by unconscious forces; in this their psyches are fundamentally similar. Yet while neurotics are inhibited in their actions, "primitive men, on the other hand, are *uninhibited:* thought passes directly into action."[3] Freud hence concluded the book with a bad pun from Goethe: "In the beginning was the Deed."[4] This pun points to the disagreement voiced in the meager correspondence between Breton and Freud; the former sought (and it was no joke) to return the modern world "through pure psychic automatism" to precisely these uninhibited and immediate beginnings.[5]

The Fuegian Indians, whom Darwin ranked so far down the evolutionary scale that he used them to illustrate our descent from monkeys, have frequently been seen to exemplify, in their present lives, the manner in which civilized "Man" lived "in the beginning."[6] Hand-in-hand with this racist ranking went the anthropological conviction as to their uninhibited, act-oriented nature. Samuel Lothrop, for instance, wrote a monograph on the Fuegians in 1928, and in it he characterized their languages (none of which he could actually speak) as at once deficient in abstract vocabulary and all the more immediate in their application to the physical world.[7] Nor did such fantasies, contemporaneous and even contributory to surrealism, end so soon. Bruce Chatwin employs similar notions to praise the Yaghan language.[8] The traveler has finally arrived at Haberton, where the Bridges family took up their eventual seat, having first settled the region as missionaries over a century before Chatwin's 1975 visit. Sitting on the family's porch, his own mission almost over, the para-ethnographer proceeds to read evolutionary anthropology into Thomas Bridges's extraordinarily poetic dictionary of Yámana terms: "the concepts of 'good' and 'beautiful', so essential to Western thought, are meaningless unless they are rooted to things. The first speakers of language took the raw material of their surroundings and pressed it into metaphor to suggest abstract things."[9] Thus Chatwin, condemned to wander through meaningless abstractions, measures the distance we have fallen from the sensual, still innocent environment of these "first speakers of language," the uncorrupted Fuegian Indians whose recent passing he mourns (too hastily).[10]

This Edenic fantasy of native linguistic immediacy slides swiftly into images of indigenous receptivity to the hollow magic of Western things. Rosemary Coombe has written of how the reputed "excessive corporeality" of Native and African Americans has been used to lend life, indeed, to "embody" the trademarks of Western commodities (such as the Inca brand Pear Juice I discovered in the "Ona Kiosk" in Ushuaia).[11] Fuegian Indians have, likewise, often been seen to lack the self-reflective secular consciousness that would disenchant their immediate responses to such products. "Rooted in things," such people are, in firstcontact literature, readily seen as impressionable enough to believe in what Lucas Bridges ironically termed the "white man's magic."[12]

Son of Thomas and one-time host and prime informant of Samuel Lothrop, Lucas Bridges was no stranger to the magic of ethnographic encounter. Writing of the early 1890s, the period of first contact, Bridges gives the following account of Fuegian gullibility in the face of "a certain magic soap, the miraculous effects of which the manufacturers have been too modest to claim for themselves."[13] A Selk'nam Indian living on the Bridgeses' coastal property had been away for some time. In the Indian's absence, his Fuegian wife gave birth to a boy with remarkably fair hair and blue eyes. Bridges, describing this incident in the late 1940s, hastens to add that his own eyes are brown. On returning, the husband discovered the "incredible transformation" of his child, while his wife "attributed the miracle to a cake of magic soap that had been given to her by [Bridges's] sister, Alice."[14] Initially quite dark, the child had been miraculously washed white by the fantastic soap. The husband, Bridges tells us, was not merely satisfied, but indeed overawed by these wonders, so much so that the colonist, finding the spirit of it all somewhat contagious, now dreams up the following End of the World advertisement: "I suggested to Alice that we should take a photograph of the happy trio and send it to the manufacturers, in case they wished to use it as an unsolicited testimonial to the merits of their wonderful product. Alice, however, thought that it would not be quite the thing, so the photograph never went to Messrs. Pears."[15]

It is, in fact, not so far from Breton to Bridges. However strange the contrast, there is a direct parallel between the colonial soliciting of this "unsolicited testimonial" and the "psychic automatism" which impelled the surrealist search for the unmediated reality of a commodity-driven world. Derived from the same anthropology of primitive immediacy, uninhibited by "the dictates of reason," the surrealist mission projected itself into precisely that purported subjectivity.

Of course, this self-imposed disinhibition was bound to seem stagy and even stupid the moment the novelty had worn off, as it had so clearly in the Ushuaia of 1996. Yet the primitivist imagining that projects such unreflective immediacy *onto others* is well and truly alive. Witness that same primitive present recapitulated in contemporary depictions of the "schizophrenic" subject of contemporary popular culture.[16] Overwhelmed by an "absolute proximity to and total instantaneousness with things, this overexposure to the transparency of the world," such a subject seems as sutured to the unbelievable things of secular modernity as any Fuegian Indian.[17]

The surrealist, the primitive, the post-structuralist "schizophrenic": these are the sort of people who would enjoy dancing at Ushuaia's Disco Dalí. If you asked (but the whole trick is not to ask) they might even consent to becoming figures in an "unsolicited" Chatwinian travel anecdote.

Holding People to Their Words

To hold myself to my offhand thesis, that the God of the disenchanted is reflected in the ozone-blind eyes of winged sheep, and to force myself to take it seriously: that would be a true act of *salvage ethnography.* This would necessitate a rather unusual approach to the offhand images I found littered through the works of Chatwin and Benetton and repeated in my fieldwork. A more popular method of critical garbage disposal would read the naturalization of hierarchy into such self-superior anecdotes, reducing the word to the successful functioning of power/knowledge.

Yet the very prevalence of such throwaway and denigrating images makes me suspect that they betoken something more than the simple stamping of self-superiority—something much more like a necessary supplement to one's being. To me this is suggested, above all, by the momentary anxiety, the tinge of bad faith that I quickly repressed whenever repeating the "We're just like sheep" anecdote to other travelers in the field. A part of me knew—and didn't need to know—that at the same time that her words made her seem so naïve, this package tourist was laughing at herself too. To follow my thesis through, seriously, requires that I unknit the very texture of this desire to colonize and flatten out the space of the Other's self-distance.

Jokes can, after all, be pushed too far. The reaction of my Ushuaian friend Horacio to Christian the Swiss surrealist made that clear enough. The humor, grounded in well-soiled European images of elsewhere, of television sets at the End of the World, simply does not survive the transplant to Tierra del Fuego. The simple truth is that the province's special tax-exempt status makes it cheaper for Phillips-Fox to ship the parts down from Buenos Aires, have them assembled at the Fuegian television factory, and then freight the completed sets back. Migrating TV sets are only so funny to someone who lives in Ushuaia and has a hand in making them such everyday items across the nation. Nor is there anything eccentric or amusing about the fact that *El Fin del Mundo* is stocked with all the latest electronic commodities, sells Guinness, cooks in microwaves, receives MTV, etc.—if you live there and take occasional advantage of the duty-free shopping to update your stereo.

This fact was brought home to me while watching *Yaktemi, Mi Tierra*, the documentary Alberto Quesada made for the local television station, which he showed me one night on his VCR. *Yaktemi* is a Yámana word which translates as *Mi Tierra*—My Land. Less a story than a series of impressions, *Yaktemi* circled between snippets of indigenous mythology, local history, and reflections from present inhabitants, some of whom were now watching with us.[18] The camera moved back and forth through encounters, images, and voices, casting passing glances at certain key Ushuaian landmarks on the way: the church spire, the town hall, Calle San Martin, the Malvinas war monument. These places kept reappearing from different angles, tracing the pathways of collective memory and taking me back to the streets I was treading daily as I visited friends, hung out in libraries, drank coffee, and settled into the everyday mundanity of the End of the World. This is not the province of travelers' jokes, which have little time for well-worn cultural surfaces.

Such jokes seem, on the contrary, to rely on *holding people to their words*, on taking Tierra del Fuegians in person to be the same people as they are on the page—or rather on the footpath and the street sign. Take away Alberto's caressing camera and, to the foreign *flâneur* walking down Calle San Martin, the signs of everyday life make the people who live by them seem strikingly dumb. Walking down the main street you pass the Videomania store, with Disco Dalí on one side and Big Harbor Travel on the other—a sign outside reads "We take you wherever your imagination suggests." Pass Casino Argentina on the left and you come to the intersection of San Martin and 25 de Mayo, where a large (in local, provincial terms) billboard veers over the street, showing a pair of jeans on a half-missing body: "UFO basics: Most of the world's most famous people wear them. If you care about your looks you will too."

As if these indicative signs weren't enough, there are *indios* everywhere: from Farmacia El Indio at one end of the town to the Ona Kiosk (where you can buy Inca Pear Juice) at the other. Agencia de Viajes Tolkeyen, meanwhile, has an Indian head decorating its decal, perhaps in honor of Chatwin and the nomadological clientele he continues to inspire. None of this trash has any place in Alberto's video, nor does he spend any time filming the local Surty Sur supermarket, at the far end of the street. Masses pass every hour through the turnstiles of this, the largest supermarket in Ushuaia, in seeming indifference to the fact that they are currently experiencing what the banner above the entrance proclaims as "The Pleasure of Shopping": *El Placer de Comprar!*

To believe in such signs, and not simply just follow them, you would have to be a Swiss surrealist. This fact is apparent the moment you survey the critical literature on advertising. Judith Williamson's *Decoding Advertisements,* one of the best works in the field, often seems stunningly naïve because of its assumption that the subject of ideology is a fundamentally sincere being who finds him- or herself in the mirror images offered by ads for jeans worn by half-missing people, slick vistas of overseas adventure, and unsolicited testimonials to all-powerful brands of laundry soap. For Williamson, advertising is an ideological system that "creates structures of meaning" in much the same way as religion or art.[19] In fact, it is directly parasitic of such structures, for it works by "hollowing out" the signifiers of preexisting ideological "referent systems" (she gives the example of surrealism) and inserting the product within them.[20] Nor does the hollowness end here. Many advertisements are characterized by the absence of a subject. Such voids, Williamson argues, draw the reader in, offering you the opportunity to find yourself there and become complete and one with the product. By offering the inaugurally split subject illusions of obtainable unity and identity, advertisements are not merely selling us things—"they are selling us ourselves."[21]

But can one really buy this theory of the billboard as iconostasis? Isn't the true "hollowing out" effect of advertising the way it empties such discourse of all possible believability? The subject of a Pears' Soap commercial is almost compelled to disbelieve in the empty signs he or she follows anyway.[22] Of course, the problems with reading "false consciousness," in Williamson's Marxist phrase, into popular culture are probably too obvious to bother critiquing here.[23] Perhaps less obvious is the fact that attempts to analyze advertising through a Foucauldian discourse theory are open to the same critique. The presupposition of a truth-seeking, faithful subject leaves the critic looking very like the naïve subject he or she seeks.

This may seem harsh on Foucault, who doubtless would never have gone so far as to attack Benetton for the "truth claims" behind its advertising images.[24] Nor is the fundamentally faithful subject of *The History of Sexuality* (a history, incidentally, that ignores the ambiguous power plays involved in sexual jokes, innuendoes, and humor) a constant in Foucault's work. Many of his earlier writings sought to bracket the subject out of debate altogether.

In "Politics and the Study of Discourse," he wrote of a mode of analysis that would seek to trace nothing more than "the law of *existence* of statements."[25] That is, it would simply set forth the "manifest appearance" of the statement itself, "without referring the facts of discourse to the will—perhaps involuntary—of their authors."[26] Such an *archaeology* of discourse allows for a subjectivity that is not immanent in the words it speaks—indeed, that is irrelevant to the words it speaks. It would thus assemble the "set of rules which at a given period and in a given society" decree "the limits and the forms of the *sayable*."[27] Hence one could present the archaeology of advertising discourse, or of Tierra del Fuegian tourist jokes, erasing the entire unwieldy issue of the subject's intentional relationship to the "truth effect" of his or her discourse, highlighting the superiority of the stupid signifier over Man, that "face drawn in sand at the edge of the sea."[28]

Effacing the subject's role in determining the sayable certainly buries a few of the problems associated with politics and the study of discourse. By holding subjects to their words, the archaeologist wipes out all of the intersubjective dynamics integral to interpretation itself—which doubtless has its uses, though it cannot erase the fact that articulating someone else's "sayable" is as much an act as drawing faces in the sand. Reducing comments like "We're just like sheep, aren't we?" to the "manifest appearance" one finds in them is not so dissimilar to the interpretative act whereby one projects a dummy subject behind such words. The parallel is not simply in the "hollowing out" effect both desubjectifying strategies occasion. The archaeological articulation and the tourist joke are united because in both instances the "limits and the forms of the *sayable*" are articulated by the Other as interpretant. For it is the Other who perceives my words and holds me to his or her statement of them.[29]

That is what constitutes the radical exteriority of discourse; that the depth, the interior dimension, the intelligence or naïveté of my words has little to do with me. It is projected onto them by the Other who owns my representation as a speaking being.[30] "What matter who is speaking?" Foucault writes, as if inscribing his own monument, "someone has said."[31] It matters greatly, for it is the Other who speaks the interiority of that discourse of his, and who has the power to hold him to the surface of his words. There is a politics of discourse that I need to study here, for this is how you plaster someone's face onto a Benettonian billboard, as an advertisement of naïve Otherness.

The Disenchantment of the Reenchantment of Modernity

The automatic, unreflecting, surrealist subject seems, as I have argued, an appropriate face to plaster there, particularly now that techniques of surrealist visual expression have become so much a part of advertising.[32] This appropriation seems to have contributed, more than anything else, to the routinized status of surrealist visuality. The banalization of the surrealist project has gone hand-in-hand with a forgetting of the movement's radical political dimensions. René Magritte, for instance, a lifelong Communist party member, was, all the same, posthumously proclaimed the "patron saint of advertising" by the 1984–85 *International Annual of Advertising*.[33] In spite of his political convictions, Magritte often found himself working, for financial reasons, in advertising. Thus he acquired an unwonted sainthood for a religion in which he actively disbelieved. The ironic posthumous power of Magritte's disowned identity as consumerist saint might seem a far more accurate image of subjectivity than the uninhibited and dispossessed revolutionary being which was the goal of Bretonian automatism. Yet an archaeology of Magritte's advertising apotheosis would throw away its own critical potential were it not to focus upon the hegemonic act whereby his "manifest appearance" is squeezed of all political dimensionality.

In this historical, contestatory manner one might attempt to revisit and reinflate the political intentions driving the surrealist search for uninhibited immediacy, which, particularly in the person of Breton, now seems so earnest as to be laughable. Seeking to project such a history back from Sloterdijk's cynical present, one might imagine that such an embrace of the immediate simply reflected the spirit of the times. A similar earnestness can be noted in the work of Walter Benjamin, who, while maintaining a certain critical distance, celebrated surrealism for the closeness with which it sidled up to the repressed revolutionary energies of the commodity culture it sought to overthrow.

In "This Space for Rent" Benjamin charged his prose down the zeitgeist's one-way street of uninhibited revolutionary action. So he attempted to claim for critique the striking immediacy of the new fiery-red neon culture: "Only fools lament the decay of criticism. . . . Today the most real, the mercantile gaze into the heart of things is the advertisement."[34] The ability to reflect carefully on one's own words was, Benjamin claimed, simply the dead residue of a "world where perspectives and prospects counted and where it was still possible to take a standpoint."[35] Advertising was "no longer a matter of correct distancing. . . . It abolishes the space where contemplation moved."[36] Revolutionary critique was to hurl itself into precisely this uncontemplative void of pure presence, to burst modernity into the life which its "mercantile gaze" at once robbed of humanity and retooled with a glimmer of redemption.

It is intriguing to contrast the massive moving pictures Benjamin conjures up on the advertising billboard he sees in the late twenties with its contemporary counterpart in Ushuaia. The UFO jeans advertisement, far from hitting its viewer "between the eyes with things, as a car, growing to gigantic proportions, careens at us out of a film screen," is about as moving as a jeans commercial.[37] Is this simply a matter of contemporary routinization, as the world becomes increasingly disenchanted with the mass media advertising which Williamson could still see, back in the seventies, as the modern equivalent of religious imagining? Such a (thoroughly un-Benjaminian) narrative of progressive disenchantment is disrupted by the "dialectical image," the montage shock of contrasting this purportedly naïve recent past with its irony-laden predecessor: the distance and obvious disbelief with which Lucas Bridges represents the naïve Other finding himself in an "unsolicited testimonial" for Pears' magic soap at the very beginning of the twentieth century.[38] Reading Bridges, it is as if such disenchantment were already there at the beginning of the world-wide mass advertising which is supposed to have replaced prior systems of testimony and belief.

Should one, on the other hand, buy Benjamin's narrative of a modern reenchantment which, in the interwar period poised between these two anecdotes, found momentary faith and feeling in the signs and things of an otherwise unbelievable modernity? Can one fail to recognize, in such a wishful one-way vignette, the hollowed-out, dummy subject of belief whose existence is always a "matter of correct distancing"? The surrealist face that finds itself in the billboard's "Space for Rent" is always someone else's face. Such a face is made to wear a spontaneous and unmediated relationship to the signs of the everyday world. It can then figure in overly earnest notions of popular culture—not to mention the primitivist anecdotes which such critical characterizations so frequently recall.

This is scarcely fair to Benjamin, whose surrealist inspiration led him to theorize the "destitution" and obsolescence locked within the temporal coordinates of the commodity itself, as shall be apparent in the following chapter.[39] Yet for the moment I want to hold him to his one-way words and to let those earnest words resound in the strikingly uninhabited "space for rent" that follows.

I stumbled across Cafe Dalí in the tedious town of Punta Arenas, the place where Chatwin's Great-Uncle Charley lived during an earlier epoch of colonial adventure. Across from the local Benetton outlet, the cafe is an uninviting and nondescript place. Cheap still lifes hang from the off-pink walls. The sticky menu features a potted Dalí biography. The list of disinterested dates and achievements concludes with the following: "He published numerous books about art and philosophy and through these works this great painter opened the doors of dreams and the imagination. We can live these dreams in reality today by enjoying—in his artistic name—a delicious cup of Cafe Dalí coffee."

The place smells. The tables are empty. The coffee is crap. Enjoy your surrealism.

Notes

1. André Breton, "The Surrealist Manifesto," cited in Rosemont, "André Breton," 23.

2. Freud, *Totem and Taboo*, 43–224.

3. Ibid., 224.

4. Ibid. Marx quotes the same pun to claim, of the fetishism of commodities, that "owners of commodities think after the manner of Faust: 'In the beginning was the deed'—action comes first. They have acted before they have thought" (*Capital*, 61).

5. For a brief and revealing account of their correspondence, see Cohen, *Profane Illumination*, 57–61.

6. Charles Darwin, *The Descent of Man*, 919–20. Throughout Darwin's works, the Fuegians are treated in a derogatory manner. The scientific racism of *The Descent of Man* seems simply the refinement of the more emotive utterances one finds elsewhere, e.g., in the December 18, 1832, entry in *Charles Darwin's Diary*, 119–20. Notwithstanding such moments, it is worth remembering that Darwin was, at other times, quite ambivalent about the validity of extending his biological theories to the analysis of human society. For Darwin's various, contradictory opinions on this subject, see Greene, "Darwin as a Social Evolutionist," 95–128. For a survey of the ideas of those "Darwinian" social scientists who were more than happy to socialize evolutionary time in his name, see Fabian, *Time and the Other*, esp. 1–36.

7. See Lothrop, *The Indians of Tierra del Fuego*, 50, 121.

8. *Yaghan*, a word used in older texts to indicate the coastal Fuegians, who called themselves Yámana, was the Selk'nam term for them. Those interior-dwelling Fuegians, on the other hand, are often called *Ona* in the colonial texts. I use their autodenomination, *Selk'nam*, in preference.

9. Chatwin, *In Patagonia*, 130. Jon Stratton has drawn my attention to the similarity

between Chatwin's linguistic musings and the theory of the poetic origin of language put forth in Shelley's *A Defence of Poetry*. In describing what he sees as the child's immediate mimetic relation to the objects of the world, Shelley claims that the "savage (for the savage is to ages what the child is to years) expresses the emotions produced in him by surrounding objects in a similar manner," that is to say, for both, "language and gesture, together with plastic or pictorial imagination, become the image of the combined effect of those objects, and of his apprehension of them" (27). Poetry, for Shelley, is a kind of linguistic recapitulationism, for it is "connate with the origin of man" (26). The "copiousness," on the other hand, "of lexicography and of grammar are the works of a later age" (30–31). The parallels between Shelley's and Chatwin's ideas are more than coincidental. Stratton has read Shelley's ideas into the history of empiricist language theory, a theoretical stance which—with its Crusoe-like insistence on the notion of language as a "fundamentally individual thing, a function of the individual mind" in its response to the world—has ever informed the English literary, critical, and philosophical tradition. See Stratton, *Writing Sites*, 99.

10. Descendants of the original Fuegians still live in Ushuaia, Punta Arenas, and, particularly, Puerto Williams. In that last town I visited the indigenous settlement at Ubika Village, where I interviewed Ursula Calderón.

11. Coombe, "Embodied Trademarks," 208. In this article Coombe borrows heavily from Taussig's *Mimesis and Alterity*. For Taussig's analysis of such depictions of the heightened "sensuousity" and mimetic dexterity of the uncivilized, see particularly his chapters on Darwin's visit to Tierra del Fuego (70–99).

12. Bridges uses this phrase when describing a "primitive" (i.e., to us, at the beginning of the twenty-first century) "magic lantern" slide projector. E. Lucas Bridges, *Uttermost Part of the Earth*, 284.

13. Ibid., 219. The anecdote is printed in full in the appendix.

14. Ibid., 220.

15. Ibid.

16. Baudrillard, *Ecstasy of Communication*, 27. In claiming that irony is impossible in this hypermodern world, Baudrillard follows the logic of this "total instantaneousness" to the letter (54).

17. Ibid., 27.

18. Quesada and Kuniger, *Yaktemi*.

19. Williamson, *Decoding Advertisements*, 12.

20. Ibid., esp. 131–34. In this respect see also Carrick, "The Surrealist Image."

21. Williamson, *Decoding Advertisements*, 13. Her reading of Lacan's mirror stage has much in common with contemporaneous usages in film theory. For a compelling critique of such approaches, see Joan Copjec, "The Orphopsychic Subject," in *Read My Desire*, 15–39.

22. I have no wish to echo the advertising industry's claim that the ability to distance oneself from such messages is grounded in the economic subject's rational ability to make

"consumer choices." Writing of this "circle of manipulation and retroactive need," Adorno and Horkheimer rightly claim that "anyone who doubts the power of monotony is a fool" (*Dialectic of Enlightenment*, 121, 148). By the same token, I am by no means denying that there might exist people who truly do believe in the unbelievable discourse of advertising (nor do I deny that certain Selk'nam might have expressed wonder at Bridges's things). The interesting question, however, is why those who do *not* believe have such a desire to talk and laugh about those who apparently do.

23. Williamson, *Decoding Advertisements*, 10.

24. Giroux does so in "Consuming Social Change," 20–26.

25. Foucault, "Politics and the Study of Discourse," 53–72.

26. Ibid., 59.

27. Ibid.

28. Foucault, *Order of Things*, 313.

29. For further exploration of these dimensions of discourse, see Zizek's discussion of Paul Grice's work on the structure of intentional meaning in *Tarrying with the Negative*, 77.

30. Of course mastery over the Other's words is itself illusory. As John Searle pointed out, in amending Grice's findings, these intersubjective plays of intentionality should not be overevaluated: "Meaning is more than a matter of intention, it is also a matter of convention" ("What Is a Speech Act?" 145). Searle's distinction is more or less useful for setting forth my point of departure from Foucault's archeological practice. The theory of the speech act which he sets forth in *The Archaeology of Knowledge* focuses exclusively on the conventional operation of such contextual speech (see 79–106).

Archaeology reads the enunciation for the conventions which structure it, but brackets out what Searle terms "intention," the field of discourse which I would prefer to define, with Foucault, as "interpretation . . . the violent or surreptitious appropriation of a system of rules" (Foucault, *Language, Counter-Memory, Practice*, 151). Of course, Foucault is fully aware that his archaeology is constituted in the archaeologist's very refusal to think through "interpretation." It is precisely through this refusal that one obtains, in the conventional forms of enunciation itself, "an intrinsic description of the monument" (*The Archaeology of Knowledge*, 7). Herein lies the point of my critique: a disagreement with the very possibility of separating convention from interpretation. In my Fuegian archive this impossibility assumes the following form: the "intrinsic description" of the "monument" which I shall discover amid the beached rubbish in Tierra del Fuego arises in the *interpretation* of "intrinsic description" itself.

31. Foucault, "Politics and the Study of Discourse," 72.

32. For the appropriation of surrealism by advertising, see Williamson, *Decoding Advertising*, 131–34.

33. Quoted in Carrick, "The Surrealist Image," 50.

34. Walter Benjamin, "This Space for Rent," in *Reflections*, 85.

35. Ibid.

36. Ibid.

37. Ibid.

38. For an analysis of the role of shock in Benjamin's writings, see Cohen, *Profane Illu-mination,* 180–86.

39. Walter Benjamin, "Surrealism; or, The Last Snapshot of the European Intelligent-sia," in *Reflections,* 182.

3

Out-of-Date Theory

The Future Perfect Tense

The civic equivalent of Cafe Dalí must surely be the two-meter-high marble pyramid I found dumped on the foreshore at Ushuaia. "The Philco Time Capsule," I read, my face reflected back to me in its black mirror surface, "Not to be opened until the 2nd of October, in the year 2492." The pyramid is flanked on one side by a white wall, intended as a place for reflection and set with plaques commemorating various national heroes. On its other side stands an awkward statue to the Selk'nam, whose many corpses paved the way to this present. The future, present, and past fantasies of the Argentine nation-state are thus plotted here, on the edge of town, in this out-of-the way and unvisited Plaza de Mayo. People I asked had to think twice before they could even remember it existed.

Such civic disinterest brings me back to Benjamin, for whom "no face is surrealistic in the same degree as the true face of a city."[1] Whose face would find its true reflection here, in this plaza of washed-up state trash, all centered upon a ridiculous black marble pyramid? A pyramid which, I read on, contains six video laser discs, recorded with three months of television broadcasts from late 1992, along with the messages of five hundred Argentines: "This material was made to last 500 years, to show to the world of the future a part of the life and the thought of our era." Yet if it were made to last so long, why does this monumental trash already seem so ephemeral and unloved? Why, in reading these lines, is my true reflection distorted by the spray-paint seal—*Jose B. Te Amo Jennifer B. 25/11/95*—that stamps its surface with public indifference?

How should one read these amorous lines? As the victory of private passion over the towering stupidity of national history? Such a reading would be almost as trite as that given by the British traveler who, having also found his way to the monument, laughed to me about mad Argentine nationalism. The strength of such reactions (for they are mine too) causes me to stop and to stare some more. The very emptiness of public statues gives them a strange power over their subjects: according to Robert Musil, monuments in fact call to be defaced.[2] Michael Taussig has likewise argued that state iconography requires the "desecration" that graffiti and laughter release for its semiotic completion.[3] The strangely compelling power of such state signifiers causes me, in pausing, to turn my attention to the weirdness of the signification itself.

Why would the Argentine state, allied with Phillips-Fox, the multinational television manufacturer, choose a pyramid—an Eastern icon of colonial conquest as much as ancient mystery—to encapsulate the message it sends to the future? Why send a laser-disc-laden pyramid to 2492, a pyramid which, the inscription continues, "when the twentieth century has become but a rumor, will stand here like a traveller through time"?

Doesn't this time capsule represent a fantasy of the present's colonization by the future—a fantasy to be realized in 2492, to coincide with the millennium of American conquest, when an ancient culture—that is, the present, the Argentine Tierra del Fuego of 1992—will finally reveal its mysteries? Under the imaginary gaze of its future *conquistadores,* the Fuegian present turns into the future's past. Through this same phenomenon—the *Reconquista* of 2492—the white inhabitants of modern Ushuaia, as much as the video technology embodying them, suddenly seem strikingly primitive. It is as if the pyramid, by invoking the future's presence, serves to loop the present into the true past. I am suggesting that the Philco Time Capsule, this "traveller through time," is actually traveling backward, not forward, availing itself of the future's imaginary gaze to place contemporary Tierra del Fuego into the past. Note how, in this future perfect primitivization of the present, those laser discs take on their true pyramidal role as magic native engravings, video-embodied souls of the dead. The true reflection to be found in the Philco Time Capsule is that of the exotic colonial inhabitant of the primitive present, whose ancient video technology can take on its truly fetishistic and surreal face only when made primitive by the *conquistadores* of the future.

The future perfect—the "I shall have been"—is also one of the most powerful tools of cultural critique. The critical employment of this tense gives a dramatic tension to many of Benjamin's formulations. Only from the futuristic perspective that would view the neo-imperial present in the same dramatic way we view the atrocious colonial past can one see that "the 'state of emergency' in which we live is not the exception but the rule."[4] The present continuous tense of everyday tragedy is itself the catastrophe. Such is the unsettling message of the Angel of History, from whose future, but backward-looking perspective the everyday outrage takes on monumental proportions: "Where we perceive a chain of events, he sees a single catastrophe which keeps piling wreckage upon wreckage and hurls it in front of his feet."[5] Yet the Angel cannot dive down, like the historical materialist, to find glints of revolutionary possibility within this "pile of debris."[6] His very perspective is held in place, indeed, is supported by the "storm" of progress that blows him along "homogenous empty time" into the future.[7] The Angel of History is divine and inhabits, however involuntarily, the future, which is why he must make the people of the present wear their wreckage, why he must hold them to their words.

The homogenous empty time through which the Angel is blown is also the temporal condition of the Philco Time Capsule. To "remember the future" is, in both instances, to adopt the anamorphotic perspective from which the present suddenly loses its hold on time and becomes Other to itself.[8] The subject becoming Other thus travels through the future perfect into the past that is the primitive present. The Angel shows such a subject his or her own *barbarism* in the "pile of debris" that is the present continuous tense of the everyday. The time capsule finds the *primitivism* of the present in the future's out-of-date technology. Whether through critique or through monumental garbage, the "true face" that finds itself there is pushed out of the ambivalent present and into the one-dimensional past, revealing the tendency trash has to suddenly slip into history and take one unawares.

Everything That Melts into Air Rains Down Somewhere Else

The surprise this occasions is odd, for rubbish is made of history. The massive waste piles that characterize capitalist modernity have their historical origin in the "constant revolutionizing of production," the ever-expanding commodification and destitution of matter which still today "chases the bourgeoisie over the whole surface of the globe."[9] Yet when Marx claimed that "all that is solid"—in the face of such overwhelming forces—"melts into air," he failed to add that the waste product of such activity always reappears in other places, at other times.[10] Patagonia, for instance, is currently being slated as a poor enough place to be used for the dumping of the Northern Hemisphere's nuclear waste.[11] Yet the historicity of rubbish lies not simply in the specific, and thoroughly colonial, circumstances through which one can explain its origins, expansion, and eventual destination. For there is a historicity, a temporal indexing, in the very nature (*sic*) of garbage itself, as Benjamin portrayed so vividly in his *Passagen-Werk*.[12] That same commercial erethism, which Marx diagnosed in the *Manifesto,* creates a progressive temporal narrative through which the life of the consumer commodity, as fashion, is endlessly emplotted—alongside the garbage that is its death mask.[13]

It is important to note the unconscious manner in which this veritable philosophy of history comes into being, immanent within the actions of social agents. For while Henry Ford, in 1916, may well have claimed that "History is bunk" (i.e., rubbish), that same rubbish, regardless of what those who discard it might think, is history too.[14] The historicity immanent within a commodity produced on Fordist production lines surfaces in Bruce Chatwin's bemused depiction of his Patagonian encounter, in the 1970s, with a still-running 1920s Dodge.[15] The commodity reveals its historical indexation, as a sign of "our" industrial infancy, in its primitive present appearance among the "underdeveloped." It is not, however, that Chatwin necessarily intends the recapitulationist discourse his encounter evokes. Indeed, history seems stamped more on the car itself than on his page. Such inadvertent practices put an interesting slant on Marx's much maligned evolutionary dictum for the advance of capital: *De te fabula narratur* (of you this story will be told).[16] It is rubbish itself—and not those like Ford who believe themselves the masters of history—which comes to speak the inexorability of this encroaching *fabula.*

This commodity-time is, as Taussig has argued, deeply run with intimations of primitivism and colonialism.[17] The Philco Time Capsule moves back (inasmuch as it moves forward) through five centuries to perform an imaginary act of future colonization. In this imperial manner it discovers the primitivism of the commodified present. The video technology that Ushuaia's future *conquistadores* (and their attendant *antropologos?*) will find so out-of-date is here illuminated by its fetishistic position within the shrine of everyday life—as seen from the "allochronistic" perspective of that present's hierarchically poised future.[18] For Chatwin, on the other hand, the physical path he travels into the "underdeveloped" Third World grants him, as representative of that world's "inevitable" future, a perspective on his own culture's recent past. The primitive present of contemporary Argentina is hence seen to reenact the prehistory of contemporary Europe, while Chatwin himself, for all his supposed nomadism, is doing no less than unthinkingly reenacting the theory of racial recapitulation, one of the most monumental of nineteenth-century metanarratives.

If the time capsule's movement through time suggests a similarly colonial hierarchizing of relations to Chatwin's movement through space, such projections fall well within the trajectory of what Johannes Fabian described as a veritable theory of "time travel."[19] To flesh out this now highly unfashionable theory will allow me to resume my search for the naïve Other of my travel anecdotes. It will also take me back to the surrealist investigations I discarded—too hastily—in the previous chapter.

Derived from the biological theories of Ernst Haeckel, racial recapitulationism held that the organic (ontogenetic) growth of the individual child recapitulated the racial (phylogenetic) evolution of humankind as a whole ("ontogeny," as the phrase went, "recapitulates phylogeny"). The white child, that is to say, behaves much like adults did in our prehistory and proceeds to shoot up through the subsequent stages of human history till arriving at that summit of racial maturity, the nineteenth-century bourgeois body.[20] Racial evolution, in this construct, was held to be a fundamentally singular process, encompassing all the varieties of human culture within the same trajectory. By the same token, this process was seen as decidedly uneven. The new nineteenth-century science of anthropology served to attest to this unevenness, in its presentation of "primitives." Cast as "backward" and "underdeveloped," such people were seen, much like the white child, to recapitulate the early stages of human development. Europe's geographically distant Others were hence regarded as living exemplars of the racial child who became "father" to the "man" of modern Europe.

These recapitulationist notions soon spread beyond biology and anthropology to have an enormous influence on a whole range of sciences. Many of Freud's clinical works, such as his book on jokes, are structured around them, as is the quasi-anthropological *Totem and Taboo*.[21] Such texts are steeped in the "allochronism" of early anthropology, a mind-set which led, as Fabian has argued, to a veritable "spatialization" of time within the human sciences.[22] Nor did this "reading of time on the clock of the globe" end at the academic's armchair. Recapitulationism was carried out into the field, to mold the structure of the travel experience itself.[23]

European movement through space to other lands hence became the equivalent of movement back through time along a homogenous developmental schema. In this way, the medieval pilgrimage, once directed toward the experience of enlightenment in European centers of knowledge, was turned on its head to make such ritualized self-discovery a function of foreign travel. The anthropological pilgrim, in the modern world, journeyed back "to places where man was to find nothing but himself" in the present-as-past features such a *conquistador* from the future could read recapitulated in the face of his or her primitive Other.[24]

As I stated in the previous chapter, the Fuegians, since Darwin, have constantly been relegated to the lowest rung of the human evolutionary ladder.[25] In this tradition, the Fuegians were seen to represent Europeans at their most racially primitive, infantile, and uncivilized. The ethnographer, journeying to the End of the World, was traveling in time as much as through space to revisit the primitive infancy through which "civilized Man" had long since passed. Samuel Lothrop's 1928 ethnography was, for instance, written with the express aim of "recreating a vista of life in Europe . . . many thousands of years ago."[26]

Lothrop claimed, by evolutionary analogy, that the Fuegians shared many features with the Tasmanian Aborigines.[27] Sir Baldwin Spencer, famed for his research among the "world's most primitive inhabitants" of Australia, followed in Lothrop's footsteps in pursuit of this same claim. He arrived to conduct ethnographic research in Tierra del Fuego in 1929, only to die shortly thereafter. In a eulogy appended to Spencer's Fuegian field notes, Sir James Frazer wrote that the Australian Aborigines "have survived to our times as if on purpose to hold up to us a mirror of the life of man as it was in ages long before the dawn of history."[28] The Fuegians, added R. R. Marrett, another of his eulogists, offered "analogies . . . that Spencer must have wanted to examine at close hand."[29] The commensuration, quantitative in essence, postulated here between the Australian Aborigines—whom Marrett claimed "remain culturally in a state of arrested childhood"—and the equally primitive Fuegians reveals something of the rigid evolutionary schema imposed upon such diverse people. Thus European time travelers sought to recapitulate themselves.

Objet Trouvé — The Obsolete Self

Bruce Chatwin journeyed to both Tierra del Fuego and Australia to find nothing (but himself). Yet the emptiness of that finding is relieved in the neocolonial cuteness of seeing the past of his own culture relived in the primitive present of contemporary Patagonia. The archaeology of such trashy anecdotes reminds me of the continuing cogency of recapitulationist findings, for all their theoretical desuetude. It allows, furthermore, for a reassessment of the surrealist *objet trouvé*, whose revolutionary potential Breton discovered in the 1920s, at the same time that Chatwin's Dodge would have seemed so thoroughly up-to-date. Indeed, to paint surrealism as commodified and dated, as I did in the previous chapter, is to partake of the very powers of obsolescence it sought to tap.

For Benjamin, the flashpoint of surrealism's revolutionary potential lay in its research into the *objet trouvé*, the out-of-date commodity encountered by chance at Parisian flea markets. Such researches disclosed something of the "atmosphere" of the everyday, the forces of life and desire packed within these once fashionable objects.[30] The way presence leaked from these old things served to make palpable, in the breach, the extent of one's own historical investment. In this way Breton was, for Benjamin, "the first to perceive the revolutionary energies that appear in the 'outmoded,'" the first to comprehend how "destitution . . . can be suddenly transformed into revolutionary nihilism."[31]

In his monumental *Passagen-Werk,* Benjamin sought to redeem the power, only visible in its desuetude, of such ordinary, oblivious objects.[32] These discarded objects served, like dreams, like surrealist images and automatic writings, to reveal the "collective unconscious" of the nineteenth century. For the *objet trouvé,* having lost its oneiric power over the collective, could nonetheless be wielded, by force of the very "atmosphere" it exudes, to make the collective recognize "precisely this dream as a dream."[33] A critical illumination of these dreams of the past would cast light on unconscious structures which persist into the present: "It is at this moment that the historian takes upon himself the task of dream interpretation."[34] Through a dialectical *presentation* of the past, the historical materialist would seek to shake the slumbering body of the present, to awaken it from its fetishistic dream-reality.[35]

The "illumination" of the collective subject's fantastic investment in such objects took place in the very site of their destitution, as one would find on revisiting "the first factory buildings, the earliest photos, the objects that have begun to be extinct."[36] Alert to the historical power of such insights, Taussig has offered a strikingly contemporary—yet displaced—site for such "profane illumination." Taussig finds his anthropological *trouvé* in "the 1930s and 1940s cars, the 1950s telephone systems, the prewar Singer sewing machines, the mechanical typewriters" that one now encounters in "Third World" travels.[37] Such contemporary commodity encounters spark magic from their siting in "underdeveloped" countries; "defined in advance as backward and always lagging behind," such places are "exemplary of the recently outdated."[38] Here one witnesses not simply the disrupture of the commodity's presence but the staging of its ever-present primitivity, its fetishistic nature in the Other who holds the West's recent past in his or her living hands. The evolutionary discourse which garbage itself speaks provides the temporal registers through which revolutionary potential sparks.

Both Benjamin and Taussig make clear, however, that this "profane illumination" is only potentially revolutionary. Unless harnessed to a dialectical project which aims to "win the energies of intoxication for the revolution," this *objet trouvé* illumination is more of a "trick than a method."[39] Such undialectical trickery is nowhere more apparent than in the travel anecdote *topoi* of the present, through which northern travelers to countries like Chile and Argentina ("defined in advance as backward") try to harness the "atmosphere" of Third World obsolescence. The anecdotes they coin, whether in half-hearted travelogues or in cynical Benetton catalogues, invoke that developmental schema to recapitulate the West's erstwhile commodity enchantment through its tricklike discovery in the past-as-present eyes of the enchanted Other. The dialectical potential of such a future perfect perspective is apparent here, as the historian as dream interpreter seeks, with an anguished flapping of wings, to awaken the present to an understanding of the fetishistic forms which structure its everyday movements.

To redeem such dreams from the anecdotal trash pile would be the task of any serious salvage ethnography. Yet this is where I still come against a certain earnestness in Benjamin's ideas. Does not this understanding of "destitution" and recapitulated desire presuppose an originary moment of presence during which one truly found one's face—"This Space for Rent"—in the billboard, magic soap, and jeans commercial, from which one could then be awakened? The preceding two chapters have focused on the always already disbelieving subject such objects seem, at the very height of their fashion, to leave so unimpressed. The "rhetoric of presence" accorded the fundamentally unbelievable discourses of consumerism has here been repeatedly found in the mouth of a dummy primitive subject. This all-believing Other has always seemed to exist somewhere else, where the people are more backward and naïve, or at some other time, when they truly did believe—a time and a place like Tierra del Fuego.

Even there, the attempt to find such naïve subjects seems forced. The Philco Time Capsule turns the Tierra del Fuegians of the present into the sort of primitive people whose things are direct conduits of their desire, but only by anamorphotically flattening them into the past, denying them the fleshed-out ambivalence of the present. If the time capsule is the repository of the present's dream about itself, its most dreamlike quality would be the fact that its trivial and ridiculous status causes people not merely to ignore it but even to stamp their seal of indifference on it. I disown my dreams, which is why I cannot be awakened from them. Benjamin has actually characterized such a self-possessed state in his description of *Jugendstil:* "the dream that one is awake."[40] But what of the dummy subject who dreams in the space of your disbelief? Could this be the dream that you are awake and that someone else is dreaming in your stead?

Indeed, one of the central tenets of Freudian dream interpretation states that, in dreams, the neurotic frequently projects his or her "sick personality" onto someone else.[41]

Monolithic Theory

In an attempt to convey the size and elevations of the monumental Fresh Kills rubbish dump on Staten Island, the aptly entitled best-seller *Rubbish! The Archaeology of Garbage: What Our Garbage Tells Us about Ourselves* features a comparative scale model of the Pyramid of the Sun at Teotihuacán.[42] I can think of no better illustration of the way garbage reopens the monumental metanarratives of the past.[43]

If this illustration is merely a joke (on a weak connotative level at that), its very offhandedness necessitates that the salvage ethnographer take it seriously. In like manner, I think we should read quite seriously John Kenneth Galbraith's joking claim that the reason Karl Marx had such a limited reception in the United States was the confusion his name caused for people more used to the Marx brothers.[44] For all the silliness of this idea, there is a strange cogency to their being grouped under the same name, as is apparent from the way the Marxist among them characterizes the commodity form of social organization: "When I say that coats or boots or what not are related to linen as the general embodiment of abstract human labor the statement seems manifestly absurd."[45] Yet, he continues, "it is precisely in this absurd form" that social relations are mediated under capital.[46]

Doubtless for this reason, Benjamin could describe the "moment of waking" from the commodity dreams of the past as the moment "in which things put on their true—surrealistic—face."[47] Both Freud and Marx, for all their irredeemably nineteenth-century attitudes, seem in some way resuscitated through such "trash of history" (and anthropology).[48] It is as if a little bit of rubbish—a bad joke—followed far enough can, like a surreal Möbius strip, suddenly open out into one of these out-of-date monoliths.

Outlook on the Future

Lucas Bridges's anecdote—the Selk'nam's testimonial to the "wonder worker" powers of Pears' Soap—offers another throwaway opportunity for dialectical redemption. It comes from the most famous text on Tierra del Fuego, the auto-biography which Bridges wrote in the late forties and entitled *Uttermost Part of the Earth: Indians of Tierra del Fuego.*[49]

Born in Ushuaia in 1874, this "legendary *indio blanco*" (white Indian) grew up among the Yámana Indians on his father's Anglican mission, playing with them and becoming fluent in Yámana, English, and eventually Selk'nam and Spanish too.[50] His story is all about managing such diverse codes and orders of representation in order to maintain the sheep farming project that his father's mission became. In managing his family's finances, Bridges, unlike so many whites around him, sought to maintain his humanity too. The colonist is famous today for the refuge, work, and succor he provided the Selk'nam throughout the genocidal period of colonization which, beginning in the 1880s, lasted well into the first decade of the twentieth century.

If Bridges's assistance necessarily occurred on the properties he and his family had carved from indigenous land in the first place, the complex quality of his empathy is apparent in the following passage from his autobiography. He and the Selk'nam Talimeoat stand on Mount Spion Kop and, back in 1901, gaze off into the colonial future. "'*Yak haruin*' ("My country")," Talimeoat says with a sigh, leading Bridges to the following future perfect reflection: "That sigh followed by those gentle words, so unusual for one of his kind—was it caused by a vision of the not far distant future, when the Indian hunter would roam his quiet woods no more; when the light wraith from his camp fire would give place to the smoke from the saw-mills; when throbbing engines and hooting sirens would shatter forever the age-old silence?"[51] "Powerless to stop the inevitable encroachment of civilization," but "determined to do my utmost to soften the blow of it," Bridges should be respected for these albeit doomed efforts.[52]

Bearing down from that future, I, on the other hand, am going to flatten Bridges to the page. I will treat this "magic soap" anecdote, torn from its humane context, as a time capsule buried in the late nineteenth century and suddenly subjected to the unforgiving gaze of the past's future. In this contained space I am going to take Bridges's text and hold him rigorously to his words, denying him all the distance, understanding, and irony one allows one's friends in the present.

To treat his text in such a one-dimensional manner is perhaps simply to turn on its hagiographic head the lifeless portrait of the *indio blanco* which you see in the tacky tourist venture now run from his old *estancia* at Haberton. But, instead of demonizing the colonist, attacking the imperial discourse he obviously at times expresses, the words to which I wish to hold Bridges are his jokes. This is the point at which those dead monuments of high theory might come back to life, as I focus on the things Bridges clearly regarded as trash even back then, at the beginning of mass world consumerism. I may seem to be turning my own argument on its head here, for it was just such archaeological violence—*holding people to their words*—which I rejected in the previous chapter and, indeed, analogized to the crassest of travel anecdotes. Yet there is method here. To force the defenseless Bridges to wear his rubbish should force me, in turn, to open out the monumental implications of my suspicion that the words to which I hold the Other, in such scenarios, are really my own words, even though I have always already disowned them.

Notes

1. Walter Benjamin, "Surrealism," in *Reflections,* 182.
2. Musil, *Posthumous Papers of a Living Author,* 61–64. The title of Musil's book manifests the future perfect perspective I am grappling with here.

3. Taussig, "On Desecration."

4. Walter Benjamin, "Theses on the Philosophy of History," in *Illuminations,* 248.

5. Ibid., 249.

6. Ibid.

7. Ibid., 254.

8. Orlan, cited in Adams, *Orlan,* 89. For a discussion of anamorphosis, see Lacan, *Four Fundamentals,* 67–119, esp. 85–97. For a succinct, if reductive, commentary, see Jay, *Downcast Eyes,* 357–70. Lacan invoked the future perfect to describe the constellation of prospective and retrospective temporalities within the expressions of the unconscious. My usage here, *mutatis mutandis,* is not dissimilar. On Lacan and his debt, in this regard, to Heidegger, see Bowie, "Psychoanalysis and the Future of Theory."

9. Marx, *Communist Manifesto,* 36.

10. Ibid., 36.

11. Taylor, "Outlaw State," 285.

12. For the fullest exposition of this project, see Buck-Morss, *Dialectics of Seeing.*

13. See also Taussig, *Mimesis and Alterity,* 232–33.

14. *The Concise Oxford Dictionary of Quotations* (London: Oxford University Press, 1964), 87.

15. Chatwin, *In Patagonia,* 30.

16. Marx, *Capital,* xlix, which continues: "A country in which industrial development is more advanced than others, simply presents those others with a picture of their own future." For a brief critique of such notions, focusing upon the infantilization of Indian civilization within this progressivist schema, see Nandy, *Intimate Enemy,* 11–18. A pertinent, albeit only partial corrective to such cogent criticisms can be found in Balibar's *The Philosophy of Marx,* 80–112, and, indeed, as Balibar points out, in Marx's own final writings on Russia. Claude Lefort claims that the homogenizing and retrospective category of "pre-capitalist" is actually innate to the thought-forms of capital itself ("Marx," 139–80). The moment debate is shifted away from the social Darwinism Marx at times articulated to the discourses he diagnosed as innate to capital itself, critiques like Nandy's seem more and more misplaced.

17. Taussig, *Mimesis and Alterity,* 232–33.

18. I take this term from Fabian, *Time and the Other.*

19. Ibid., 39.

20. For an overview of the biological context and some of its extrapolations and effects, see any of the many writings by Stephen Jay Gould on the subject, e.g., *The Mismeasure of Man,* 113–22.

21. Freud, *Jokes;* Freud, *Totem and Taboo.*

22. Fabian, *Time and the Other,* 19.

23. Ibid.

24. Ibid., 6.

25. For all the racism of his biologization of Fuegian social organization, Darwin can-

not be blamed for *initiating* this trend. James Cook, for instance, also claimed, "Of all the Nations that I have seen," the Fuegians "were certainly the most wretched" (*Voyage of the Resolution,* 600). Yet for Cook, Fuegian wretchedness is *not* indexed to an evolutionary schema wherein it could be read as the recapitulation of his culture's own prehistory. A certain schematism is apparent in the work of Johann Reinhold Forster, who traveled with Cook and claimed, "I believe the nations inhabiting the frozen extremities of our globe to be degenerated and debased from that original happiness, which the tropical nations more or less enjoy" (*Observations Made,* 192). This notion of backward-sliding degeneration is still worlds away, however, from Darwin's evolutionary schema.

26. Lothrop, *Indians of Tierra del Fuego,* 204.

27. Ibid., 16.

28. Frazer, "Introduction," 1.

29. Marrett, "Memoir," 45.

30. Benjamin, "Surrealism," 182.

31. Ibid., 181–82.

32. For this brief exposition I am indebted to Buck-Morss's *Dialectics of Seeing* and also to "City as Dreamworld and Catastrophe," 3–26.

33. Buck-Morss, "City as Dreamworld," 6.

34. Benjamin quoted in ibid.

35. I am borrowing Benjamin's "body politic" metaphors here. For the originals, see Buck-Morss, *Dialectics of Seeing,* 272.

36. Benjamin, cited in Taussig, *Mimesis and Alterity,* 231.

37. Taussig, *Mimesis and Alterity,* 232. As will be apparent, this insight has had a large influence on this book.

38. Ibid.

39. Benjamin, "Surrealism," 182, 189.

40. Benjamin quoted in Buck-Morss, *Dialectics of Seeing,* 272.

41. Freud, *Interpretation of Dreams,* 410.

42. Rathje and Murphy, *Rubbish!* 5.

43. Actually the following passage comes close. Describing their initial forays into the field in Tucson, Arizona, Rathje and Murphy write, "The garbage itself was an unknown world—everything learned about it was new—and thus held the fascination that a trip up the Congo in the nineteenth century would have"(*Rubbish!* 59).

44. Galbraith, *History of Economics,* 240.

45. Marx, *Capital,* 49.

46. Ibid. I can imagine Louis Althusser being interpelated by Groucho, that other Marxist. Althusser: "Knock! Knock!" Groucho (opening door): "You look like Louis Althusser." Althusser: "But I am Louis Althusser." Groucho: "No wonder, then, that you resemble him so much!" Apologies for the above to Zizek, who quotes the original Marx brothers' joke in "How the Non-Duped Err," 85.

47. Benjamin, "Konvolut N," 9.

48. Ibid., 5.

49. E. Lucas Bridges, *Uttermost Part,* 219–20.

50. Ibid., 5. The quote is actually from the English Adventurer A. F. Tschiffley, whose (unsolicited?) testimonial to Bridges forms the preface of the volume.

51. E. Lucas Bridges, *Uttermost Part,* 336–37.

52. Ibid., 337.

4

A Time Capsule

Containing an Unsolicited Testimonial to Future Generations

Growing up as the "third white native" of Tierra del Fuego, Lucas Bridges passed an idyllic childhood on his father's mission at Ushuaia.[1] The idyll was cruelly interrupted in the mid-1880s when an epidemic suddenly broke out among the Yámana. Inadvertently brought by a visiting ship, the disease wiped out, almost in entirety, the mission's nonwhite native population. In the wake of this tragedy Thomas Bridges renounced the mission and moved his family to the private property he obtained at Haberton, on the south coast. Shortly thereafter he died too.

Now, in the early 1890s, Lucas Bridges must awaken from his enchanted childhood and take up the colonial mantle. The decade into which he comes of age is rent with racial violence. Having settled the northern part of the island, the *estancioneros* are now moving into the lands of the interior-dwelling Selk'nam. Progressively dispossessed, if not murdered in the process, the Selk'nam are continuously pushed south. In this suspicion-laden environment, full of projection and counterprojection, Lucas and his brothers are initiating relations with the Selk'nam, learning their language, and so once more playing out the theater of first contact. At this point I want to interrupt Bridges's narrative and focus on one bad joke. For it is at this moment that the miracle of Pears' Soap occurs.

The "white man's magic" leads a naïve Selk'nam to give an "unsolicited testimonial" to the fantastic power of the civilized commodity: Pears' Soap has the power to make his child an *indio blanco* too.[2] This miracle, Bridges implies, is little more than a sleight of hand on the part of the Selk'nam's less than naïve wife. Yet the colonist, ever his father's son, wishes to uphold the marriage sacrament. He sees no alternative but to play along with the wife's deceit. So Bridges tells the *indio* that his child has indeed been washed white by the "magic soap": "The proud father was so impressed by these wonders that he came seeking another cake of soap. Suspecting that he wanted to try its effects on himself and might be foolish enough to doubt his wife's story if the experiment failed, I hastened to tell him that the particular cake of soap given to his wife by my sister must have possessed some special virtue not to be found in any other tablet. He went away disappointed, but satisfied."[3] There is clearly a deep reserve of missionary motives inspiring the colonist's irony, dissimulation, and disbelief. Only through such ulterior motives—for the sake of the deluded Other—could Bridges be inspired *to pay lip-service* to a miraculous power in which he has no actual faith.[4]

It is precisely such pretextual grounding which I want to erase in this past encapsulation of the colonist's words. Rather than let Bridges fetishize his cake and disbelieve in it too, the time capsule's future perfect perspective must flatten out all such maneuvering between the self and the language it speaks. Bridges's nuanced text will here be reduced to his proposal to facilitate an "unsolicited testimonial" to the fetishistic power of his own culture's magic. I am going to hold Bridges to his suggestion that a "photograph of the happy trio" be taken and sent to Pears to complement its advertising campaigns.

To concentrate on the casting—however joking, half-hearted, or disowned— of a pair of the "world's most primitive inhabitants" within this advertisement opens up a rather strange question.[5] Why would a backward, deluded Indian be set up to witness the power of the civilized commodity?

The question is even more significant if one recalls that the name Pears had, by the early 1890s, become almost a metonym for advertising itself, much like Coca-Cola, McDonald's, or, indeed, Benetton is today. An early pioneer in advertising, Pears received enormous "name recognition" among English speakers for its widespread newspaper advertisements, which featured "testimonials" from famous people. In this respect, the Selk'nam's "unsolicited testimonial" accords with that of other witnesses to the holy power within this commodity. At the other end of the earth, some years previously, Henry Ward Beecher had testified in the company's newspaper advertisements that "if cleanliness is next to Godliness, soap must be considered a means of Grace."[6] Pears merges with Bridges here, both pioneers in soliciting such testimonies, while their informants' heartfelt words enshrine the otherwise disenchanted product of capitalist industry with divine power. The analogy between Beecher's article of faith and the Selk'nam's fetishistic fantasy in fact intensifies the question. Why is such religious testimony invoked in preference to any scientific proof or academic authentication? Why does the massively successful formula for selling the latest consumer commodities in the most civilized countries seem so primitive that a Selk'nam Indian can find his way into it?[7] What does it mean to take Bridges's bad joke seriously?

Marx and Taussig on the Turn

The fact that an ultraprimitive Selk'nam Indian is presented in this throwaway anecdote as a natural witness to the divine power of the Western industrial product plunges me straight into what Karl Marx termed "the mystery of the fetishistic character of the commodity."[8] At issue here is the status of the anthropological "turn" Marx executed at the end of the first chapter of *Capital*, in which he attacked the bourgeois economists for their naturalization of the commodity form. "All the mystery of the world of commodities, all the sorcery, all the fetishistic charm which enwraps as with a fog the labor products of commodity production is instantly dispelled when we turn to consider other methods of production."[9] Through such a strategy, Marx sought to make the historical specificity of this supposedly "universally valid" mode of production palpable.[10]

Taussig quotes this same passage to explain his turn to consider how peasants undergoing rapid proletarianization in Columbian sugar plantations and Bolivian tin mines comprehend encroaching market realities.[11] For these people, whose world, in the 1970s, is not yet "market organized," but rather "market dominated," their labor relations appear fundamentally unnatural, alien, and even evil. To these peasants, the sugarcane of the plantations becomes "the terrible Green monster," "the Great Cane," the "God of the landlords," an animated being that is said to slowly devour the men who bring it to life.[12] They patently fetishize those very forces which we unconsciously fetishize, revealing the subordination of people to things, which to us is so naturalized as to be either invisible or, if noted, regarded as "universally valid" and morally neutral.

The anthropological turn Taussig executes here is not Marx's. The latter clearly had no wish to consult medieval peasants—or, for that matter, nineteenth-century South Americans—for their opinions on Western commodities. His turn was intended to illustrate the overt manner in which relations of social domination occur in other systems of production. Such an illustration would serve, in contrast, to show up the nonuniversal nature of bourgeois domination by commodity. Taussig's aim, in representing a precapitalist fetish of *our* things, is hence the same as Marx's: the defetishization of bourgeois social relations. The patent Indian fetishism of the capitalist plantation product as evil, barren, and sterile is represented in his text in the aim of revealing and even dispelling the latent fetishism of things within the Western world of commodities.

Yet this strategy—the representation of their fetish of us and our things—is far from necessarily critical or, for that matter, defetishizing. It is a classic ploy of advertising, as much as a favored site for the colonial travelogue.[13] Bridges adopts a parallel tactic to advertise, in all anecdotal levity, the fetish power which his cake of soap has in primitive eyes. The turn that both Taussig and Bridges engage unites them to the extent that they tap a certain power, one critical, the other anecdotal, in their representations of such fetishistic indigenous representations of the power of the capitalist commodity. Indeed, the "terrible green monster" and Pears' magic soap could well be different sides of the same coin, one face diabolical, the other divine.

Taussig says as much himself in his later work *Mimesis and Alterity* when he turns to discuss the Third World *objet trouvé*. In such situations, the "turn" to other methods of production, like the surrealist "trick," may lead to situations wherein "the magic and necromancy of the commodity is not so much dissipated as fortified."[14] *The Devil and Commodity Fetishism* is perhaps best read as an attempt to wield, much more than dissipate, the power its author finds in the eyes of the Other. These travel anecdotes and advertisements, on the other hand, seem simply to observe, enshrine—yet not take on—"the mystery of the world of commodities."[15]

What Mystery?

But what mystery can one discern behind such potentially defetishizing anecdotes as Bridges's magic soap, here still on the level of a "trick"? Clearly such anecdotes reflect more than simply the whimsical humor of one Lucas Bridges; examples abound of the way the "world's most primitive" inhabitants are seen to fetishize the "white man's magic." Captain James Fitzroy, Bridges's predecessor in this field, could even generalize that there is "something absorbing in observing people displaying childish ignorance of things familiar to civilized man."[16] What, then, is the so-absorbing primitivist magic that such anecdotes conjure up, revel in, and fail to dispel?

The attempt to unleash the spirit driving these things will take me further into Marx's formulations in the first chapter of *Capital*.[17] The mystery, for Marx, lies in the fact that within a capitalist society social mediation loses its human face and becomes a function of the exchange of commodities.

The participants in such exchanges are, of course, simply seeking to obtain the other's commodity for their own particular—indeed, heterogeneous—uses and purposes. Yet such *use-values,* by very reason of their heterogeneity, are incapable of providing the means of commensuration necessary to facilitate exchange. It is only when each item of exchange can be taken as the objectal embodiment of so much commensurable *exchange value* that the correlation of "coats or boots or what not" as so many identical units of each other (e.g., two coats = twenty cakes of Pears' Soap = three and a half boots) can at all occur. As the "general equivalent," money seems to perform this quantifying function all on its own, at a remove from commodities.[18] Yet in doing so, it is simply a stand-in for the principle of equivalence which effectively pertains to each and every commodity (two coats = twenty cakes of Pears' Soap = three and a half boots = two dollars). The unit of equivalence is, as the bourgeois economists discovered, "abstract human labor."[19]

Commodities, then, have a twofold character, as "transcendental or social things, which are at the same time perceptible by our senses."[20] We exchange objects "perceptible by our senses" to obtain our own specific uses. Yet the secondary layer of that process lies in the "transcendental" way in which the commodities simultaneously "confront each other" and render each other commensurable as abstract stores of value.[21] Value measures the amount of labor time "socially necessary" under current social and technological conditions for the manufacture of any given commodity.[22] Not that this is immediately apparent. "When I say that coats or boots or what not are related to linen as the general equivalent of abstract human labor, the statement seems manifestly absurd."[23] Yet, "it is precisely in this absurd form" that labor relations occur under capital.

In describing this social confrontation of things (twenty cakes of soap = three and a half boots) taking place over and above the meeting of their makers, Marx presents the scenario whereby "a social relation between human beings" is enshrouded with "the semblance of a relation between things."[24] "Things . . . control them, instead of being controlled by them," for it is value itself, as "transcendental" soul to the commodity's palpable body, which ultimately mediates the labor product, regardless of the use to which those human beings might wish to put it.[25] This system of social mediation, for all its modernity, partakes of "theological subtleties" more akin to the "nebulous world of religion," a world in which "the products of the human mind become independent shapes, endowed with lives of their own and able to enter into relations with men and women. The products of the human hand do the same thing in the world of commodities."[26] This secular fetishism is of the hand, not the head; it pertains not to the beliefs of the individual, but rather to the beliefs implicit in his or her actions. No one, in the act of exchange, imagines that they are thereby abstracting and equating human labor and, furthermore, treating it as the spiritual substance of the object in question. This is precisely Marx's point: "They do not know that they are doing this, but they do it."[27] As Alfred Sohn-Rethel puts it: "In commodity exchange, the action and the consciousness of people go separate ways. Only the action is abstract; the consciousness of the actors is not."[28] This "unconscious" fetishism acts, Slavoj Zizek adds, on the level of an "as if" postulate.[29] In capitalist societies we act *as if* we believed that social relations were subordinate to the "transcendental" interactions of our commodities, *as if* it truly were those things which control us, not vice versa.

A Solicited Testimonial — Native Reticence

Marx's argument takes a further step at this point, as he considers the bourgeois economists who have gone so far as to translate the metanarratival abstractions of such unconscious fetishism into postulates of science. For having discovered the determination of the magnitude of value in abstract labor, they proceed to regard "as universally valid" this "truth which is in fact true only for one particular form of production."[30] There are, then, two forms of fetishism here, both sides of the same coin: an unconscious *as if* postulate pertaining to one's acts and also an intellectual manifestation of this material fantasy, the uncritical translation of the forms of this "real abstraction" into the epistemological figures of bourgeois science.[31]

In according fully fetishized powers to Pears' magic soap, the native informant whom Bridges presents clearly fits into neither of these categories. In his patent faith in the Western thing he is neither *unthinkingly* fetishizing this commodity (acting through his exchanges *as if* he fetishized it) nor *intellectually* universalizing the historically specific category of value. The Selk'nam's blatantly primitivist advertisement of the "white man's magic" has no place in Marx's argument—unless in the articulation of the anthropological "turn" I mentioned above. If I am to follow Marx in my attempt to unravel the significance of this offhand anecdote, I need to find a link between the Taussigian turn, in the service of critique, and Bridges's seemingly tireless capacity, in the service of anecdote, to find the fetish in primitive eyes. For what becomes apparent, the more one holds Bridges to his offhand anecdotes, is the relentlessness with which he manages to find further instances of native naïveté in the face of the Western thing.

As with the mystery of the cake of soap, such scenarios are always explained away by the exigencies of cross-cultural interaction, the demands of the present moment. A future perfect perspective must necessarily flatten out such self-distance to find the repetition structuring its particular pretexts and evasions. Take another example: the miracle of modern science which Bridges performs in 1900, a few years after the advent of magic soap on Fuegian shores.[32] The Selk'nam have just treated Bridges to a display of their shamanistic powers. Now the colonist, in response, sets up a "magic lantern" (i.e., a slide projector). The projection of a

picture of Bluebeard terrifies the Selk'nam and many try to flee. Bridges's attempts
to persuade these "proven warriors" that the picture is not real fail, for "Unfortunately the Ona [Selk'nam] word for 'picture' or 'shadow' was the name of one
of their ghosts, so the assurance that this was only a picture would have been no
better than telling a frightened child that it was only a bogey-man."[33] Bridges is
forced to put the projector into the only—fetishistic—language that the Selk'nam
can understand. His unenchanted words (*magic lantern* among them) are perforce made magical by their translation into the idiom of a "frightened child."
Indeed, the way Bridges's wares are forced to find their Fuegian equivalence in
the body of the Other's magic is a persistent theme in his pages. It is as if the
disenchanting narrative of modern rationalization is being run in reverse here,
in these first-contact commodity encounters at the Uttermost Part of the Earth.[34]
Not that the colonist claims any investment in this. In such situations Bridges is
merely—a fact he ever stresses—reporting to us the Other's fetishistic response
to his everyday objects.

Yet the colonist himself lays out the material a salvage ethnography can seize
upon to pull his disbelief out from under him. After all, it was Bridges who solicited the Other's magic in the first place. A few pages prior to this shamanistic
display: "I told Houshken that I had heard of his great powers and would like to
see some of his magic. In order to impress him, I told him we would show them
some white man's magic in return."[35] Bridges cites motives of defense in setting
up this magical exchange, a need to mystify the natives with an impression of
white power. Yet there seems something strangely desirous in all this: "Houshken did not refuse my request, but answered modestly that he was disinclined,
the Ona [Selk'nam] way of saying that he might do it by and by."[36]

Some may accept Bridges's claim that he was acting out of strategical reasons
and buy into his anthropology of Selk'nam reticence. Yet there are numerous other
such scenes within his book and the literature of his contemporaries that reveal
not simply a Western delight in witnessing the indigenous witnessing of Western magic but even an outright demand for such scenarios. Such desire is nowhere more apparent than in the breach. Samuel Lothrop, for instance, an ethnographer and erstwhile guest of the Bridges family, mentions that travelers have
often been confounded by "the indifference of the natives to the wonders of European civilization."[37] Clearly their expectation was quite the reverse. As a pre-
lude to introducing the miracle of the cake of soap, Bridges himself writes of the
Fuegians' "apparent ingratitude" when given Western things.[38] Both writers proceed to state that this indifference is actually only an effect of "native reticence"—
the silence of an excess of awe, which mutely attests to the Fuegians' belief in the
sacral qualities of the secular thing. Yet isn't there something excessive in this very

reading of indigenous indifference? Both writers seem to want not only to find the unsolicited testimonial in whatever way possible but also to erase their own desire to solicit it.

The Object You Have Found Is Not the *Objet Trouvé*

What seems apparent is that the colonist, in holding these Selk'nam to their words—or rather their (i.e., his) translations of his words—is really holding them to his own words. It is he who wants them to fetishize his things. This projection is intricately woven into the evolutionary scale which makes the Indians primitive and childlike in the face of the paternalistic future he brings to their lands. Infantilized in this manner, the Selk'nam are perfectly poised to recapitulate, in *objet trouvé* anecdotes about "magic lanterns," the awe and mystery with which their white interlocutor might once have regarded such objects of the everyday.

The example Taussig uses for his Third World reworking of Benjamin's "profane illumination" is very similar: Nanook of the North, the "world's most primitive inhabitant" at the other end of the world, whose fantastic response to Robert J. Flaherty's phonograph has been cause for the white man's anecdotal wonder ever since.[39] The history of the "optical unconscious" of Western modernity in *Mimesis and Alterity* presents many such parallels to my antipodean encounter with what Zizek has termed the "unconscious of the commodity form."[40] Yet Taussig is not—quite—talking of commodity fetishism.[41] His argument deals with the physicality of mimesis, which, repressed by modernity, reappears in the colonial "organization of mimesis" that projects such repressed sensuality onto the body of the primitive. Hence the so-common primitivist conclusion that, in Bridges's words, "Natives are often good mimics."[42]

In the twentieth century, Taussig continues, the machinery of mechanical reproduction serves to open up a new "optical unconscious." Yet by intimating that primitivist mimetic capacity, such novel technology appears strikingly primitive itself. These two projective primitivisms run into each other in those first-contact colonial vignettes in which natives appear amazed at the "white man's magic" embodied in technology such as the phonograph. In such scenarios, pioneers like Bridges and Flaherty appear "masters of these wonders, that, after the first shock waves of surprise upon their invention and commercialization in the West, pass into the everyday. Yet these shocks rightly live on in the mysterious underbelly of the technology—to be eviscerated as 'magic' in frontier rituals of technological supremacy."[43] The profane illumination of such *objet trouvé* situations derives from the shock of the new they once elicited. Through the primitive present of the Other, these anecdotes recapitulate the magical primitivism of the technology's initial Western presence.

The problem I have with this argument is once more the presupposition that objects such as the phonograph really did initially occasion the sort of shock and surprise that is then recapitulated in Third World commodity encounters. It strikes me that the "magic lantern," for instance, has always been surrounded with quotation marks. Even if such inventions did once inspire awe, stagy testimonials to items like Pears' magic soap were clearly *never* meant to elicit belief, awe, or wonder. Such commodities have always already been redolent of the "destitution" which for Benjamin held such revolutionary promise. While this begins to veer from the terrain of Taussig's argument, it does raise a striking question. Why would Bridges, through the naïve testimonial he solicits from these representatives of the early infancy of his own culture, seek to recapitulate the fetishistic faith that was never his to begin with? (For, in fact, Bridges is not holding these Indians to his own words at all.)

The Critique of False Consciousness

The fact that, for Bridges, the fetish is never felt on any conscious level draws me further into Marx and into the Benjamin who conjured up the following: "The XIX Century: a time space [*Zeitraum*] (time dream [*Zeit-traum*]) in which individual consciousness maintains itself ever more reflectively, whereas in contrast the collective consciousness sinks into ever deeper sleep. . . . This is what we have to pursue, in order to interpret the nineteenth century in fashion and advertisement, building and politics, as the consequence of [the collective's] dream countenance."[44] In the collective but individually disowned "time-dream" one can finally find the fetish impelling Bridges, who in the "time-space" of his own conscious perception has absolutely no faith in it.

The collective "time dream [*Zeit-traum*]" exists as a separate world within the very confines of the "time space [*Zeitraum*]" of the individual's everyday existence. I propose to read this dialectical doubling of the self-same reality as an illustration of the split between the unconscious discourse of one's hand—the "time dream" implicit in one's actions—and the conscious discourse of one's head.[45] In this I am returning to Sohn-Rethel's postulate of a separation between action and consciousness in exchange.[46] Through Sohn-Rethel, Zizek has attempted to disinter such a privately disowned, publicly enacted "dream countenance" to argue that "belief, far from being a purely mental state, is always *materialized* in our effective social activity."[47] This is certainly the case under capital, in which the fetishistic "fantasy which regulates social reality" is a material discourse latent in our actions, not our minds.[48] It is here, in the transindividual realm of the Benjaminian "time dream," that one discovers the "unconscious of the commodity form."

Bridges need have no conscious faith in the fetishistic manner in which he, as colonial capitalist (and predecessor to the Benetton farmers now working the same region) equates sheep, labor, and other commodities to further his family's finances. His actions do it for him. Regardless of the disbelief he expresses in his accounts of native fetishism, he, in his unthinking actions as an agent of capital, has already treated these "palpable" things as "transcendental" indexes of "abstract human labor." Hence he affirms, however unwittingly, Sohn-Rethel's startling interrogation of the abstraction enacted in the exchange of commodities: "Can there be abstraction other than by thought?"[49]

The commodity, Sohn-Rethel argues, is an "abstract *thing,*" even though this "is a contradiction in terms."[50] Through such a contradiction-in-terms Sohn-Rethel takes issue with Althusser's insistence that the production of consciousness takes place only within thought.[51] Within the very act of exchange are philosophical postulates completely removed from any state of consciousness. During the moment of exchange, for instance, we act as if the material status of the commodity remains unchanged. This invisible postulate of a separation of the sphere of exchange from that of use creates a set of further philosophical postulates as to the unity and commensurability of matter in abstract time and space. The atomicity of matter, its separation into substance and accident, the notion of abstract movement, and even the idea of strict causality can all be read into the "real abstraction" enacted within the exchange of commodities.

Nor do these thoughtless abstractions simply remain hanging in the air. Sohn-Rethel proceeds to argue that they provide the pre-thought form to the abstract figures of bourgeois epistemology. The structures through which the idea of evolution makes sense—the "homogenous empty time" and space into which Tierra del Fuego was plotted—arise from their prior hypostatization within the act of exchange.[52] Through such a reading of the "real abstraction" and the scientific categorization he sees as its manifestation, Sohn-Rethel stages a strikingly radical return to Marx and his historical materialist method. In the classic formulation of *The Eighteenth Brumaire of Louis Napoleon:* "It is not the consciousness of men that determines their social being, but, on the contrary, their social being that determines their consciousness."[53] So Sohn-Rethel turns to the Kantian critique of empiricism, which led the latter to locate the categories cast up by Newtonian science in an a priori realm of pure understanding. Sohn-Rethel grounds Kant's argument—while simultaneously unsettling it—by articulating a historical dynamic in which apriorism figures as a misrecognition of the "second nature" implicit in the commodity form. In according such provenance, neither empiricist, idealist, nor apriorist, to the "laws of nature," Sohn-Rethel proceeds to define science as the "self-encounter of nature blindly occurring in man's mind."[54]

It is worth reiterating the dialectical and materialist nature of this argument. There is nothing post-structuralist in this fundamentally uncanny image of nature's blind self-encounter, a simultaneous act of recognition and misrecognition that is *both true and false at the same time*. Compare those critiques of universalizing "truth claims" which so ceaselessly expose the inadequacy of *any* scientific discourse's claim to truth. It is not merely that such a skeptical self-consciousness misrecognizes the universalism of its own utterance (as Hegel put it, "it proclaims an absolute vanishing, but the pronouncement *is,* and this consciousness is the vanishing that is pronounced").[55] Even if it could vanish from its own utterance, such a critique would misrecognize the *social* truth of Newtonian science, its imbrication in the "real abstraction" of commodity exchange. To attack its epistemological adequacy, and yet leave its commodity origin intact, is to fail to critique it. As Dipesh Chakrabarty writes, commenting on the post-structuralist persistence of the (recapitulationist) master narrative that is History, "Analysis does not make it go away."[56]

Could Sohn-Rethel's definition of science be valid for anthropology too? If so, it provides a way to reread the mired anthropological concept of fetishism itself. The primitivist concept of fetishism from which Marx drew was derived from Charles De Brosses's highly dubious geographical and temporal universalization of what he saw in the eighteenth century as a manner of thinking "that has none other than a common base, and that is no more than the accessory of a general religion diffused through the most distant parts of the Earth."[57] It is not surprising that Jean Baudrillard takes issue with the "moral and rationalistic" connotations of this "great fetishist metaphor," attacking the presupposition he sees in it of a nonalienated truth of the object (his understanding of Marx's category of "use-value").[58] For Baudrillard, the term *fetishism* should be used in its Freudian sense to indicate the pursuit of that mythical object which promises to suture the lack in the subject.[59] This mythical object might well be use-value itself, or, his analysis continues, here approximating my Benetton catalogue, the consumer commodity we all apparently seek so religiously.

Yet for all their falsity, the distinctions between essence and appearance, use-value and value, particular and universal are written into the very practice of exchange itself. They are *both true and false at the same time*. It is Baudrillard himself who, in his own words, falls into the "subtle trap of a rationalistic anthropology."[60] There is little difference between his critique of the notion's essentialist presuppositions and Bridges's patent disbelief in a magic power he knows cannot be true. As Zizek makes clear, both have missed the point: "The illusion is not on the side of knowledge, it is already on the side of reality itself, of what people are doing."[61] On any conscious level the fetish is fundamentally false—yet such a finding is itself false the moment one's attention turns to the discourse of people's actions, wherein the fetish finds its truth. The Lacanian phrase puts the matter succinctly: "The real fools are those who are not fooled."[62]

A Marxian Slip

Commodity fetishism has nothing to do with false consciousness, unless one uses that term to mean that any consciousness is necessarily false in its comprehension of a fetish which is, by definition, not a matter of consciousness. This still leaves open the question of Bridges's desire to find his fetish (which is not his fetish) in the Fuegian primitive. Zizek's reading of Marx and Sohn-Rethel, which I have largely followed to this point, leads me—turning the tables on Zizek himself—to the argument that will answer this inquiry.

Zizek invokes Sohn-Rethel to complexify Sloterdijk's characterization of the cynical present. For, far from representing any "end of history," such a split between acting and thinking has always been innate to the social reality constituted by capital.[63] It is not simply, Zizek proceeds, that under capital our thoughts run at a remove from our actions. In the act of exchange—when commodity A ("coats or boots or what not") finds, like a good Hegelian subject, its value and measure of equivalence in the body of commodity B—we humans effectively think through the commodity, delegating our intersubjective dialectic to the Other embodied therein. That is to say, in Zizek's words and italics, "*the things (commodities) believe in their place,* instead of the subjects."[64]

Such a situation reflects the potential "objectivity of belief," its radical exteriority to consciousness and immanence within actions. Zizek gives the example of a Tibetan prayer wheel; you merely have to spin it and it does the praying for you. Go through the motions and it (by extension, the commodity) will believe in your place. He then supplements this anthropological example by citing Lacan's observations on the role of the chorus in Greek tragedy. In psychoanalysis one's most intimate beliefs and emotional states can be "delegated" to others without losing any of their sincerity. Lacan, in his analysis of *Antigone,* states that it is not that the chorus *stands for* the audience, but rather that it *stands in for* them, experiencing their emotions for them: "The emotional commentary is done for you. . . . Therefore you don't have to worry; even if you don't feel anything the Chorus will feel in your stead."[65] So too with commodities, states Zizek; even if you don't feel anything like a fetish toward them, the commodities will believe in your stead.

Zizek then goes on to contemporize this example, making a revealingly Marxian slip in the process of giving his "modern" variant: "But to avoid the impression that this exteriorization, this transference of our most intimate feeling, is simply a characteristic of the so-called primitive stages of development, let us remind ourselves of a phenomenon quite usual in popular television shows or serials: 'canned laughter.' . . . The Other—embodied in the television set—is relieving us even of our duty to laugh—is laughing instead of us."[66] Zizek suddenly brings me back to Bridges here in referring to the expectation of primitivity that arises on consideration of such delegated beliefs. Intimating "the so-called primitive stages of development," exotic Tibet and ancient Greece are appropriately matched with Tierra del Fuego here, as civilizations in which the Other seems primitive enough to believe for you.

The anthropological turn Zizek executes, in placing a contemporary television set in their vicinity, only serves to underscore, in spite of his argument as to the modernity of such ideological delegation, the intimations of primitivity it evokes. Nor is this simply a matter of primitivization by association. Taussig argues that the machinery of mechanical reproduction, such as the television, is suffused with primitivist imaginings, and he explicitly includes automata (such as the machine for "canned laughter") within this claim.[67] In claiming that commodities/things believe for us, Zizek both personalizes and inadvertently primitivizes those things. It is as if the "profane illumination" he engages here, in this surprising leap to embrace canned laughter, travels not forward, but rather back in time, illuminating a similar primitive present to that encapsulated in the video-laden Philco Time Capsule. That delegated belief, in the meantime, attaches itself to the automaton/primitive confronted with the Western commodity, and they, Bridges's Fuegians, start to believe in our stead.

Zizek has the things themselves speak the beliefs which Sohn-Rethel saw implicit in our actions and then manifested in commodity science. My twist on this argument is to claim that the fetish also manifests, *quite literally as a fetish,* in those colonial representations where primitives take on the role otherwise delegated to these objects of our disbelief. In this manner the primitive Selk'nam provide the "canned fetish" that supplies the faith in Pears' Soap, a faith otherwise embedded in the act of exchange and outside the realm of capitalist consciousness. Sohn-Rethel sees an intellectual fetishism in the misrecognition of commodity forms that is science, the "self-encounter of nature blindly occurring in man's mind." In like fashion, the fetish manifests itself, as an externalized property of the Other, in these fantastic first-contact commodity anecdotes.[68] Such humor could be defined as the self-encounter of fantasy "blindly occurring in man's mind" and visibly projected outside, to make up the fetishistic *nature* of the Other. Following the Marxian distinction between first and second nature, these anecdotes should then be read as evidence of a *third nature*—the fetishistic belief in commodity magic projected out from our actions and made to seem natural to us, insofar as it appears a property of the (deluded) Other in our stead.

This brings me to the final "subtle trap of a rationalistic anthropology." Both De Brosses and the imperialist anthropology that succeeded him were, contrary to Baudrillard, correct to universalize the "great fetishist metaphor" through all the homogenous geographical and temporal coordinates of Enlightenment science. A simple instancing of the utterly diverse times and places in which one can find such anecdotal encounters—where the native believes in our magic for us—is enough to prove that. The rationalistic anthropology did not fail in universalizing the fetishistic illusion, but rather in misconstruing its attribution, to focus on an all-purpose primitive Other in the place of an all-colonizing fantasy form. The fetish, for all its disembodied displacement, is clearly Western in "nature."

It belongs, furthermore, to the present, as I shall try to show in the following chapter, when I attempt to drive these time capsule conclusions home.

Notes

1. E. Lucas Bridges, *Uttermost Part,* 67.

2. Ibid., 219–20. See the reproduction of this text in the appendix.

3. Ibid., 220.

4. Not to mention at the instigation of the deluding Other, the *indio*'s wife. The gendering of illusion and disbelief in this anecdote could be compared to Anne Chapman's fieldwork and rewriting (i.e., gendering) of Bridges's and Martin Gusinde's ethnographic data. Chapman asks whether the Selk'nam women did indeed believe in the divinity of the characters of the *Hayn* initiation ritual. Thinly disguised as spirits, Selk'nam males performed a myth of origins in front of a captive (literally—the expression of disbelief in this "dramatic illusion" was reportedly punished with death) female audience. Chapman, *Drama and Power,* 146–56.

5. I am focusing my reading of this anecdote on its testimonial structure, regardless of its particular "white washing" content. In doing so I leave uncommented the other history which calls to be written here: the racist equivalence between indigeneity and dirtiness so prevalent in late colonialism. The campaign to make a previously (till the mid-nineteenth century) superfluous item like soap a national necessity both relied upon and reinforced racist rhetoric. See Vinikas, *Soft Soap, Hard Sell.*

6. Ibid., 93.

7. These questions are quite deliberately naïve. After all—to step out of the time capsule for a moment—when a critic claimed in the thirties, as a rejoinder to Beecher's claims, that by then cleanliness had actually replaced godliness, he was merely voicing the skepticism

that has always been concomitant, and indeed integral, to advertising. Vinikas, *Soft Soap, Hard Sell,* 93. Claims such as Beecher's do not need to be believed to be compelling.

8. Marx, *Capital,* 43.

9. Ibid., 50.

10. Ibid.

11. "My strategy is to view certain fantastic and magical reactions to our nonfantastic reality as part of a critique of the modern mode of production" (Taussig, *The Devil and Commodity Fetishism,* 10).

12. Ibid., 122.

13. There are numerous such passages in E. Lucas Bridges, *Uttermost Part:* e.g., the "magic lantern" incident, 284–87; the Selk'nam encounter with money, 483; and the passage in which a group of Selk'nam wonder how a thermos flask can work without visible fire and conclude that "it is white man's magic," 512. For another Fuegian example, see Juan Esteban Belza's account of the Selk'nam awe at the bridles, mounts, and horses (as if all such objects and organisms were one to them) of Ramon Lista's surveying expedition of 1886–87 (*En la Isla del Fuego,* 172). (By the time of this wondrous encounter Lista's party has already killed twenty-eight Indians in "self-defence"; projective wonder thus walks hand-in-hand with projective aggression. See Belza, 167–70.) For a contemporaneous fictional example (but what is fiction in this respect?) from another "world's most primitive" place, see Rider Haggard's extraordinary 1885 account of first contact between his party of English adventurers and the lost tribe of Kukuanaland in *King Solomon's Mines,* 101–9. Captain John Good here removes his false teeth and brandishes them in the air as a way of terrifying these primitives (while Allan Quatermain frightens them with "the magic tube that speaks," i.e., his rifle, 103). "I see ye are spirits" says their would-be attacker, exemplifying the way such anecdotal scenarios often reveal an indigenous fetish not merely of the colonizers' things but of their persons as well (in this instance, it is as if the magic power of rifle, false teeth, and monocle act to suffuse the adventurers' British bodies with fetish power too). For a few of the many other examples that can be found of this first-contact fetishism of the "white man's magic," see Taussig, *Mimesis and Alterity,* 193–255. For even more nineteenth- and early-twentieth-century examples, see Coombe, "Embodied Trademarks." Examples from the "world's most primitive" places of this century will be found in the following chapter.

14. Taussig, *Mimesis and Alterity,* 234.

15. Marx, *Capital,* 50.

16. Fitzroy quoted in Taussig, *Mimesis and Alterity,* 76.

17. Marx, *Capital,* 47.

18. Ibid., 47.

19. Ibid.

20. Ibid., 45.

21. Ibid., 11.

22. Ibid., 7.

23. I am stressing the nonessentializing aspect of use-value here, in line with Dipesh

Chakrabarty's usefully recuperative reading of "real labor" and "precapitalism" as categories of erasure, which burst at the seems with "the traces of what they themselves cannot
enclose" ("Marx after Marxism," 451). Yet, however useful such readings are in bringing
Marx back into the post-structuralist debate, I think that one has simultaneously to stress
the changes which capital does indeed effect upon the reconstitution of these initially
heterogenous realms. "Real labor" becomes, through its subsumption by capital, more
and more like "real labor."

24. Marx, *Capital,* 45.

25. Ibid., 48.

26. Ibid.

27. Ibid., 47.

28. Sohn-Rethel, *Intellectual and Manual Labour,* 30.

29. Zizek, "How Did Marx Invent the Symptom?" 18.

30. Marx, *Capital,* 48.

31. Sohn-Rethel, *Intellectual and Manual Labour,* 77.

32. E. Lucas Bridges, *Uttermost Part,* 284–87.

33. Ibid., 287.

34. Rationalization and disenchantment were, in Weber's analysis of modernity, inex-
orably linked. See Gerth and Mills, "Introduction," 51. For Marx, on the other hand, the
disenchantment of *patently* fetishistic relations of domination runs hand-in-hand with
the *invisible* reenchantment of fetishistic relations among commodities. See *Capital* 29,
n. 1, in which Marx invokes Hegel's "reflex categories" to depict the fetishistic relation of
king and subject before proceeding to rediscover them in the dialectic of Commodity A
and B at the kernel of capital.

35. E. Lucas Bridges, *Uttermost Part,* 284.

36. Ibid.

37. Lothrop, *Indians of Tierra del Fuego,* 92.

38. E. Lucas Bridges, *Uttermost Part,* 218.

39. On Nanook, see Taussig, *Mimesis and Alterity,* 200–207.

40. Zizek, "How Did Marx Invent the Symptom?" 16.

41. I am, contra Taussig, reading technologies such as the phonograph for their fetishistic role as consumer commodities. Ultimately, the impetus to produce ever new and more
advanced consumer items like the phonograph owes to the outlet they provide for the
objectification of labor time. For, far from being simply some consumer-driven or scien-
tifically inspired fetish of technology per se, the trajectory of technological development
falls very much within the trajectory of capital. There are two sides to this phenomenon.
With regard to the production process, capital necessitates constant technological innovation, for new technology effectively allows entrepreneurs to produce products of the
same value as their competitors, with less labor. Such price-related profits are, however,
short-lived. The moment innovations are generalized across the field, the value of the
product (given that value is a measure of "socially necessary" labor time, i.e., of the industry standard) readjusts to the new technologically enhanced level. The innovation is

now rendered necessary, but valueless. A system based on value, that is to say, necessitates continual technological change and yet is constitutively incapable of deriving any value from it. My understanding of the above owes much to Postone's *Time, Labour, and Social Mediation*, 286–385. Turning to the consumerism attendant upon this inexorable self-expansion, innovations in that realm clearly have a very different function to the industrial developments which Postone charts. Yet here too the goal of production is *not* use, in any sense of the word, but rather the production of value. Markets need to be created simply so as to facilitate more production. For this reason (from magic lantern to cinema to TV set to VCR, etc., etc.) there must ever be more and more innovation in consumer technology. Whether in the realm of production or consumption, the regime of valorization that is capital necessitates a never-ending series of "miracles of modern science." Both the factory and the household are united in this contradictory "progress," which is why Postone's "trajectory of production" runs so parallel to the Benjaminian timeframe of consumer trash which I articulated in the previous chapter. Just as Postone invokes the figure of Sisyphus to characterize the "dialectic of transformation and reconstitution" operative at the level of production, so does Benjamin call upon this mythic figure of "eternal recurrence" to describe a landscape run with consumer commodities and ever-new technology (Postone, *Time, Labour, and Social Mediation*, 298; Benjamin quoted in Buck-Morss, *Dialectics of Seeing*, 103, 108). Both these schemata of hellishly unending technological progress are ultimately a regressive function of the fetish of commodities at capital's core.

42. E. Lucas Bridges, *Uttermost Part*, 52. On the "organization of mimesis," see Taussig, *Mimesis and Alterity*, 59–70.

43. Taussig, *Mimesis and Alterity*, 208.

44. Benjamin quoted in Buck-Morss, *Dialectics of Seeing*, 272.

45. Could one read the "shock" of the new in Benjamin's *One-Way Street*, which I precipitously critiqued in chapter 2, through such a doubling of commodity reality? "Shock" could then be read as the traumatic blow which, like an operation under anesthetic, batters the social body in the individual mind's absence (for the metaphor, see Buck-Morss, "Aesthetics and Anaesthetics," 3–41). How subjunctively does Benjamin intend the following *as if*: "Here one lives *as if* the weight of the column of air supported by everyone had suddenly, against all laws, become in these regions perceptible" ("Imperial Panorama, a Tour of German Inflation," in *Reflections*, 75; my emphasis). Compare Marx, referring to the proletarian uprising, which he saw as the secret (ever on the verge of unveiling) of the nineteenth century: "But although the atmosphere in which we live weighs on everyone with a 20,000 pound force, do you feel it?" ("Speech at the Anniversary of the People's Paper," in *Selected Works*, 427).

46. I am, at the same time, running against the grain, where it can be discerned, of Benjamin's text and drawing it back to a material base. Benjamin is far more Freudian in his analysis of these "dream forms" of the "collective consciousness"; for him they redound with the social body's transindividual *wishes* for utopian life forms. For Adorno's criticisms, see Buck-Morss, *Dialectics of Seeing*, 110–59, 277–84.

47. Zizek, "How Did Marx Invent the Symptom?" 36.

48. Ibid.

49. Sohn-Rethel, *Intellectual and Manual Labour,* 17.

50. Ibid., 19.

51. Ibid., 15, 20.

52. Georg Lukács argues, similarly, that this commodified second nature "reduces space and time to a common denominator and degrades time to the dimension of space" ("Reification," 88). His argument obviously correlates to Sohn-Rethel's on many points. Postone privileges Lukács's work (with criticisms), on the grounds that Sohn-Rethel's exclusive focus on the "exchange abstraction" necessarily leads him to downplay the mediating role of labor in capitalism. Postone, *Time, Labour, and Social Domination,* 156 n. 90, 177–79. These criticisms, which I find persuasive, do not affect the validity of Sohn-Rethel's reading of the material origin of these categories (so much as shift their base, from exchange per se to the exchange of labor).

53. Karl Marx, *The Eighteenth Brumaire of Louis Napoleon,* in *Selected Works,* 317.

54. Sohn-Rethel, *Intellectual and Manual Labour,* 75. In a sense he thus mirrors Emile Durkheim's pathway "midway between classical empiricism and apriorism" to the "social origin of the categories" in *The Elementary Forms of the Religious Life* (25, 33). Yet to arrive at this theory, Durkheim is forced to transhistoricize a mode of categorical constitution (*society as God*) which, in its Marxist analogue (the fetish of commodities) is pegged to the historical trajectory of capital and could well function differently under other modes of production.

55. Hegel, *Phenomenology of Spirit,* 125.

56. Chakrabarty, "Postcoloniality and the Artifice of History," 2.

57. De Brosses quoted in Assoun, *El Fetichismo,* 21. Assoun is citing De Brosses's 1760 work, *Du culte des dieux fétishes ou Parallèle de l'ancienne religion de l'Egypte avec la religion actuelle de Négritie.*

58. Baudrillard, "Fetishism and Ideology," 89.

59. See Sigmund Freud, "Fetishism," in *Standard Edition,* 5:198–205.

60. Baudrillard, "Fetishism and Ideology," 89.

61. Zizek, "How Did Marx Invent the Symptom?" 32.

62. For an analysis of this phrase, a translation of the title of Lacan's twenty-first seminar, *Les non-Dupes Errent,* see Zizek, "How the Non-Duped Err," 69–88.

63. Sloterdijk, *Critique of Cynical Reason,* 82.

64. Ibid., 34.

65. Lacan, *Seminar VIII,* 252, partially quoted in Zizek, "How Did Marx Invent the Symptom?" 34–35.

66. Zizek, "How Did Marx Invent the Symptom?" 35.

67. Taussig, *Mimesis and Alterity,* 212–20. Hence the irony of the title of Eric Michaels's *The Aboriginal Invention of Television in Central Australia.*

68. Sohn-Rethel, *Intellectual and Manual Labour,* 75.

5
On the Rebound

Back to the Present

Bridges's time capsule testimony has turned into a pyramid-sized theory of commodity fetishism. A piece of joking trash, flattened into the past, has provided a point of theoretical focus for the anamorphotic gaze that sought to hold him to his words. Those words were never his to begin with. In focusing upon this self-absence, I found the true fetish behind the Benjaminian *objet trouvé* in a past that never accorded it any conscious belief, but nonetheless acted as if it did. Thus these graffiti hieroglyphs offered the spell that would summon Karl Marx's theory of commodity fetishism back from the dead. Those words were never his to begin with, though the Fuegians were well placed to own them—a discarded canned fetish—for him. The supplementation which the deluded Other afforded his disbelieved discourse seemed simply *third nature* for primitives at the Uttermost Part of the Earth.

To carry these insights forward into the neocolonial present brings into relief the homology between the structure of Bridges's anecdotes and those Chatwinian and Benettonian sites I have investigated. In such scenarios the "underdeveloped" are held to a similarly fetishizing faith in the Dodge cars, Coke cans, and jeans commercials of the "Future." The material discourse of the Western anecdotalist's actions is thereby recapitulated through the developmental time-space coordinates that project Third World Others into their observer's primitive past. Whether at the end of the nineteenth century or on the verge of the twenty-first, "the backward" have always been there[1] to fetishize the otherwise unbelievable things of the self-styled "Present."

Yet insofar as these insights tune me back into the television set with which I began this book, they appear all the more surreal. Canned laughter does not end where I left it in the last chapter, laughing away in the place of the viewer. The striking thing about this stagy mechanism is the way it serves to excite the viewer's laughter in response to a canned emotion which was initially so difficult to muster. In his book on jokes, Freud identifies a similarly intersubjective structure behind the curious fact that jokes are characterized by an "urge to tell" them to someone else.[2] The teller, Freud explains, can access the pleasure of his [sic] joke only when it is embodied in the Other. Yet it is not merely that the Other laughs for us, in the manner of Lacan's Greek chorus. Laughter is infectious by nature; when the Other starts laughing for us, we catch the spirit and laugh in return, "attaining the laughter that is impossible for us by the roundabout path of the impression we have of the person who has been made to laugh."[3]

A similar response is evoked by the canned fetish that the Fuegians offer Bridges. Not only do these Fuegians do what Bridges cannot—fetishize his things for him. They force him to mimic back those delegated beliefs, to play out—"on the rebound," as Freud would say—the fantasies in which he has no actual faith.[4] In response to the Fuegian husband's demands, Bridges pretends that the soap truly does have magic (albeit particular) powers. With the miracle of the "magic lantern," the Selk'nam language itself forces Bridges to bespeak his fetish; "unfortunately the Ona [Selk'nam] word for 'picture' or 'shadow' was the name of one of their ghosts." By fault of translation, the colonist finds himself compelled to play along with the Selk'nam fetishism of his things, compelled to respond to, and in terms of, the other's magical comprehension.[5] On the rebound, Bridges becomes as fetishistic as any indio (as indeed he is).

What is happening here? As I argued in the previous chapter, it was Bridges himself who engineered these exchanges of cross-cultural magic. To take into account his rebounding response, one would have to say that it is as if he wants to be solicited to play along with that "unsolicited testimonial" which he has already so desirously elicited from the Other.

As I attempt to bring my time capsule findings back into the present, this extraordinary behavior makes for an intriguing question: How can Bridges engage in such blatant self-encounters and yet remain blind to his own role in them? The trajectory of the previous chapter underlines the significance of this question. In flattening the colonist into the primitive colonial past, I denied him the textual ambivalence and distance with which I treat the self-absent words I myself mouth as I visit Tierra del Fuego "just to say I've been there." Bridges's self-absent wish served to cast the Fuegians in an "unsolicited testimonial" to the magic of Western things. In taking this subjunctival fantasy for an indicative statement of fact, I sought, like a Foucauldian archaeologist, to hold him to this throwaway image. Yet something seems to have surfaced from these bald statements in spite of all the violence I inflicted upon them. The more I proceeded in the previous chapter, the less this archaeological procedure seemed necessary. Bridges's desire for the Other's supplementary fetishism seemed almost to break through the surface of his statements, for all the fact that the fetish they conveyed was so obviously not his.

This paradox becomes even more mysterious as I now attempt to read an intersubjective dimension to the colonist's words. Bringing laughter, and all the ambiguity that would usually imply, back into the picture has the same strange effect of making him appear even more blatant in his desires. In mimicking back the fetish he has so recently delegated to the Other, Bridges seems to want *to hold himself* to those words.

This is even more apparent in the following anecdote. Bridges has just splinted the broken collar bone of one of his Selk'nam workers. The operation is a success, but the Indian, all the same, keeps soliciting extra treatment. The splint, Bridges explains, is "too simple"; the Indian wants to see some real white magic. The colonist then remembers a bottle of iodine which he has in the house: "so I took Teëoöriolh along there and applied the tincture lavishly to the injured part. What a marvellous balm that was! So red and scented! Teëoöriolh went away rejoicing, and was back at work again within a few days. Soon the fame of this wonderful medicine of mine spread throughout the country. The Indians would come with the most flimsy excuses for a touch of this magic paint, which was regarded not only as a cure, but as a preventative against any possible pain or accident in the future."[6] Bridges pretends to believe in his own disbelieved fetish for the psychosomatic sake of the Other. In the process, Teëoöriolh's immodest faith in the miracle of rejuvenating iodine solicits a twofold rebounding response: firstly, the acting-out that has the colonist pretend to the Indian, *on the rebound,* that he believes in the modern medicine he dispenses; secondly, the ironic representation of this very incident to us. Relaying the fetish to us, Bridges adopts a native voice and, through it, mimes the primitive wonder he describes: "What a marvellous balm that was! So red and scented!"

What pretext could be strong enough to sanction such desirous mimicry of these projective primitives? Such an anecdote manifests the same disjuncture in the unity of thinking and being that, in Sohn-Rethel's texts, seemed so startling and challenging. For Bridges, however, the acting out of a doubly-displaced and doubly-disbelieved subjectivity seems simply *second nature* on the edge of the capitalist periphery. The "as if" postulate that has him, as colonial capitalist, act *as if* he truly believes in commodity forms and fetishes is echoed in the *as if* scenarios he enacts with these primitives, in which he acts *as if* he fetishizes the Western commodity even though he so clearly does not. His disbelief, as it manifests itself in the very act of exchange, comes full circle in this polar manifestation of the disbelief with which he mimicks back, *on the rebound,* that fetishism that was never his in the first place. How is this possible? Surely such a vertiginous exchange of displacements should make perilously plain the colonist's absence from himself. How can Bridges play so willingly into this fetishistic primitive-present, as if it were indeed his own?

Time Out: This Sudden Laugh from Where?

In trying to understand how Bridges can misrecognize his own imbrication in such projective identifications, I am drawn back to the *objet trouvé.* According to Benjamin, the *objet trouvé,* in the hands of the surrealists, constituted more of a "trick than a method."[7] There is, as I noted in the previous chapter, a clear analogy between Bridges's blind witnessing of "the white man's magic" and the anthropological turn through which critique seeks to avail itself, through the eyes of the Other, of similar self-insights.

So what distinguishes "trick" from "method"? Taussig's awareness of these risky parallels is clear in *Mimesis and Alterity,* in which he describes the recapitulative laugh that takes the Western observer on seeing indigenous images of the West and its things: "There is an element of colonialist mastery in this laughter . . . but there is also the possibility that this sudden laugh from nowhere registers a tremor in cultural identity, and not only in identity, but in the security of being itself."[8] There is the potential here, according to Taussig, for a "novel anthropology . . . of the West itself as mirrored in the eyes and handiworks of its others."[9] His way of turning "trick" to "method" involves isolating and redeeming just such double-edged moments. Through grasping such "mimetic excess," in all its trickery, and propelling it into a crazy state of "mimetic vertigo," Taussig strives to weave a text in which the imbrication of First World and Third World, self and Other, mimesis and alterity spin in a dizzying whirl. Such vertiginous interchanges will allow for the formation of new postcolonial subjectivities that are neither self nor Other so much as ineradicably entwined in each other.[10]

Lucas Bridges's text holds me in my tracks here, forcing me to investigate precisely that "element of colonialist mastery" which Taussig so suddenly leaves behind. For now that I have returned my findings to the present, the question that these anecdotes beg is clear: Just how does the master manage so continually to misrecognize the Otherness he embodies in the course of these blatant projections?

In watching Teëoöriolh, and then in representing him to us, Bridges mimes the latter's motions by becoming Other within the very texture of own skin. Why does the veritable "mimetic vertigo" this encounter whirls up not cause any "tremor in cultural identity" for him? When it comes to tremors in the "security of being," the master, laughing at himself in the place of the Other, all of a sudden seems not at home. This self-absence, far from causing any mimetic anxiety, is, on the contrary, converted into the self-superior "sudden laugh from nowhere." How does one explain the vanishing trick, and indeed the method behind this so stupid, but also clearly so clever, misrecognition of mastery? How does one explain how the master, on finding his fetish through the agency of the Other, then mimics that fetish back, *on the rebound,* and with such excess? Why, that is, would one ever need to redeem such obvious anecdotes?

Ethnographic Surrealism on the Rebound

The question is cast into interesting relief, if we turn to the film which is probably the closest contemporary analogue to Bridges's magic soap anecdote. *The Gods Must Be Crazy* opens with a Coke bottle falling from the sky upon a tribe of idyllically innocent Bushmen, another group of "the world's most primitive inhabitants."[11] By becoming at once property, technology, and even a medium of exchange, this *ur*-thing of capitalism causes chaos in their primitive paradise. Indeed, it could be the "terrible Green monster" of Taussig's sugarcane fields. The Coke bottle, unbottled by the native's magical comprehension, thus releases its genie, in its primitive characterization as "the evil thing." At least these are the words of the South African voiceover narrator, who in this way imitates the imagined voice of the otherwise inarticulate Bushmen. So he describes their encounter with modernity, as they run to dodge a "big animal" (i.e., a car), while—marvel of marvels!—a "great flying bird" passes overhead. *The Gods must be Things,* for through this very voiceover the white narrator mimes out to us the *third nature* fetish which he finds, Coke bottle incarnate, in the eyes of the Other.

I remember watching this film ten years ago, laughing sudden laughs from nowhere and finding nothing unusual in the narrator's (and, by extension, my) patent reveling in this blatant mimicry of "their" fetish of our "crazy" things. To personalize the matter like this brings to mind the rather obvious fact that I was laughing, and beyond Taussig's "tremor . . . in the security of being," for the simple tautological fact that I was laughing. Jokes, that is to say, allow one to become Other precisely on the grounds that they will not be taken seriously.

This fact can easily be ignored when one looks at the now lifeless utterances of an old colonial era. It is rather harder when the narrator is an anthropologist sitting next to you, in a tourist restaurant in Ushuaia. Eric was on a brief holiday, relaxing from fieldwork in Brazil. We ate a bad pizza together and disagreed about the need for objectivity over dessert. Later he smiled and handed me a pamphlet advertising Haruwen. "Perhaps you could do some of your research there," he laughed into another drink, as I read a brochure for this cultural theme park, a place where you can ride horses, use canoes, and "experience life just like the real Indians of Tierra del Fuego." That is how the ethnographer becomes Other at the Uttermost Part of the Earth: going, in all ironic spirit, to a ethnographic theme park, experiencing, in quotation marks, "life just like the real Indians," and then drunkenly advertising it to me.

As my analysis of Bridges suggests, such primitivist anecdotes are far from trivial in their implications. These are, of course, precisely the moments which serious historians and ethnographers do *not* bring back home in their cultural baggage. They themselves realize this; the disregard such mimetically excessive anecdotes occasion is less a function of their obscurity than a consequence of their *blinding obviousness*. Jokes are disregarded for the very fact that they are jokes. Our blindness to them is predicated upon their utter visibility. The fact that I know I am joking and not being serious allows me to ignore the monumental implications of the discourses I call into action, allows me to disregard the scenarios in which I place myself. As in the experience which I proceeded to relate to the anthropologist, responding to his tipsy tale of mimetic excess with a sloshed history of my own:

> I'm in Chilean Tierra del Fuego, buying an old man's story with boomerang lessons. It's a genuine model, real factory-made. I brought it from home to make sure I return. The old man is Scottish. He came here as a child. He has never, in all his sixty years in Tierra del Fuego, seen a boomerang. Though he *has* seen plenty of UFOs.
>
> I was talking to the old man as part of my research, my ethnohistory of the white colonial subject traveling through time to Tierra del Fuego. I don't know why I mentioned to him during our desultory interview (he was born too late, he told me, to know anything about the Indians) that I had a boomerang back at the hotel. "And it really comes back?" he kept asking.
>
> So suddenly we're walking out of town and over to the sheepfields. Now I'm the native informant, teaching the foreigner something about our plastic, factory-made, and stolen culture. I hurl the boomerang into the air, it revolves around us and then returns into my hand.
>
> "You're a real *indio*," the old man tells me, in his lilting Scottish accent. I'm laughing under my breath, while he proceeds to launch my boomerang in turn.

Paranoid Projections

If these throwaway researches of mine, conducted in Melbournian cinemas, Ushuaian pizza parlors, and Chilean sheep paddocks, suddenly draw Bridges's ancient jokes closer to my world in the present, the parallels this brings to mind do create a "tremor" in my "cultural identity." The other "element of colonialist mastery," in such recapitulative laughter, and the other reason why it needs to be redeemed is the index it offers to the projective structures of far more brutal colonial realities. These realities must be brought into the present too and made to appear an indicative attribute of such mastery.

Taussig quotes from Adorno and Horkheimer's "The Elements of Anti-Semitism" to characterize the savage underside of the history of the senses he sets forth. Adorno and Horkheimer's characterization of the "morbid projection" structuring the "mass paranoia" of fascist anti-Semitism relies on a similarly recapitulative structure to the anecdotes about Nanook, Houshken, and Teëoöriolh quoted above.[12] Sniffing out Jews, they write, allows anti-Semites to mimic the very behavior they impute to the Other:

> The civilized individual may only indulge in such pleasure if the prohibition is suspended by rationalization in the service of real or apparent practical ends. The prohibited impulse may be tolerated if there is no doubt that the final aim is elimination—this is the case with jokes or fun, the miserable parody of fulfillment. As a despised and despising characteristic, the mimetic function is enjoyed craftily. Anyone who seeks out "bad" smells, in order to destroy them, may imitate sniffing to his heart's content, taking unrationalized pleasure in the experience. The civilized man "disinfects" the forbidden impulse by his unconditional identification with the authority which has prohibited it; in this way the action is made acceptable.[13]

This "organized control of mimesis" is, for Adorno and Horkheimer, integral to capitalist modernity. Taussig sees a similar structure manifest itself on the nineteenth-century Tierra del Fuegian frontier.[14] The genocidal invasion was, he argues, empowered by such paranoid projections. By availing themselves of "the savagery imputed to the Other," Fuegian colonists managed to rationalize their own brutality, a brutality they then "mimicked on the body of that Other."[15] Eliciting native response, and then responding in turn, such a "colonial mirror of production" propelled the ever-escalating dynamic of savagery which would eventually lead to the virtually Indian-less Tierra del Fuego of today.

Only a decade before Bridges witnessed Houshken fetishize his magic lantern, Julio Popper, an early pioneer in the use of photographic technology, staged the famous photo that is now, more than anything else, emblematic of the civilized brutality that cleared Tierra del Fuego for sheep-farming capital.[16] The image shows a quartet of uniformed men; one of the killers, probably Popper himself, stands with the naked body of a dead Indian at his feet, while the others stare off in the distance for more.[17] "We answered their aggression with our Winchester rifles," Popper claimed during the public lecture in which he described how he, and the twenty uniformed men under his command, invaded Selk'nam territory.[18] It is the uniforms, I think, that have made this image so famous. They seem to signify the "unconditional identification" with civilized authority through which such savage aggression can be "disinfected." Made to seem a natural property of the primitives upon whose bodies such violence was projected, "the action" was "made acceptable" and hurled back as an answer to what Popper termed "their aggression."

"These same Indians" wrote Ramon Cortés in 1896, explaining the counterattack during which his men killed four Selk'nam, "have robbed a good number of animals in the last few weeks, and just for pleasure they destroyed two miles of barbed wire."[19] The importation of sheep, begun almost at the same time that Lucas Bridges was born, led to the fencing in of the north of the island and the fencing out of any viable lifestyle for the Selk'nam. Fenced out as well by the legal discourse that denied them any grounds on which to invoke the right to self-defense, those "same Indians" reenacted the violence done to them. Cortés took ninety prisoners during this attack. Two of his men were last seen leading seven of these Selk'nam prisoners in chains toward the boat that would take them to the missions. These two henchmen, slaving for Christ, were found some time later, one decapitated, the other disemboweled, his hands and face covered with wounds from the knife he had tried to ward off.[20]

If such counter-"counterattacks" added impetus to the "mimetic vertigo" with which the "colonial mirror of production" cast up aggressors and reprisals on either side, this optic was clearly in favor of the colonizer. From the official perspective, the land was always already white. Any indigenous response to an invasion that legally never occurred could only proceed from what José Menéndez, owner of the properties on which the above events occurred, described in a newspaper interview as the Indians' "incomprehensible rapaciousness."[21] Half a century later, when Fernando Durán published his laudatory history of Menéndez's company, the Sociedad Explotadora de Tierra del Fuego, this fantasy of a primordial indigenous aggression led him to praise the manner in which the early colonists "heroically defended their property against the attacks of Indians and the elements."[22] Thus again, white aggression was "disinfected" and made to seem a natural property of the savage Other.

Explotador means both "exploring" and "exploiting," a typically unintention-al irony cast up by the paranoid mimesis integral to such enterprises. The un-canny colonial doublet of cannibalism/capitalism, repeated in various ways throughout South American colonial history and counterhistory, made its shift-ing presence felt here too.[23] Whereas Darwin called the Fuegians "cannibals" in 1833, for José María Borrero, writing almost a century later, that epithet belonged in truth to the Frenchman Monsieur Maistre, the "degraded trader of human flesh" who sought to make money by enslaving these "cannibals" and exhibiting them as such in chains in Europe.[24] To Borrero, Maistre himself, far from excep-tional, is merely representative of the other so-called "*primeros pobladores*" (first populators) like Menéndez and his Sociedad Explotadora. These men, bringing with them the wonders of money, barbed wire, and guns, were in truth the "*prim-eros despobladores*" (first depopulators), the murderers of an entire race.[25]

This same equation of capitalism and cannibalism can be found in Marx too. His doubled-edged anthropology led him, in *Capital,* to claim sardonically that "there is a natural foundation for surplus value," inasmuch as there "is no natu-ral obstacle" to its appropriation.[26] In this it is as "natural" as cannibalism, for there is no "natural hindrance in the way of one who should propose to nourish himself by consuming another human being's flesh."[27] This passage is capped with an extraordinary footnote, in which Marx claims that "according to a recent cal-culation [whose?], in the parts of the world hitherto explored [which?], there are at least 4,000,000 cannibals."[28] At least one of them, to put this projection back in its place, would have to be Don José Menéndez, described with such unin-tentional irony, in the newspaper article quoted above, as a "self-made man."[29]

Menéndez, and his fellow "self-made" *despobladores,* made themselves rich on the surplus value of local Chilean and Argentine labor, skimming its properties into the tinned mutton which, in Sir Baldwin Spencer's words, "you probably buy and appreciate under the designation of 'Best Canterbury.'"[30] The assault upon the Indians' bodies, on the other hand, still outside the "natural" self-nour-ishing circuit of capital, was far more manifest in its End of the World workings. "The prohibited impulse," Adorno and Horkheimer write, "may be tolerated if there is no doubt that the final aim is elimination." Bridges rationalized his in-volvement in the patent fetishism of commodities for missionary motives, to further the advance of civilization, which, for all his occasional ambivalence, he could only but treat as inexorable. His murderous co-colonists rationalized their patent savagery through a not dissimilar future perfect wishfulness; merely tem-porary phenomena, these momentary excesses would end with the "elimination" of the Indians' "incomprehensible rapaciousness." Wearing such pretexts like uniforms, colonial killers like Popper's quartet set to the slaughter, earning, according to the popular accusation that persists to the present, a pound a head for helping to eliminate the savage Other.

At times, such pretexts wore very thin indeed, as in the case of Mr. Bond, one of Menéndez's henchmen, a self-styled "Indian killer." Mr. Bond, Borrero writes, passing the horror on to his reader, would tell "with pride and always as a special joke" a story which is to this day repeated throughout Patagonia.[31] Again and again I heard it repeated, this *ur*-incident of Fuegian colonization: "The killers were paid one pound sterling for each pair of ears they delivered as proof." I almost had to put my hands to my own ears, as the story, with all its monstrous oral violence, continued: this arrangement had to be changed when it was brought to the patrons' attention that certain Selk'nam had been sighted, earless, yet still alive. Certain killers, somewhat "weak of heart," had relented and left the Indians alive—yet taken their tokens all the same. Since that time, the pound sterling had been paid only on receipt of a head or the testicles or the womb or some other vital organ. "This story Mr Bond tells on occasions like a joke, and always with the greatest naturalness."[32]

Whatever the veracity of this joke (it is unverifiable, but by no means necessarily apocryphal), I am intrigued by its very definition as a "joke," albeit only in the mind of the clearly psychopathic Bond. How can this forced equation of one Fuegian corpse to one English pound be so hideously evocative, to rephrase the matter, as to bear repeated retellings, if only under the ideationally mimetic pretext of excoriating the colonists of the past? This numericization of genocide—for it is this which these macabre retellings stress—touches on something. The joke here must lie in the index this anecdote provides to the inhuman accounting structuring the restructuring of Tierra del Fuego into terms suitable for, and indeed accountable to, capital.[33]

In this sense, Mr. Bond's joke is the patrimony of more than just his immediate company. Those other entrepreneurs in Tierra del Fuego—humane men like Bridges, as much as local capitalists like Popper (who, on settling in the region, began to campaign in the Indians' defense)[34]—were, in their unthinking enterprises, engaged in a similarly brutal operation. In this sense, Juan Esteban Belza has a point in downplaying the colonists' blame for the genocide, attributing it to the diseases the whites brought, to psychopaths like Bond, who can be found in any society, and above all, to the fantastic atmosphere of the time, the "*neurosis colectiva*" that now makes it so difficult for a reasonable historian like him to discern what really happened.[35] In this very statement, Belza reveals why empathetic exonerations of the atrocious past like his are so dangerous. It was reality itself, the *neurosis colectiva* integral to the very act of colonization, that was psychopathic. Reality itself was as genocidal as the Mr. Bonds or Julio Poppers whom the victors' history now tries to make exceptional to the rule they actually serve to emblematize. Such exceptional incidents are in themselves symptomatic of a far more encompassing narrative—the colonial reduction of the Fuegians to capital, the genocidal "*liquidacion de cuentas*" (settling of accounts) which formed the unconscious counterpart to enterprises such as Bridges's or Menéndez's.[36]

The First Time as Farce

From such a perspective, to the Angel of History flying backward from this atrocious past into the present, the indicative parallel between Bridges's anecdotes and Mr. Bond's bad joke is all too clear. Of course, it is not that jokes like Bridges's were causative of the slaughter, even though they share the same structure of rationalized, unconscious immersion in Otherness. Yet inasmuch as these jokes point to the structures of capital, and the brutal *liquidacion de cuentas* it settled upon the island, they need to be read as parallel phenomena. Both, from this perspective, are in on the joke, which is no joke at all. The fundamentally estranging connection I am articulating here, between the "colonial mirror of production" and what Adorno and Horkheimer described as "jokes or fun, the miserable parody of fulfillment," estranges me in my possession of the present too. It is easy to distance oneself from the pathological violence of that colonial generation. Yet when it is humor itself which proves symptomatic of the structures empowering such occurrences, I am drawn back from Bridges, his bad jokes, and his genocidal era. I am suddenly pinned to my own disowned and self-parodied travels through the postcolonial present.

What can I say? This uncanny feeling underscores the difficulty of taking humor seriously, the difficulty of attributing it to the one-dimensional past, of analyzing it in the ambivalent present. Writing the ethnohistory of Fuegian colonization and its current recapitulation in tourism, I feel the overwhelming temptation to invoke that formula, now so old and naïve, that reads historical repetition "the first time as tragedy, the second time as farce."[37] The quickest way to disabuse oneself of such a narrative is to turn to the photograph album in which Julio Popper's "Indian Killer" self-portrait appears.[38] Popper had a wild (this word seems appropriate) sense of humor.[39] One photo, taken during this same murderous expedition, shows one of his soldiers pointing with a saber at a disheveled and empty Selk'nam lean-to. "In search of ethnographic treasures" runs the caption. Another shows a mound of dirt with a stick in it. The caption reads, "Post box." Yet another reveals smoke rising from a distant fire and bears the caption "Ona telegraph line."

Compare a recent issue of Benetton's *Colors* magazine on race, whose opening

pages begin with photos of excessive racial violence, capped with the headline
"We're Looking for Trouble."[40] This is followed by a table of racial insults, which
are indexed to photos of the various peoples thus insulted; the pretext of elimi-
nating racism allows the editors to revel in articulating it. One entry even features a Yámana Indian.[41] On another page you find a TV set advertised under
the banner "The Universal Language of Phillips," the very company whose Philco
Time Capsule drew me to Bridges in the first place.[42] What is for me most trou-
blesome, however, is the inclusion, alongside such open obscenities, of an article
featuring a critical analysis of the economics of race, underdevelopment, and
poverty that, in any other context, I would probably respect.[43] It is as if critical
self-awareness is "business as usual" too. What can I say?

> The boomerang loops back and forth in ever-decreasing spirals before re-
> turning to my hand—genuine Australian plastic. The old man and I sit down
> on the grass and he begins to talk.

> "What do you think of these UFOs then?" he asks me. "Have you seen one?
> I've seen a few, you know. There is life out there. We're from out there too
> you know—originally." He tells me of a local abduction: "Someone was taken
> aboard by the aliens, they performed all sorts of experiments on him, you
> know. Not that they would have done anything bad—just a few experiments.
> They are, after all, more intelligent than us, and surely a more intelligent
> being would do nothing bad."

> Suddenly I realize that I am at last hearing a history of race relations in Tier-
> ra del Fuego.

> "Imagine what it would be like," the old man begins to joke, "if the aliens
> abducted me while I was out throwing the boomerang." He leaps up, and
> suddenly assumes a boomerang throwing pose: "They'll think I'm an *indio*,
> won't they?"

Reflexive Awareness Meets with Mimetic Vertigo

So the self becomes Other at the Uttermost Part of the Earth. Surveying a similar range of colonial scenarios, Taussig's project, in *Mimesis and Alterity*, aims at
"creating reflexive awareness as to the mimetic faculty."[44] Such a project would
catch the self becoming Other in the "sudden laugh from nowhere" evoked by
these throwaway anecdotes: Lucas Bridges's magic soap, the Bushmen's divine
Coke bottle, Julio Popper's indigenous mailbox. In this manner Taussig seeks to
foment awareness of the way Popper and those who laugh with him exceed the

limits of their rational identities, the way they actually identify with the primitivism they project onto the Other. In trying to bring Bridges's bad jokes into the present, I asked the naïve question why such obvious anecdotes need to be redeemed in the first place.

The first answer to this question was that these so indicative jokes are—by definition—read otherwise. Too obvious to be read so obviously, they are treated subjunctivally. Not being statements of fact, these fetishistic revelations of the "white man's magic" are not taken seriously. The deadly serious, indeed imperative, answer to this question emerged as I turned to recapitulative structures of far more brutal dimensions: the genocidal savagery which the colonist projects onto the primitive Other and then mimicks back, *on the rebound.* Both these mimetic structures are, I argued, symptomatic of capital's civilizing advances. As such, they both need to be taken as symptomatic of realities that must be changed. The hegemonic force (but also the critical potential) of such interactions lies in the *blinding obviousness* with which they indicate that *reality itself cannot be taken seriously.*

This fact is, yet again, particularly apparent in one's interactions with the projective past. Bridges knows, and he is not just joking, that there are times when it is important not to be yourself when dealing with the Selk'nam. Acting Other to himself creates no "tremor . . . in the security of being," for the security of being in colonial Tierra del Fuego is so evidently dependent on *not being yourself.* Throughout Bridges's narrative, he stresses the dissimulation and the fakery he must perforce enact to manage not simply his family farm, but, in the process, the transition from the cultural code of civilized Englishman to that of primitive Selk'nam. So Bridges describes how, during a period of great unrest, recrimination, and even mutual massacre among the Selk'nam, he has the old man Kilehehen adopt him as son, making him in truth the *indio blanco* others call him. This protective mimicry is rationalized by Bridges's desire to shield Kilehehen's daughter from a would-be abductor—a role that would be expected of a brother, yet seen as interference and even provocation from a stranger.[45] This motive allows Bridges to become *indio,* yet to distance himself from his own adoption of and into the Selk'nam and their customs; through such a pretext he can separate that part of himself that will imitate the Other and thereby forestall any internal change in his identity.

The unjoking expectation that he *not be himself* in his relations to the Selk'nam carries over into his jokes and, indeed, forms their most serious component. Bridges is far from hiding the fact that in such encounters he is playing along, *on the rebound,* with "their" commodity fetishism. His Otherness to himself at such moments is not repressed so much as *stressed.* Hence the disavowal that he so constantly performs upon his anecdotes, wherein the magic of soap, lantern, and all-curing iodine, all of which is *third nature* to the Other, is simultaneously, and so adamantly, revealed to his readers as fake and hollow. Bridges's need to point out to us readers the hollowness of the "white magic" in which he pretends to believe is only paralleled, in its repetitiveness, by his fixation upon the necessity of such dissimulation. Both before and after such encounters, Bridges's text stipulates the ethical imperative of such dissimulation, invoking either pragmatic or altruistic motives at all times. In this manner he can always become Other, yet be pegged so tightly to the self he thinks he is and thus never swoon to the "mimetic vertigo" that would have him really become Other.

Taussig is too hasty in setting aside such literally "schizoid" pretexts for becoming Other.[46] He aims to unrepress the wild mimetic plasticity prone to the "temptation by space" which Roger Caillois described in his article "Mimicry and Legendary Psychasthenia."[47] For Caillois, becoming Other is a terrifying, vertiginous, and ultimately a-functional faculty of being. Bridges feels no such fear and can, on the contrary, always fall back on the Darwinian rationale for mimicry that Caillois rejects, to justify his acting as *indio blanco* in the interests of his own survival among the Indians, if not for the sake of their betterment as well. Through such pretexts, Bridges puts himself beyond the perils of that Pascalian/Althusserian ideological slide whereby, through acting it out, you effectively internalize and become your outward belief: "Kneel down, move your lips in prayer, and you will believe."[48] The colonist's *lip service* to his Selk'nam identity is anchored to a missionary aim to preserve the Fuegians from their own discord. Such pretextualization justifies his open self-splitting, while allowing him to snap back into himself at every moment.

Compare this with the notion of a mimicry that takes you out of yourself and has you become Other beyond the point of rationalistic return. "Many of the natives were great mimics," Bridges states, introducing the story of Yekaifwaianjiz, a Yámana who shows his (perilous) mimetic talents in his response to a visiting party of French scientists. "Some of the habits and little tricks of speech that he had noticed in the visitors and had taken pains to imitate . . . grew on him as time went by. At every opportunity when talking he would spread his hands, palms upwards and towards his hearer, and drawing backwards, shrug his shoulders with a gesture a comedian might well have envied. Eventually these ultra-French motions became so natural to him that he could not have avoided using them even had he tried."[49] This unrationalized mimicry-out-of-control is so clearly a property of the Other, and not of Bridges, that his controlled mimicry seems in contrast proof of his civilized and rational status. Indeed, contrary to Taussig's argument, it seems that Bridges's "reflexive awareness as to the mimetic faculty" is the very thing which ultimately, and paradoxically, allows him to become Other so excessively.[50]

The paranoiac mind-set that allows one, through whatever particular pretext, to become an *indio blanco* and at the same time stay oneself is not something one simply shakes off. Nor, as Adorno and Horkheimer make clear, can one just laugh it away. The unsettling humor they force me to face unsettles me by shifting the rationalizing focus away from the colonist's specious strategies for survival. Such pretexts seem so clearly a property of Bridges, his generation, and *not* me. Indeed, it seems simply *second nature* to find such naïve pathology in the past, in the facile anecdotes of an otherwise serious colonial capitalist with a mission. It seems simply *second nature* to hold such a colonist to his words, whether humorous or otherwise.

Yet Bridges knows—and here I am forced to see myself in him—that when acting *on the rebound,* to whatever degree of mimetic vertigo, he quite literally is not himself. Indeed, knowledge of one's own imbrication in this process is no necessary corrective. To know that you are fighting fire with fire or meeting fetish with fetish by no means stops you from continuing to play into such a reality. Far from alerting Bridges to his own mimetic excess, such knowledge in fact allows him to carry out Kafka's "wish to be a red Indian" all the more excessively: being adopted into an Indian family, experiencing, in quotation marks, "life just like the real Indians," and then advertising it to us.[51]

Later in These Pages . . .

Such a destiny is foreshadowed—and I think the irony is intentional—in the following passage at the very beginning of Bridges's book: "Even as a child, I was obsessed by a passionate longing to explore those ranges of mountains that hemmed us in and join the wild tribe of which I had heard such fantastic tales from our Yaghan [Yámana] playmates. Later in these pages it shall be told how I realized that ambition."[52]

Later in these pages it shall be told how I—driving my analysis beyond the *blindingly obvious* lures of the present—catch the colonist's "sudden laugh from nowhere." The present's "reflexively buffered" reality cannot be taken seriously. Yet the "possibility" that such a laugh might nonetheless unsettle "the security of being" remains.[53] In pursuit of this possibility I will revisit, and attempt to reclaim, the *self-defeating* critical potential of the recapitulationist structure through which these paranoid projections plot themselves.

The present cannot be taken seriously. This final project will launch me into the future—by way of the past.

Notes

1. Where? Tierra del Fuego is, of course, not the only End of the World. See Lindstrom, *Cargo Cult,* for its fascinating archive of European and Australian tales of millenarian commodity worship in Vanuatu. There is a moment in Greenblatt's *Marvellous Possessions* which is worth citing in this regard. As a gesture to a realm beyond his own text, Greenblatt gives an anecdotal account of the group of otherwise exotic Balinese whom he saw, in his travels in the late 1980s, watching a video recording of one of their own temple ceremonies. For Greenblatt such a "utopian moment" brings out "what you almost already have, what you could have—if only you could strip away the banality and corruption of the everyday—at home" (7, 25).

2. Freud, *Jokes,* 194.

3. Ibid., 209.

4. Ibid.

5. E. Lucas Bridges, *Uttermost Part,* 287.

6. Ibid., 219.

7. Walter Benjamin, "Surrealism," in *Reflections,* 182.

8. Taussig, *Mimesis and Alterity,* 226.

9. Ibid., 236.

10. Ibid., 254, 237.

11. Uys, *The Gods Must Be Crazy.* I am grateful to Vera Mackie for drawing my attention to this (albeit awful) film, which served to crystallize many of my ideas on this subject. See also, in this regard, the staging of first contact in Dimond, *Papua New Guinea Patrol.* In this Australian documentary, yet another group of "the world's most primitive inhabitants" fetishize Australian commodity magic and, in the process, the heroic bodies of the Australian colonial forces. "Surely these strangers are mighty men!" the narrator exclaims in voiceover, thus miming the message of the apparently inarticulate Other. Thanks to Amanda Samuels for showing me this (again, truly awful) film.

12. Adorno and Horkheimer, *Dialectic of Enlightenment,* 192.

13. Ibid., 184.

14. For the most involved explication of this concept, see Taussig, *Shamanism, Colonialism, and the Wild Man,* 3–135.

15. Taussig, *Mimesis and Alterity,* 87.

16. The photo was already famous in 1937, when Braun Menéndez came to comment on it in *Julio Popper,* 38. As a descendant of the island's most famous sheep magnates, Braun Menéndez has a vested interest in casting doubts on the veracity of this photo and, by association, the extent of his ancestors' atrocities. His main target in this is Borrero's *La Patagonia Tragica,* an anarchist tract from the late 1920s, still unpublished in Chile, though widely circulated in semi-illegal photocopies. Braun Menéndez correctly points out that the photo was not taken "in full flight" by Salesian missionaries, nor did any such observers succeed (as Borrero thinks) in catching the killer in the act. On the contrary, the photo was taken by Popper's own men. It could not, furthermore, have been taken "in

full flight" for the simple fact that such an instant shot was not, in 1886, technologically possible. So Braun Menéndez attempts to undercut an image famous for its "exposé status" through the specious assertion that it represented nothing more than an act of staged self-exposure on Popper's part. Yet for all the speciousness of this argument (for the fact is that Popper did indeed commit the murder, however artificial the proof), there is a certain strange power in Braun Menéndez's unmasking of Borrero's rhetoric of unmasking.

17. First published in a Salesian missionary journal, this image appeared in Borrero's text (ca. 1927) and then circulated the academic world through its reproduction in Martin Gusinde's canonical 1931 ethnography, *Los Indios de Tierra del Fuego*. The photo is visible in all of the regional museums of Chilean and Argentinian Tierra del Fuego, as well as in the Musée de l'Homme in Paris. In a particularly repulsive development, it is now even available as a postcard in some of the tourist shops of Punta Arenas.

18. Popper quoted in Lewin, *Quién Fue el Conquistador Patagónico Julio Popper*, 102. This book constitutes an expanded edition of Lewin's earlier *Popper, un Conquistador Patagónico*.

19. Cortés quoted in Belza, *En la Isla del Fuego*, 307.

20. For the details of this incident, see Perich, *Extinción Indigena*, 105–8.

21. "They steal for the pleasure of stealing, and enjoy destroying other peoples' property" (José Menéndez interviewed in *El Diario* [June 13, 1899], a Buenos Aires newspaper cited in Perich, *Extinción Indigena*, 116).

22. Durán, *Historia*, 10.

23. For a (disturbingly rare) anthropological attack on the Western fantasy of primitive cannibalism, see Arens, *Man-Eating Myth*. Political rhetoric, on the other hand, has often drawn its power from the unmasking of this lie. For some examples of the anticolonial counterattribution of "cannibalism," see Escudero, "The Logic of Biosphere," 1–25; Paul Harrison, *Inside the Third World*, 273–79; and Johnson, "Tupy or Not Tupy," 41–60.

24. Darwin quoted and refuted in E. Lucas Bridges, *Uttermost Part*, 33–36. For Maistre's story, see Borrero, *La Patagonia Tragica*, 27, and Perich, *Extinción Indigena*, 47. An even more extraordinary version can be found in Popper, "Tierra del Fuego," 435–48.

25. Borrero, *La Patagonia Tragica*, 20, 28.

26. Marx, *Capital*, 555.

27. Ibid.

28. Ibid.

29. Perich, *Extinción Indigena*, 115.

30. Spencer, *Spencer's Last Journey*, 52.

31. Borrero, *La Patagonia Tragica*, 21.

32. Ibid.

33. Compare Darwin explaining, after his first encounter with the Fuegians, how they will need to learn how to be "natural" if they are to compete with Europeans in the survival of the fittest (until such time, the Europeans will "labour under a cruel disadvan-

tage"): "if these barbarians were a little less barbarous, it would have been easy, as we were superior in numbers, to have pushed them away and obliged them to keep beyond a certain line; but their courage is like that of a wild beast, they would not think of their inferiority in numbers, but each individual would endeavour to dash your brains out with a stone" (*Charles Darwin's Diary*, 134). Darwin laments the inability of these too barbarous "barbarians" to organize reality into the supposedly natural calculus that allows one to tabulate and be tamed by the superiority of numbers. It is as if the primitivist precondition to peopling that Fuegian barrenness with things requires that the Fuegians learn to cower before such *market forces*.

34. See Popper, "Tierra del Fuego."

35. Belza, *En la Isla del Fuego*, 307, 314.

36. Borrero uses this phrase to describe the massacre of Patagonian workers during the 1921 anarchist uprising. See *La Patagonia Trágica*, 120 n. 3.

37. Karl Marx, *The Eighteenth Brumaire of Louis Napoleon*, in *Selected Works*, 315.

38. This unpublished photo album lies in storage in the Popper file at the Museo del Fin del Mundo (Museum of the End of the World), having been initially given in 1887 to Juarez Celman, then president of Argentina, and later passed into the hands of Armando Braun Menéndez, who donated it to the museum. Many thanks to Oscar Zanola, the museum's director, for placing the album at my disposal.

39. See, for instance, Popper's extraordinarily baroque attack upon Maistre, the cannibalistic Frenchman who exhibited Fuegians as cannibals at the World Exhibition in Paris ("Tierra del Fuego").

40. *Colors 4: Race*, Spring–Summer 1993, 2–3.

41. Ibid., 11. Compare Mr. Bond, who, as Borrero states, "in pure sarcasm named his property '*El Tehuelche*'" after the local tribe he was so instrumental in slaughtering (*La Patagonia Trágica*, 21).

42. *Colors 4: Race*, 17–18.

43. Ibid., 52–54.

44. Taussig, *Mimesis and Alterity*, 254.

45. E. Lucas Bridges, *Uttermost Part*, 392.

46. I take this phrase from Sloterdijk, *Critique of Cynical Reason*, 82.

47. Caillois, "Mimicry and Legendary Psychasthenia," 70.

48. Pascal paraphrased by Althusser in "Ideology and Ideological State Apparatuses," 127.

49. E. Lucas Bridges, *Uttermost Part*, 115.

50. Taussig, *Mimesis and Alterity*, 254.

51. Kafka quoted in ibid.

52. E. Lucas Bridges, *Uttermost Part*, 66.

53. Taussig, *Mimesis and Alterity*, 226.

6

To Recapitulate

They Were Not My Words

"I crossed over into Fireland," Bruce Chatwin writes, fording the straits for the first time.[1] In between describing the dingy ferry, the trucks it carries, and the distant oil rigs on the horizon, the traveler embarks on an enchanting intertextualized survey of the footsteps and voices which have preceded his. Named for the fires Magellan sighted on its shores, Tierra del Fuego has had a long history of European imaginings.[2] Even prior to Magellan, the Nuremberg cartographer Martin Beheim had already mapped out the rhetoric which European colonists were later to stamp upon the island in person: "In this Upside-down-land, snow fell upwards, trees grew downwards, the sun shone black, and sixteen-fingered Antipodeans danced themselves into ecstasy. WE CANNOT GO TO THEM, it was said, THEY CANNOT COME TO US."[3] It is fascinating to compare Chatwin's invocation of these imaginary geographies with James Boon's deconstructive history of European representations of the island. Surveying texts ranging from Pigafetta through Hawkesworth, Darwin, and even up to Carl Sagan, Boon critiques these pseudo-ethnographers for their untenable claims to representational transparency.[4] Such "exaggerations" of indigenous culture offer little more than allegorical representations of their observers' own cultures.

Chatwin is worlds away from Boon. For the traveler, an absurdity such as Beheim's serves simply to carry his meaningless narrative through all the mundanity of ferry crossing, passport stamping, and conversing with local oil engineers. Such unbelievable stories are quite literally necessary to provide the local color, imagination, and fantasy that Chatwin himself, in all his skepticism and futility, cannot muster. These age-old and naïve fantasies serve—precisely as the "exaggerations" Boon seeks to expose—to tide the traveler over to Tierra del Fuego.

I have been drawn to similar strategies throughout this book, as much as during the offhand travels it documents. The trash of travel has led me into the recapitulationist realms of surrealist research, as I attempted, in Taussig's footsteps, to follow the *objet trouvé* out beyond its European home. Such redemptive activities ran parallel with a set of disturbingly analogous behaviors: unsolicited testimonials to the magic of white commodities, which reclaim for advertising the primitivity of the present; unsolicited projections of indigenous savagery, which rationalize for colonial capitalism the savagery then "mimicked on the body of that Other."[5] Throughout, these time capsule revelations have suggested a mode of mastery which, in holding others to their words, in fact holds them to its own words.

Indeed, the master's Otherness may be there on the very face of things. This is apparent in the "reflexively buffered" manner in which Chatwin, himself a master recapitulationist, revisits the relics of his past. Beheim's Antipodean discourse provides the traveler with a meaning which he can mimic as he moves through the same terrain, traveling back in time, in body, if not in spirit, with his European predecessor. This ironic cultural recapitulation is paralleled in the personal regression through which Chatwin reexperiences a childish belief in his search and the unity it promises him. Both these ethnic and familial strains converge in the person of Chatwin's Great-Uncle Charley, the turn-of-the-century colonist who once seemed "a God among men" to the awed and infant Chatwin.[6] The loss of the fragment of "dinosaur" skin symbolizes the loss of this childish wonder and awe—emotions which Chatwin will then come to seek, in the mid-1970s, in the real Tierra del Fuego. As he enacts this pathetic realization of his childhood dream, he finds his quest for truth mediated through a grown-up knowledge of the farcical inevitability with which this "ridiculous" quest will lead to failure.[7] He seeks all the same, letting Great-Uncle Charley answer the question *What am I doing here* for him.

The other heroic pre-text is provided by Lucas Bridges, whose trail Chatwin traces from Ushuaia to Haberton and into the interior. *Uttermost Part of the Earth* was, he writes, "one of my favorite books as a boy."[8] Now leaving the Bridges family property at Haberton, Chatwin recalls a favorite passage (the very passage which I cited in chapter 3, on the threshold of my own time capsule):

> In it he [Bridges] describes looking down from Mount Spion Kop on the sacred Lake Kami, and how, later, the Indians helped him hack a trail linking Haberton with the family's other farm at Viamonte.
>
> I had always wanted to walk the track.[9]

And so he does. And so did I.

A Mute Witness

To let Bridges answer for Chatwin answering for me will, to follow this hierarchy down to its end, take me to the Fuegians, who, in such a temporal schema, so consistently answer to and for their self-styled masters.

From citing Bridges's backward outlook on the "not far distant future" at the end of chapter 3, I have traced a similar ventriloquism through the *Uttermost Part of the Earth*.[10] The colonist's jokes, I argued, serve to script the Selk'nam with faith in a fetish which is in fact his. Translating back for the Other, Bridges avails himself of a doubly-disbelieved, rebounding mimicry. It was this structure of projective identification which I began to draw into the self-distant forms of the anecdotal present. Bringing such humor face-to-face with its own self-distance, I asked the all-too-obvious question: How can the master fail to see his role in these blatant projections? "Colonialist mastery" is, in truth, not so easily unmastered; its Otherness is predicated upon the "reflexive awareness" which should by all rights disarm it.[11] Yet the fact that such findings, far from breaking the trajectory of my analysis, actually serve to maintain it alerts me to the necessity of looking to whatever it is that persists beyond such self-knowledge.

That is why Yekaifwaianjiz, the mimic-out-of-control who, in Bridges's portrayal, seems simply beyond all meaningful speech, is such a lucky find (*objet trouvé*) for me. When he turns to describe Yekaifwaianjiz, Bridges for once cannot quote any of the Other's enchanted words as his own. That this mute Fuegian provides his European audience with such a "sudden laugh from nowhere" suggests that his wordless gestures, nonetheless, follow the same perceptual course as the everyday commodity encounter anecdote. They should, therefore, allow me to follow through my questioning of the master's place in these projective identifications without, for once, being caught up in the self-reflexive (false-conscious, self-conscious, or otherwise) vertigo of attempting to fix his relation to the Other's words, which are in fact his, which were never his to begin with. Shorn of all fetishistic overlay, these preverbal mimetic relations may instead reveal something of the naked structure, provenance, and staying power of the "sudden laugh from nowhere."

To elicit such testimony I want to turn to the theory of "ideational mimetics" which Taussig cites from Freud's book of jokes. "One tries out the very shape of a perception in one's own body," Taussig explains, weaving this striking Freudian model of perceptual mimesis into his own theory of representation.[12] In what follows I shall investigate how the mimicry of a Yekaifwaianjiz might fit into Freud's models. These century-old ideas will hopefully serve to illuminate the fetish-free face of "colonialist mastery" that finds itself in Bridges's labile complexion, as he laughingly takes in Yekaifwaianjiz's excesses through the "ideational mimetics" of his own body.[13]

Freud's Comic Naïveté

According to Freud, it is the "comic of movement" which makes Yekaifwaianjiz's excessive motions funny ("a gesture a comedian might well have envied") to their European observer.[14] This mode of humor relies on the internal and quantitative comparison that an observer makes between his [sic] empathetic imagining of the Other's exaggerated movements and his memory of the expenditure these movements would normally require. The surplus that arises from this preconscious comparison, the "*Differenz*" (a purely quantitative term in German) between one's empathetic muscular enervation and the actual cathexis of energies typically required is then converted by the percipient into laughter.[15] For Freud, this internal perceptual/mimetic apparatus is particularly operative when the observer looks at "a child or a man from the common people, or a member of certain races" (perhaps an Indian from the Uttermost Part of the Earth?).[16] Using their bodies so much more in expressing and perceiving, such people are all the more likely to spark off a comic response in their educated male observers. The more intellectual and civilized you get, the funnier the unrepressed physicality of the Other's mimetic behavior. Yet far from intellectual, this comic dimension arises from the subject's own internal mimetics, from the *Differenz* they allow him [sic] to experience—in the flesh.

This biological theory of a quantifying economy in psychic expenditure is, on the face of it, quite crazy and even seems comic itself. Deliberately reading Freud against himself, Rey Chow invokes the theory to illustrate the structural hierarchizing of visual relations between the modern male subject and his Others. Turning to the humorous automation of workers in *Modern Times,* Chow argues that Freud's hierarchical categories are in themselves symptomatic of a modern power structure: the Other's consignment to the status of visual object, of automaton. She ties this analysis into a gendered reading of Freud's theory of the uncanny: "The two arguments intersect at the notion of the automatized Other, which takes the form either of the ridiculous, the lower class, or of woman."[17]

While Chow's seems a valid critique of Freud, who may well have believed in the virtue of the hierarchy he thus diagnosed and/or symptomatized, it brushes over one startling fact. The inequality underwriting this hierarchization of visual relations is not, according to Freud, actually what makes the comic comic. The "dehumanized" relations Chow sets forth often provide the framework for comic perception, yet it is not this dehumanization itself which is funny.[18] Freud is adamant on this point, stressing more than once that "the feeling of superiority bears no essential relation to comic pleasure."[19] A "comparison," on the other hand, "is indispensable for the generation of this pleasure."[20] Stage comedy, for Freud, is proof of this. A comedian can be deliberately excessive in his [sic] motions, and thereby be comic. Whether the audience members consider the comedian inferior to them, equal, or otherwise is irrelevant to the laughter he provokes.[21] A civilized comedian acting out, in all reflexive self-consciousness, the same ultra-French actions as Yekaifwaianjiz can be just as funny.

If Freud is right, then the "element of colonial mastery" in the laugh with which one watches the ignorant Yámana overact the intelligent Frenchman actually has little to do with mastery. The feelings of self-superiority one may derive, retrospectively, from such comic scenarios are not merely delusory. They are irrelevant. They are irrelevant to a pleasure which arises from the internal perceptual mimicry of the Other's exaggerated movements. The master is not laughing at his supposed superiority so much as imagining himself in the body of the Other. If this is so, then the naked face of "colonial mastery" is nowhere near as simple as its hierarchical posturing suggests.

While Freud's quantifying biologizations seem irredeemable, the hierarchizing, contrast-oriented structure he discerns in them deserves to be salvaged for the mute insight it provides into this two-faced comic mastery. As I proceed to bring words back into the picture—that is, as I return to Bridges's expressly fetishistic anecdotes—I will follow this Freudian method to see where it takes me beyond the impasse of the previous chapter. It takes me beyond Yekaifwaianjiz's mute testimony, for, as the very term *ideational mimetics* suggests, this mode of internal mimetic perception takes in not merely the Other's gestures but indeed their very words.

Freud opposes the category of the comic, which operates through the preconscious comparison of quantities, to that of jokes, which work through the expression of unconscious meaning. By allowing "the representation of something which cannot be expressed directly," the joke releases the energy invested in the "psychical damming up" of repressed ideas and turns that energy into laughter.[22] The way the joke thus evades the taboos of "critical reason" mirrors the way Bridges's utilitarian pretexts allow him to evade the modernist taboo on superstition and fetishism.[23] Of course there is only a structural analogy, not an identity, between Freud's jokes and Bridges's anecdotes. The discrepancy is apparent the moment one considers them in terms of their differing audiences and addressees. The Fuegians clearly are *not* party to the "sudden laugh from nowhere" which anecdotes of native testimonial occasion, as Chow's argument, critiquing similar structures, makes clear.

To take this into account, one must turn to Freud's "comic of the naïve," the category in which the preconscious, quantitative character of the comic intersects with the unconscious, linguistic nature of the joke. Naïveté, Freud notes, occurs when the person observed acts in ignorance of an inhibition in their observer. The disinhibition of the naïve person allows the observer access to the expression of otherwise repressed thoughts. In perceiving this naïveté, "we take the producing person's psychical state into consideration, put ourselves into it, and try to understand it by comparing it with our own."[24] The pleasure derived from this "comic of the naïve" is hence twofold: the pleasure we derive from the comparison of expenditure (the comic) and that which arises from our sudden access to the repressed material (the joke).

For Freud, naïve ignorance of the male observer's inhibitions is found "most often in children, and is then carried over to uneducated adults, whom we may regard as childish as far as their intellectual development is concerned."[25] I could, of course, again criticize Freud's decidedly unrevolutionary ideas here. I would have to simultaneously critique the revolutionary Breton; his notion that "childhood . . . comes closest to true life" is indeed simply the other side of Freud's hierarchical, indeed recapitulationist, structuring.[26] Yet what is fascinating in the contrast between these two is the way Freud's argument, for all its law-abiding elitism, is so much more subversive.

If his "comic of the naïve" reifies a hierarchical structure, it simultaneously describes the manner in which that structure is, in all *legitimacy,* inverted and made to contradict itself. Hearing the child's naïve words, the mature male subject mimetically imagines himself in the pleasurable position of the inferior. Momentarily inverting his position on Freud's evolutionary scale of developed and less developed humanity, he gains access to his own unconscious and repressed desires. Yet in doing so, he not only retains his status as superior; he converts the hierarchical *Differenz* into the pleasure of laughter. His sense of superiority is hence bolstered by the very mechanisms which violate it. For Freud's recapitulationist mastery is not as simple as its hierarchical language suggests.

This is apparent as I return to the scenarios through which Bridges manages to fetishize his commodities and yet not break the inhibitions of critical reason. The miracle of the magic lantern combines rationalizing pretexts with the "comic of the naïve" to allow access to "the unconscious of the commodity form": "Unfortunately the Ona [Selk'nam] word for 'picture' or 'shadow' was the name of one of their ghosts, so the assurance that this was only a picture would have been no better than telling a frightened child that it was only a bogey-man."[27] In talking down to the Other, here cast as "frightened child," Bridges coins a comic anecdote of native naïveté. He thus shores up his superior civilized position, while simultaneously accessing his own tabooed animism, the fetishism he experiences through the eyes of the Other. Note the bilocation this maneuver allows, where, as Freud states, the narrator puts himself in the position of the child, while still laughing, in all supposed superiority, *in loco parentis.* Access to such uninhibited awe, contracted out to the Other as *third nature,* but desired by the colonist all the same, is made possible through a recapitulationist structure of racial superiority. So Bridges can humorously misrecognize himself as master, for all his excessive indulgence in the fetishistic freedom of the slave.

A Revolutionary Awakening?

The recapitulationist structure of "colonialist mastery" seems to have little to do with mastery itself and everything to do with the channel it opens up for unmasterly reveling in fantasies which the colonist cannot even own as his own.

So how to make him own them? A critic such as Boon would take issue with recapitulationism for its inadequacy to the nature it supposedly represents. A similar attack could be directed against Freud for the fundamentally false analogy which he makes between his child-adult developmental schema and the evolutionist's primitive-civilized ladder of time and space. Yet Freud himself lays the traces through which one can unwrite his own texts, in his insistence that there is no necessity for such structures of superiority to be in any way true for them to allow the master access to the pleasures he locates in the purportedly inferior. To focus upon the truth/untruth of such a discursive structure vis-à-vis nature is, at best, irrelevant. The most subversive attack on recapitulationism focuses not on the concept's inadequacy to "nature," but simply on its inadequacy to itself. The dysfunctional, self-contradictory, and excessive articulations of such a structure of colonial mastery point to the unmasterful aspects of mastery, to its own persistent failure, not so much to be natural, as simply to be itself.

In this dialectical fashion, I want to return to the hierarchical, evolutionary, and outrightly imperial recapitulationist structure which I have tracked through anecdote, advertisement, and joke to this point. Far from necessarily adequate to its own self-superior logic, such a temporal schema allows a figure like Bridges to violate its rules repeatedly. The anecdotal inversion of the colonist's self-superiority has him constantly experiencing the awe-stricken beliefs of a "frightened child"; through such instances Bridges has vicarious access to those fantasies which he, as rational colonial capitalist, has quite literally grown out of. In thus *bilocating* himself, accessing the primitive/childish place of the Other and at the same time staying *in loco parentis,* Bridges himself unwrites the logic of the very structure that makes him master. This is the contradiction I want to awaken, this the "colonial mastery" I want to bring face to face with itself.

This is, however, a double-edged strategy. It needs to be seen that Bridges, in recording such encounters, is enacting for advertising precisely that recapitulative operation which Benjamin would claim for revolutionary critique. In his anecdotes of native awe, the colonist recapitulates both the primitive-present fetishes of his Indian companions and also the awe-stricken fantasies of his own childhood. He thereby misrecognizes, and yet maintains mastery over, the repressed dreaming sites which for Benjamin were spaces of potential redemption: "Every childhood achieves something great, irreplaceable for mankind. Through its interest in technical phenomena, its curiosity about all kinds of discoveries and machinery, every childhood ties technological achievement to the old, symbolic worlds."[28] The redemptive potential of such childhood dreams was, according to Benjamin, analogous to the potential energy stored within the civic dreamscapes of the recent past. In Susan Buck-Morss's paraphrase, "the out-of-date ruins of the recent past appear as residues of a dreamworld."[29] Rejecting the surrealist intoxication with dreams, the Bretonian focus on psychic automatism, Benjamin sought a grown-up "fairy tale" that would harness the revolutionary power of awakening from such wish-laden dream forms.[30] The historical materialist would aim to bring such dreams out of their discarded optative forms and into the present, to make that present tense with the imperative for change.

If only that were still possible. In Buck-Morss's reading of the cynical, post-perestroika present, this very dream of revolutionary awakening now seems an "out of date ruin of the recent past."[31] After Stalin, Benjamin's famous call for the politicization of art now seems not simply naïve and wishful, but even beyond redemption. In this tawdry present, dreams eke out a miserable existence in the form of commodified and clichéd "city-image[s]" that no one even believes in.[32] In the following, Buck-Morss could be describing travelers to the End of the World, as much as those who travel through the hopeless political landscape of the postmodern present:

> They reproduce the dream-image, but reject the dream. In this cynical time of the "end of history" adults know better than to believe in social utopias of any kind—those of production or consumption. . . . When it [the dream] is allowed expression at all, it takes on the look of children's toys . . . as if to prove that utopias of social space can no longer be taken seriously; they are commercial ventures, nothing more. Benjamin insisted "We must wake up from the world of our parents." . . . But what can be demanded of a new generation, if its parents never dream at all?[33]

Coming of Age in Tierra del Fuego

It is intriguing to turn from this disenchanted present to that naïve imperial past in which dreaming was still possible. Lucas Bridges makes just such a nostalgic gesture, in turning to describe the missionary world of his parents, the dreams of his childhood. What is so exceptional in his autobiography/ethnography is the way the colonist shares his childhood fantasies and dreams with those of his Indian companions, firstly as childhood playmates, and then later as the adults who, unlike him, somehow never quite grew up.[34] But that awakening lies off in the future, when his father dies, when the family's commercial responsibilities are abruptly devolved upon him. As an Anglo-Yámana child, his only wish is to regress, to be stolen by a wolf, to be adopted like Mowgli, to go native. "Later in these pages," writes Bridges-as-adult, and now in all irony, "it shall be told how I achieved that ambition."[35]

Yet one need read no further, for Bridges's eventual adoption into the Selk'nam is already foreshadowed in his description of the primitive awe with which he, aged five, experiences the wonders of white civilization. The Bridges family is on a journey to Haberton, the place of his grandfather's farm in England, as well as the name of the Fuegian property to which he shall eventually return. The family embarks on the Galicia, a "floating palace" to the awestruck Bridges-as-child, which takes them from Punta Arenas to an England of industrial wonders.[36] His fascination with the technological novelty he encounters there serves, much as Benjamin would argue, to tie such products of capitalist industry into the older symbolic worlds of childhood and primitivism. The farm has "a forge and a wheelwright's workshop with a circular saw driven by a water-wheel. What an enchanting place we thought it!"[37]

From here Bridges's father takes him to a railway station where a new sort of illumination is, in the late 1870s, being tried out for the first time. "People said it was too bright and would be injurious to the sight, and I devoutly hoped our sight had not been harmed already."[38] The naïveté of Bridges-as-child merges here with that of the still-timid British, afraid of electric light as if they were peasants in awe of commodified sugarcane or Bushmen faced with Coke bottles from the future. For those of us, on the other hand, for whom electric light is already second nature, Thomas Bridges's naturalizing explanation of the invention seems uncannily artificial: "Father explained that it was allied to lightning, of which we had seen plenty coming through the tropics, and that it was called electric light."[39] Profane illuminations indeed!

On the family's return to Tierra del Fuego, the visit of a team of French scientists gives young Lucas something to look up to again. The scientists' "learning, enhanced by their colored spectacles and beards of different shapes and hues, filled my boyish mind with awe."[40] It is these same French scientists who inspire Yekaifwaianjiz's uncontrollable mimicry. Meanwhile Lucas (having gained a certain self-reflection from his travels?) is learning to control his cross-cultural interactions and feels "proud" to act as translator for the scientists. As literal mediator between the Europeans and the Yámana, he thus begins his career of talking down and talking up to Others, translating the words of modern science into the primitive tongue, and vice versa. In such mediations Bridges is, of course, following in the footsteps of his rather distant missionary father, a man whom he "almost worshipped."[41] (In much the same way, the young Chatwin of the future would see his Great-Uncle Charley, a Fuegian colonist almost contemporaneous with Bridges, as a "God among men."[42])

I wonder whether Bridges was already thinking *in loco parentis* when he witnessed his father perform a miracle of medicine-giving to a Yámana who arrived and beseeched some of "the white man's magic" for his sick child. "Father gave him a little sweetened raspberry vinegar, and he went away delighted. The baby, of course, recovered."[43] Was the young Bridges full of faith in the power of white sugar water? Or was he instead learning the rationalized dissimulation that would lead, only twenty years later, to the miracle of iodine, that psychosomatic "magic paint" with the power to heal broken-boned Indians?

Of course neither Bridges nor his father could cure the Yámana of the epidemics which the whites brought in their wake. Not even a disbelieved and displaced magic can do that. In his early twenties, and now living at Haberton, Lucas has grown up to the point that encounter with the Selk'nam is no longer a youthful dream. The childish awe characterizing the "third white native" of Ushuaia's confrontation with the "white man's magic" seems to have been transferred in full to the Selk'nam. In this manner Bridges awakens into the hierarchical structure that poises him paternalistically over the previously "coeval" Indians. Not that this disenchanting fate will stop the adult Bridges ("later in these pages") from attaining his childish wish—it is at this moment that the miracle of Pears' magic soap occurs.

The Dream That You Are Awake Is the *Objet Trouvé*

In Buck-Morss's reading of Benjamin, the point of awakening from the utopian dreams of childhood has, for all its disenchantment, the potential to provide the impetus for change. The sorry contrast between such dreams and the "dystopian actuality" that one has actually grown into, might, Benjamin hoped, spark off the desire for revolutionary activity.[44]

Bridges's example (inasmuch as one can rely on his out-of-date testimony) seems to show that one can keep dreaming these very dreams of childhood, even after awakening, by channeling them through the primitive/childish, naïve Other. The critical power Benjamin and Buck-Morss wish to engage and redeem from the "nostalgia for a world which was supposed to be" is here reclaimed in the prolongation, outside of the self, of that same other world of faith and fantasy.[45] The failure of such dreams (in my materialization of Benjamin, the disenchantment of the fetishistic awe inspired by Western things) here loses its redemptive potential. It provides, instead, the pretext whereby the white man of reason can maintain and yet simultaneously deny his own open reveling in, and even advertisement of, such fantasies.

This disenchanting reenchantment may, on one level, represent the ideological recuperation whereby, in Adorno and Horkheimer's phrase, "the rebellion of suppressed nature against domination" is made "directly useful to domination."[46] Yet it does leave open a space in which to contest the very end of dreaming which Buck-Morss fears. No one stops dreaming at the End of the World; they simply send their dreams elsewhere. Such a primitive, more naïve, recapitulable place really does, in Benjamin's words, offer something "irreplaceable" for revolutionary practice. It continues to do so.

Buck-Morss is worried about the future's past that the cynical present will become. But such dream forms need not necessarily have any actual provenance in the dreams of the past, either now or in the future. As Freud states, apropos of the comic of the naïve, "none of the characteristics of the naïve exist except in the apprehension of the person who hears it."[47] Freud even argues that the repressed childhood state of bliss, to which the comic returns us through laughter, actually never existed in the sense in which we access it. The child is incapable of the comic, having no sense of the separation of self and Other through which comic comparison could occur.[48] Benjamin, it seems, understood the projective, rebounding power of such parental agendas: "Toys," he wrote, "even when not imitative of adult utensils, are a coming to terms, and doubtless less of the child with adults than of adults with him."[49] And with themselves, I want to add.

This is why Buck-Morss's description of the trivialized appearance of contemporary social dreaming—"When it is allowed expression at all, it takes on the look of children's toys"—is so revealing.[50] The infantile, discarded appearance of such dream forms seems manufactured "as if to prove" that they "cannot be taken seriously."[51] Why the need to prove this triviality? Why the insistence, stamped on the very face of these things, that they are "commercial ventures, nothing more"?[52] Can one fail to recognize in these things the same always already destitute item of fashion which, to the cynical "dream that one is awake," will always be either our contemporary trash or our amusement in someone else's naïve hands? The philosophical message stamped like a trademark on such out-of-date trash is that "commercial ventures" such as these are indeed always far more than simply "nothing more."[53]

That something more is the Benjaminian "time-dream," the discourse of which, like Marx's commodity fetishism, structures the adult's self-absent actions. Such dream forms can be taken seriously only through the anamorphotic future perfect perspective that reveals their disowned power over "reflexively buffered" cynical realities. Lucas Bridges plays with these children's toys, "as if to prove" that he himself "cannot be taken seriously." So he observes at the end of the nineteenth century, at the End of the World, the disenchanted faith and the fantasies that suddenly seem so impossible at the "end of history" one hundred years later.

In Loco Infantis

Projected onto the infant and then mimicked back by its parents as the childish discourse those adults have grown out of, the parental *agenda* (literally, "that which is to be done") manifests itself through time. However infantile, it describes the true contours of their acts. In this way, the collective's *time-dream* manifests itself in rational *time-space* at the very point where that Cartesian time-space is irrationally, and yet legitimately, doubled in on itself—in the civilized primitivism of the masterful present, in its address to the infantilized Other.

Contrary to Foucault, for whom the "political question" is the constitution of "truth itself," I am arguing that such structures have their most subversive potential for "profane illumination" at the point at which they de-constitute the truth which grounds them, turning it into falsity as their only means of staying true to themselves.[54] In his essay on epic theater, Benjamin asserts that "interruption is one of the fundamental devices of all structuring."[55] Is there not a certain fundamental interruption in the truly false structure through which Bridges-as-adult anecdotalizes his childhood awe before electric light? The profane illumination that flashes through the self-superior discourse of colonial recapitulationism takes its light from the blind spot of that same discourse. The political question arises, only to be rapidly misrecognized as a joke, at such farcical moments of constitutive de-constitution. A rejuvenated Marxism must identify such unmasterful moments of mastery and *blow them out of all proportion*.

England's claim to lie at the apex of this homogenizing developmental schema may seem set in time and space. Yet Bridges's text equates the primitive English reaction to electric light to that of the infant Bridges and even to that of the Selk'nam, who are almost coevally overawed by the "magic lantern." For a Baldwin Spencer or a Sir James Frazer, England has always been the culminating point of the evolutionary metanarrative that casts the Fuegians in the "most primitive" role. Taking on such claims, critics like Johannes Fabian and Arturo Escobar have attacked recapitulationism and development discourse for all the obvious reasons.[56] Yet they ignore the way this same England, the imperial capital of the nineteenth century, can now be so desirously posed as backward and primitive—as primitive as Tierra del Fuego—for the sake of a commodity encounter anecdote.

Revealing the backwardness which marks the very height of civilization, these anecdotes offer a white Fuegian adult, writing in the England of the late 1940s, the primitivist pleasure of the comic of the naïve. Nor does Bridges's line in humor finish here, in the nostalgically disenchanted final years before his death. It is as if he is simultaneously devolving these farcical properties onto the traveler who will follow in his footsteps. At this moment Bruce Chatwin is growing up in that same England, with the horror of Stalin and the bomb hanging over his childhood. So Chatwin foments the dream forms of the primitive past which he will then recapitulate, thirty years later, in Tierra del Fuego. Young Bruce and friends create an "Emigration Committee" that aims to evacuate them to Patagonia, the "safest place on Earth" in which to experience the end of the world.[57] Chatwin knows this from having read Bridges's autobiography, "one of my favorite books as a boy."

The cuteness of this infantile image (Taussig writes that the "very word 'cute'" suggests the "pervasive intimations of primitiveness")[58] points once more to the lability of definitions of superiority and inferiority in the hierarchized comparisons which give rise to the "sudden laugh from nowhere." Nowhere is not so easily located as one might suspect; nor is the joking present so sure of itself as not, at times, to slip perilously behind. As Freud states, stressing the fundamental independence of the comic and the feeling of superiority, one may well pretend (and pretend quite openly—like a comedian) to occupy the space of the naïve, thereby sparking off those same pleasures. Such a knowing perspective on his own simulated naïveté allows Bridges, as mature colonist and later as author, to "play along" with the unsolicited testimonial, to become, quite literally, part of the joke.

A similar slipperiness in one's movements along the time-space schema of development and civilization has this same adult Bridges become suddenly rather more perilously backward in his rustic's encounter with the monstrous metropolis of Buenos Aires. Bridges is now twenty-eight and has already witnessed—as participant observer laughing off his "colonial mastery"—the miracles of magic soap, all-curing iodine, and magic lantern. Yet having not left the island since the age of eleven, and with the prospect of the modern capital ahead of him, Bridges realizes that he has "grown as wild and apprehensive of white strangers as the wary Te-ilh of Najmishk."[59] This is the same Buenos Aires that modern travel writers, neocolonial masters to the core, never tire of labeling backward and slavishly imitative of European fashions and forms.[60] Bridges, on the other hand, is suddenly facing the future, and the horse-drawn cab which picks him up at the port gives him the fright of his life, as he is "whisked along in what seemed a confused whirl of traffic."[61] Questioned as to his obvious nervousness, the colonist "felt very small" and shamefully answered that he had not been in a coach since the age of six.[62]

Bridges, a poor *flâneur* indeed, cowers backwardly at "those awful wax figures in the shop windows. . . . So unnatural were they—and yet so human—that I could not meet their glassy stare."[63] As if regressing to the same childish perspective that was his in England, yet now in fear, Bridges cowers from the "nightmare" of a feminized modernity of mechanical reproduction. Wax shop-front dummies seem as injurious to the sight as electric light was to the English primitivized by the future only twenty years before. The Fuegian colonist's inability to face these fake women brings to mind the central position woman-as-automaton has in Benjamin's "metaphysics of fashion" in the "nightmare" Paris of the nineteenth century.[64] Bridges's self-infantilization before these dummies only foreshadows his ineptitude with the actual women he now encounters, and recoils from, in ultramodern Buenos Aires. As an inexperienced and abashed adult, Bridges declines an Argentine lawyer friend's repeated attempts to match him with the women of the capital. He recoils to such an extent that he now imagines, fifty years later, that he must have appeared "either physically or mentally deficient."[65]

The mystery and repulsion of mechanical reproduction is, in this way, thoroughly feminized for Bridges, in accord with Chow's argument. Yet in his text it is precisely his inability to cope with the Other's consignment to automaton status which characterizes *his* backwardness, inferiority, and fetishistic fear. Writing fifty years in retrospect, Bridges is effectively creating a primitive persona for himself, making himself backward to a fearfully animated, and fetishistically sexualized, inorganic modernity. He writes that "Bluebeard's unfortunate wives could not have been more varied" than the dossier of photos of eligible women which the lawyer puts before him, and from which he recoils in infantile fright.[66] Can one ignore the echo here of the primitive fear that had the Selk'nam recoil before a mechanically reproduced "magic lantern" image of Bluebeard just ten years before in Tierra del Fuego, when Bridges was still, vis-à-vis them, at the vanguard of civilization?

How Firmly Are Those Feet Planted?

It is hard to find a more striking instance of the spatialization of time which Fabian discusses than this primitivization of the "third white native of Ushuaia," as he moves out of the Cartesian time-space coordinates that have him civilized among the Selk'nam and into the future that makes him backward in Buenos Aires. Bridges's time-traveling visit to the future brings out its fetishistic characteristics through the eyes of the backward colonist, just like any of his primitivist anecdotes. He becomes backward through the same recapitulationist structure that, according to its critics, is meant to secure his possession of the present. If Caillois's "legendary psychasthenia" is terrifying for the very formlessness of being it potentiates, there is something equally uncanny in this schema of mastery.[67] Like a Möbius strip, its denial of coevalness perilously and yet logically inverts its own principles of order, dispossessing the master of his sense of self-superiority through the same structure that once gave it support—leaving him nothing to cling to but his new-found inferiority.

There is little allowance in Fabian's argument for the possibility that a colonist, or an anthropologist, might find him- or herself on the primitive end of the allochronistic scale, the whole notion of a hierarchy being, apparently, that those at the top get all the rewards. Obviously this *was* the case in Tierra del Fuego. Yet it needs to be seen that someone like Bridges only possesses the fine things of the present by virtue of the unmasterful way in which he simultaneously wallows in the fantasies he projects onto the past. His mastery over the present is inextricably linked to the hierarchical inversions that make him cower so backwardly before the fantasies he finds in the future. Bridges repeatedly *bilocates* himself within the developmental space-time coordinates of a supposedly naturalized and immanent recapitulationist discourse which stress that the only speaking position is *unilocal*. It is at these very points, where the discourse fails, that the subject finds and simultaneously misrecognizes him- or herself. These are the spaces for the true surrealization of reality.

Of course such spaces can always be uneasily redeemed by the nostalgic whimsy with which the now-married Bridges, in the 1940s, laughs at his primitive and virginal response to the feminized future back in the early 1900s. For he himself has a "reflexive awareness as to the mimetic faculty." Indeed, the ability of someone like Bridges to step out of his place in this structure and to play at being primitive, while staying civilized, is predicated upon the fact that he recognizes the contours of the terrain on which he so trivially treads. In this he is much like Freud's comedian, pretending to be physically primitive while knowing that he remains civilized. Through consciously acting out such impossible bilocations, Bridges accesses the fetishistic perspective he projects onto the past, yet keeps his feet firmly planted in the disenchanted rationality of the present.

But how firmly are those feet planted?

Notes

1. Chatwin, *In Patagonia,* 105.

2. The trope Chatwin employs here (Indian campfires to modern oil rigs) is actually a commonplace in such literature. One can find several versions of this illuminating advertisement of industrial primitivism, none of them original, in Prosser de Goodall's bilingual travel guide, *Tierra del Fuego, Argentina,* 135; Samagalski's *Chile and Easter Island;* and even the preface to this very book. For further comment, see my "Changing Channels," 29–31.

3. Chatwin, *In Patagonia,* 106.

4. Boon, *Other Tribes, Other Scribes,* 37–43.

5. Taussig, *Mimesis and Alterity,* 87.

6. Chatwin, *In Patagonia,* 5.

7. Ibid., 182.

8. Ibid., 131.

9. Ibid. Chatwin is referring to E. Lucas Bridges, *Uttermost Part,* 336–37.

10. E. Lucas Bridges, *Uttermost Part,* 336.

11. Taussig, *Mimesis and Alterity,* 226.

12. Ibid., 46, referring to Freud, *Jokes,* 252–54.

13. Freud, *Jokes,* 252.

14. Ibid., 248–60; E. Lucas Bridges, *Uttermost Part,* 115.

15. Freud, *Jokes,* 247 n. 1.

16. Ibid., 252.

17. Chow, "Postmodern Automatons," 108. On the uncanny, see Sigmund Freud, "The Uncanny," in *Standard Edition,* 17:217–52. In like fashion, Chow critiques *The Dialectic of Enlightenment* for its feminization and automatization of the supposedly deluded object-masses of mass culture.

18. Chow, "Post-modern Automatons," 107.

19. Freud, *Jokes,* 256.

20. Ibid.

21. Ibid., 260.

22. Ibid., 114, 166.

23. Ibid., 175, 140.

24. Ibid., 245.

25. Ibid., 241.

26. Breton quoted in Rosemont, "Introduction," 73.

27. E. Lucas Bridges, *Uttermost Part,* 287.

28. Benjamin, "Konvolut N," 6.

29. Buck-Morss, "The City as Dreamworld," 6.

30. Ibid., 7. For Benjamin's stance on surrealism, see Cohen, *Profane Illumination,* 173–215.

31. Buck-Morss, "The City as Dreamworld," 4.

32. Ibid., 25.

33. Ibid., 26.

34. For specific references to their adult-childishness, see E. Lucas Bridges, *Uttermost Part,* 248, 330.

35. Ibid., 66.

36. Ibid., 89.

37. Ibid., 90.

38. Ibid.

39. Ibid.

40. Ibid., 114.

41. Ibid., 94.

42. Chatwin, *In Patagonia,* 5.

43. E. Lucas Bridges, *Uttermost Part,* 83.

44. Buck-Morss, "The City as Dreamworld," 23.

45. Ibid.

46. Adorno and Horkheimer, *Dialectic of Enlightenment,* 185.

47. Freud, *Jokes,* 243.

48. Ibid., 302.

49. Benjamin quoted in Mehlman, *Walter Benjamin for Children,* 4.

50. Buck-Morss, "The City as Dreamworld," 26.

51. Ibid.

52. Ibid.

53. Ibid.

54. Foucault, "Truth and Power," 75.

55. Walter Benjamin, "What Is Epic Theatre?" in *Illuminations,* 148.

56. Fabian, *Time and the Other;* Escobar, *Encountering Development.*

57. Chatwin, *In Patagonia,* 7.

58. Taussig, *Mimesis and Alterity,* 226.

59. E. Lucas Bridges, *Uttermost Part,* 341.

60. Pico Iyer, the travel writer, cites his debt to both Chatwin and V. S. Naipaul before proceeding to imitate, in minor key, the latter's hysterical rantings about Argentine imitativeness (*Falling off the Map,* 44). Iyer thus himself appears the poor "translation" (37) that he accuses Argentina of being (i.e., of Europe), mouthing, without feeling, that

same stupid and overbearing discourse he found in Naipaul's *The Return of Eva Peron,* in which one can find the original unoriginal attack on the Other's unoriginality.

61. E. Lucas Bridges, *Uttermost Part,* 342.

62. Ibid.

63. Ibid., 343.

64. Buck-Morss, *Dialectics of Seeing,* 99.

65. E. Lucas Bridges, *Uttermost Part,* 342.

66. Ibid.

67. Taussig, *Mimesis and Alterity,* 33–43.

7

Seeing "One's Mirror Image Close Its Eyes"

Like Badly Translated Bruce Chatwins

Sergei practiced his English on me at a party one night. He told me that he worked in a "drugstore" (that's the Spanish word for it too, he said), where he sold "*puro trucho*" (utter crap) to tourists: furry penguins, *El Fin del Mundo* bumper stickers, "I've been to the End of the World" T-shirts. He did this in whatever language he could, but mainly French. French tourists flock to Ushuaia. One of them once told Sergei, laughing in broken Spanish, that the reason so many visit is that there is a TV program in France called "Ushuaia," which features people engaging in "extremes" and visiting "crazy" places. That is the sole reason they come here: to mimic the cast of this TV show, by being "crazy" and "extreme" enough to go as far as Ushuaia itself to do so. We laughed at how ridiculous these tourists were, flying all the way around the world, just to say that they had stepped into their own stupid documentary.[1]

To laugh at these French clowns, these badly translated Bruce Chatwins, is, for the ethnographer, to become them. My own documentary—this ethnohistory of the white colonial subject traveling through time to Tierra del Fuego—will be all the more critical if I translate their travel discourse back into the broken English I speak when I play at not being myself. For the subjects of travels to "Ushuaia" lie not in the truth claims which they make about the actual Ushuaia. They have no faith in their own disowned discourse ("traveling all the way around the world just to say that they have stepped into their own stupid documentary").

A Full Circle?

This maneuver takes me right back to the truth-seeking subject with which I started this book. Mimetically disciplined to become Other and yet remain themselves, these French tourists can revel in the offhand humor through which they sign their true signatures on the time capsule at the End of the World. To reinvoke Foucault in their case leaves me with no option but to turn him on his head. The idea I am tracing in the sand speaks of none other than the *falsity effect* through which the subject can ignore the significance, and indeed the symptomatic expressions, of his or her actions.

Of course, however much it rewrites the terrain, this *broken French* thesis has followed the lines of Foucault's own theoretical trajectory. As archaeologist, Foucault sought to reduce discourse to the bald appearance of the statement itself, "without referring the facts of discourse to the will—perhaps involuntary—of their authors."[2] I began by articulating colonial antecedents to this practice. Travel jokes utilize a similar maneuver—*holding people to their words*—to project the Other into the primitive present of the archaeologist's past. Such a primitivizing gaze, an anamorphotic wielding of the future perfect, is as much a "denial of coevalness" as any "imperial discourse," as much a tool of colonial advertising as of critique.

Yet if I have gestured toward an empathetic ethic of respecting the Other's right not to be taken at face value, I have consciously violated this principle precisely at those offhand moments when such a respect would be taken for granted. My archaeology of garbage has seen me scavenge through certain hegemonic texts in the history of Tierra del Fuegian colonization. I have sought precisely those offhand anecdotes which a sober-sounding ethnographer would pass over in silence. In his throwaway anecdote of magic soap, Lucas Bridges holds the Other to his own words. Effacing Bridges's ironic intention from this joke, taking his trash seriously, I stumbled upon Marx's theory of commodity fetishism.

Such a finding seemed to have monumental implications for the present. Yet the more I ran my ethnohistory into the present, the less it seemed necessary to erase the subject from his utterances. In the mimicry these anecdotes occasioned, Bridges was more than willing—*on the rebound*—to hold himself to his words, to articulate the fetish for me. Of course to project such a will into this trash is already to depart from Foucault's practice. I have done so precisely so as to investigate my own investment in Bridges's time capsule testimony. There is more to this trash than meets the eye; precisely the *falsity effect* which allows one to ignore one's own role in producing it.

These conclusions bear little in common with the truth-seeking subject who would, later in Foucault's work, find her or his sexuality in these flattened-out fields. In squeezing the "positive subject" and its "disciplined body" of any potential self-absence, the latter Foucault has power/knowledge not simply functioning and fitting its environment, but indeed producing it.[3] Such ideas do not simply strike me as incorrect, they scare me. If power and knowledge really work so well together, how does critique address that "part of us [which] welcomes the fact that reason—as instituted—has violence at its disposal"?[4] How can critique unsettle the disturbing intimation that—however awful—at least the master's rationalization of violence—"law is law"—at least this promises to ward off the *anomie* of the Other?

The *anomie* of the Other is internal to order itself. That is why it is so necessary, in Derrida's words, to render *"delirious* that interior voice that is the voice of the other in us."[5] That is why one must find the will to power's inadequacy to itself. To find the master at the very moment he gleefully stoops to being that nonidentity (the face that believes in his disowned actions) upon whose repression his rule is grounded presents a far more subversive depiction of colonial mastery. How better to pin the master to the spot than to render him "delirious" by *the same logic* that makes him master in the first place?

Return to Sender

But why should an ethnography of Tierra del Fuegian travel pivot so foundationally around Europe, its theorists, its stupid television images of the End of the World? What of that other flight path—the transpolar flight which actually took me from Patagonia, via New Zealand, and nowhere near the Northern Hemisphere, back home to Melbourne?

There is a whole natural history to be written of such polar-centric itineraries, beginning with the flora and fauna which migrated across the ancient Gondwana supercontinent and which strangely link the landscape of Tierra del Fuego and Tasmania right into the present.[6] Such a history would continue into the modern era, mapping the *second-nature* analogies drawn onto the regions' supposedly primitive inhabitants. Following the journeys begun by Cook, then Darwin, then others, this would be a history of flight and counterflight. Sir Baldwin Spencer began a long and distinguished ethnographic career in Australia, only to end his days, seeking analogies to what he sought here, in Tierra del Fuego. Bruce Chatwin followed the same path backward, tracing "journeys mapped out in our central nervous systems" from his first novel *In Patagonia* to his final book, *The Songlines,* which he set in the Central Desert.[7]

Eugenio Dittborn's airmail paintings redrew these lines of flight again, when they arrived through the mail to be exhibited in Melbourne. One of these epistles—*Airmail Painting No.49 Jemmy Button,* buttons, wool, feathers, painting, and photo silk screen on wrapping paper, 1986—featured the Yámana who was abducted by Fitzroy and then brought back to Tierra del Fuego on the *Beagle.*[8] Dittborn wrote that

> Airmail Paintings carry with them the peripheries they cross.
>
> Peripheries they cross stamped on their envelopes.
>
> Stamped on their envelopes in return for a cheap franking.
>
> In return for a cheap franking the Airmail Paintings *return to their destination* when they *fly to their origin.*[9]

I am tempted to keep moving in this direction, to mail myself to another periphery, perhaps even back home, if that were indeed to take this book further. Yet Dittborn reminds me that my home is already stamped on the envelope which contains the illusory images I convey of these travels. Its formal address simply states the dead letter of the motions I go through, the words I mouth. Cheap and frank, such postings "carry with them the peripheries they cross." They send me back to myself.

Travel Will Not Make Travel Go Away

I have sought throughout this book to make certain footloose authors wear the words they cast off into the time-space of the Other. Catching the anecdotalist's magic soap projections, returning such dead-letter words to sender, I aimed to unsettle the cynicism which a company like Benetton exploits to show its true colors to the "rest of the world."

The present has no monopoly over the supposedly epochal separation of being and consciousness. In Lucas Bridges's autobiography I found a similarly conscious disenchantment in the fetishistic world of commodities then dawning upon Tierra del Fuego. I traced the projection of these unthought fantasies through a theoretical spectrum that located them in people's actions (in Sohn-Rethel's materialist argument), in the objects themselves (in Zizek's reading), and finally (by my extension) in the primitivized Other. Bridges, I argued, indulges his disbelieved fetish, on the rebound, through those time-traveling fantasies which allow him to access it through the primitive Other.

In readdressing such recapitulationist anecdotes, I have repeatedly discovered that the subject's patent disbelief in the fantasy they articulate offers no impediment to their operation. The "real fools," as Lacan has it, "are those who are not fooled."[10]

Those who disbelieve in the discourse of power, and yet pay it lip service in the words they mouth, the actions they play out, are precisely the dupes insofar as they imagine that it is consciousness itself that counts. For Jacques-Alain Miller, this is why cynicism is "a form of naïveté": "it is naïve to deduce from the fact that the Other [for which, in my argument, read fetish] does not exist that we can erase its universal function and that only *jouissance* is real. . . . The fact that it does not exist . . . does not at all prevent it from functioning as such."[11] So Miller analyzes that unsettling Lacanian notion ("in you more than you yourself") of *extimité*, the broken French phrase Lacan latched upon to translate the Freudian *unheimlich*.[12] The alien and disowned foreign body, which Lacan sees as the essential attribute of the subject, need not have any substance to function as if it did.

To face such an uncanny face is an operation predicated upon doubt. Yet such a confrontation runs counter to the post-structuralist valorization of hesitancy, inconsistency, the "refusal to set meaning." The political move here requires not the deferral but rather the negation of that doubt—the *falsity effect*—which founds the subject's certainty.[13] A subject who doubts doubt is always in the position to discard such comfort, to take the words it mouths and the motions it goes through seriously. I do not mean to assess their truth content, a lure if ever there was one. On the contrary, I mean to line my face against the stupid TV screen that plays me back to me, completely flattened, to the point where the pixels are visible. I mean returning to the surreal TV screen with which I started this book.

There Is No Beyond the Screen at the End of the World

It would scarcely be alienating to interrupt the closure of this epic book and follow its author's flight elsewhere across the surface of the globe. For all the beyonds it proposes to the computer screen I now stare at here in Australia, it's hard to pretend that there is anything alienating in such a comforting—self-reflexive—interruption. Benjamin claimed, in his essay on epic theater, that "interruption is one of the fundamental devices of all structuring."[14] The interruption whereby I indicate my knowledge of the falsity of my own discourse, this self-reflexivity, is very common indeed, a property of "all structuring."

Is there not a stunning naïveté in the Brechtian insistence that the "common man" (for whom read Nanook of the North, at one end of the world, Houshken and "magic lantern" at the other) really needs to be alienated into seeing a beyond to the intoxication of theatrical narrative? It is the ever-visible artificiality of that framework which provides the possibility for staging intoxication in the first place. I do not suspend my disbelief, to lose myself in that Fuegian televi-

sion set. I am *suspended by my disbelief* in the reality of those images, and that is
how I can fly through the air to Tierra del Fuego and not see myself on that surrealist screen along with all those other sheep with wings.

Recalling Nanook and Houshken again on the Benetton billboard brings to
mind the Baudrillardian subject, the "common man" who is now just "a pure
screen, a pure absorption and resorption surface of the influent networks."[15]
I have argued that the anamorphotic act of reducing people to such a primitivist
faith in the words they speak and the images that cross their faces is profoundly
colonial. They are made to voice the same naïve society of the spectacle which,
from any future perfect perspective, our own unthinking actions evidence. These
primitives, common men, schizophrenics, feminized masses believe for their
observers, anchoring the comfortably alienating disbelief by which we hang suspended in midair.

Herein lies the brilliance/silliness of Adorno and Horkheimer's work on the
"culture industry."[16] It is now almost a trope among the celebrants of so-called
consumerism to declaim against the elitism of Adorno and Horkheimer's dismissal
of so-called popular culture. In fact, they argue that the culture industry, far from
unphilosophical in its workings, provides a contemporary version of "Kant's formalism."[17] In such entertainments the categorical imperative to relate "the varied experiences of the sense to fundamental concepts" is already done for you.[18]
There is a strikingly a priori element, one might recall in passing, to Sohn-Rethel's
commodity-bound presentation of Western science. The "culture industry" operates in a similar fashion; it "robs the individual of his function. Its prime service to the consumer is to do his schematizing for him."[19]

The very title of Adorno and Horkheimer's essay, "Enlightenment as Mass
Deception," underlines the silliness of its patronizing conclusion: they, not we,
are dumb enough to believe in the images projected on the screen. The point, as
Adorno and Horkheimer otherwise state, is that the screen does the job of ideological illusion for you. Like Zizek's primitivist canned laughter, the screen works
regardless of your ability to overlook its narrow frame. Yet like bad tourists, Adorno and Horkheimer get tangled up in their own "reflexively buffered" illusions:
firstly, the fantasy that the Other necessarily believes in the words projected onto
his or her face, and secondly, the notion that a critical disbelief such as theirs might
put the subject outside the ambit of such unthinking images.[20]

I must once more diverge then from the Frankfurt dream of emancipation
through self-reflection. Self-reflection—by making things so blindingly obvious—
only obscures the problem. Bridges makes patently clear his knowing possession
of what Taussig proposes as the very remedy to his paranoid colonial condition,

this "reflexive awareness as to the mimetic faculty."[21] The implicit distinction Bridges makes between his civilized mimicry and that of the primitive Yekaifwa-ianjiz hinges precisely on the colonist's ability to reflect on what he is doing. Bridges *can* see a structure to his own mimicry, whereas the Yámana is simply caught up, vertiginously, in the movements which "grew on him" beyond any control of his own.[22] It is Bridges's ability to step outside of himself which allows him to treat trivially those unserious, ironic, *self-reflectively* defused spaces in which "that interior voice that is the voice of the other in us" speaks itself.

Dispensing with such disbelief, Lacan cheekily equates these self-reflexive fantasies with Platonic idealism. "The picture," he writes, "does not compete with appearance, it competes with what Plato designates for us beyond appearance as being the Idea."[23] For Lacan this Platonic space of idealistic disbelief, the space we imagine beyond the stupid picture screen, is precisely that which founds the subject.[24] In turning back to ancient Greece to support his statement, Lacan forgets to add the anthropological finding that such primal scenes consistently employ a naïve self from elsewhere to hold up the screen.

The *Objet Trouvé* Is That Which You Discarded in the First Place?

Conscious self-reflection seems, at the end of this history of projection, misrecognition and disowned desire little more than a dream within a dream. Freud interpreted such "dream[s] that you are awake" as acts of recuperative self-censorship.[25] When you dream of yourself reflecting upon and disowning a prior dream you are actually seeking to censor the reality of your own self-alien desire: "If a particular event is inserted into a dream as a dream by the dream-work itself, this implies the most decided confirmation of the reality of the event—the strongest affirmation of it."[26]

This may seem to take my argument back once more to Foucault. Foucault would reduce the subject to that ancient and primitive cinema screen that reduces his or her words, images, and utterances to a one-dimensional surface. To do so may indeed present a true statement of the "reality of the event," a representation shorn of all the evasive and ambiguous claims of subjective desire. Yet Freud's event is none other than the expression of an unconscious wish, and its reality no less than that wish's irreducibility to the conscious surfaces of everyday waking reality.

The very act of flattening the Other, as much as the self, against the page is saturated, like greasy newspaper, with the ugliness of desire.

Beyond the Big Screen

Bridges's reflexive awareness of the artificiality of his own mimicry provides the pretext which allows him to persist in it. The true threat to his subjectivity would be if he were forced to find himself in that primitive Other who *wants* to believe so *unreflectively* in his own words and actions.

If he could see the extent of his own alienation-alienating blind faith he would be face-to-face with Mladen Dolar's definition of "the uncanny": not seeing oneself see oneself, but rather seeing "one's mirror image close its eyes."[27] The political power of such blinding insights is apparent in the Marxist analogue that immediately presents itself. What could be more uncanny than Sohn-Rethel's strikingly unreflective characterization of science: the "self-encounter of nature blindly occurring in man's mind"?[28]

Just such a negation-negating, doubt-doubting science of the uncanny impels me to face once more the surreal TV screen I stumbled over in the upside-down land at the end of the world. A rejuvenated Marxist "table-turning" would have me flatten my face—unreflectively—against precisely such self-alienating dream forms.[29] Thus I would find, with "feet solidly planted on the floor," those "transcendental as well as palpable" paradoxes of observance that have me at my most potential, at those very unrevised moments I shed to create my own self-fashioning.[30] The *unheimlich,* Freud writes, is a "subspecies of the *heimlich.*"[31] A Marxist uncanny must face a similarly alien presence on that otherwise homely screen. Thus focused, palpably, transcendentally, it must renounce the support derived from its own alienating frame. A Marxist uncanny must blow that image out of all proportions.

"We, the masters, were not home," Benjamin writes.[32] So he furnishes the empty interior of an ancient physiognomy of power with those of his readers who, already overseas to themselves, there find and fail to find themselves. There is nothing reassuring in that Benjaminian face of mine/not mine. It scares me with my own absent potential.

Notes

1. I expand upon this reading of travel as a medium of entertainment—i.e., as a phenomenon whose rhetoric is subject to similar generic laws as film or documentary (and by no means stuck in the realist mode of representation/performance)—in "Changing Channels," 29–31.

2. Foucault, "Politics and the Study of Discourse," 59.

3. For a trenchant critique of the supposed immanence of power in knowledge, see Joan

Copjec's "Cutting Up," in *Read My Desire*, 39–63. Copjec refers to Beckett's stuttering prose, the recollection of which provides a welcome reminder that *language isn't meant to work*. Beckett translated himself back into broken English too.

4. Taussig, "State Fetishism," 115: "And consider how we slip in and out of recognizing and disavowal."

5. Derrida quoted in Spivak, "Can the Subaltern Speak?" 294.

6. For a description, in paint and poetry, of these curious resemblances, see Wolseley, *Patagonia to Tasmania*.

7. Chatwin, *In Patagonia*, 83.

8. Dittborn, *Airmail Painting No.49 Jemmy Button*, 76. For an amazing read and further reproductions, see Kay, *Del Espacio de Aca*. I am grateful to Juan Davila for introducing me to Dittborn's work (and Kay's).

9. Dittborn, "Correcaminos—Roadrunner," 72.

10. See Zizek, "How the Non-Duped Err," 69–87.

11. Miller, "Extimité," 84.

12. "In You More than You" is the title of the final seminar in Lacan, *Four Fundamentals*, 263–76. *Extimité* is a neologism Lacan formed from the French word *intimité* (intimateness as much as intimacy). For comments on this terminology see the translators' notes to Miller, "Extimité," 86.

13. Barthes, "The Death of the Author," 147.

14. Walter Benjamin, "What Is Epic Theatre?" in *Illuminations*, 148.

15. Baudrillard, *Ecstasy of Communication*, 27. This may seem a radical approach to human subjectivity. The legal definition of insanity is, after all, the inability to reflect upon your own actions. Yet how much more crazy does this make the law's obverse—that sanity is, as Lacan points out, effectively defined as the ability to stand back, watch, and believe neither in yourself, your actions, nor your images? (*Four Fundamentals*, 76). To be sane is to realize that you are not the same as yourself.

16. Theodor W. Adorno and Max Horkheimer, "Enlightenment as Mass Deception," in *Dialectic of Enlightenment*, 120–68.

17. Ibid., 124.

18. Ibid.

19. Ibid.

20. Sloterdijk, *Critique of Cynical Reason*, 5.

21. Taussig, *Mimesis and Alterity*, 254.

22. E. Lucas Bridges, *Uttermost Part*, 115.

23. Lacan, *Four Fundamentals*, 112.

24. I am much influenced here by Joan Copjec, "The Orthopsychic Subject," in *Read My Desire*, 5–39.

25. Freud, *Interpretation of Dreams*, 338. For the dream-work process of self-censorship Freud termed "secondary revision," see 488–508.

26. Ibid., 338.

27. Dolar, "'I Shall Be with You on Your Wedding Night,'" 13.

28. Sohn-Rethel, *Intellectual and Manual Labour,* 75. For Sohn-Rethel's critique of the theory of reflection, see 189–93.

29. Marx, *Capital,* 44.

30. Ibid.

31. Sigmund Freud, "The Uncanny," in *Standard Edition,* 17:226.

32. Walter Benjamin, "The Image of Proust," in *Illuminations,* 207.

Appendixes

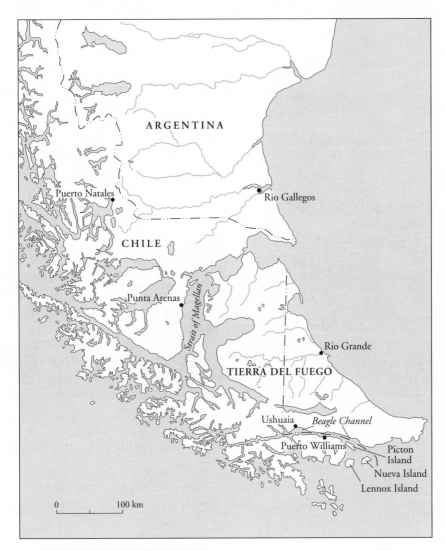

Tierra del Fuego. Map by Bill Nelson.

Ushuaia.

The Pears' Magic Soap Anecdote

I was to discover that I had yet another wonder-worker; this time a certain magic soap, the miraculous effects of which the manufacturers have been too modest to claim themselves.

One of the Ona [Selk'nam] had been working on Picton Island, frequently for long spells. During one of these protracted periods of absence his wife gave birth to a son who had fair skin and hair and blue eyes. (Here I must make it quite clear that my own eyes are brown and that, in those days, my hair was nearly as dark as an Ona's). Naturally I wondered what the good husband would say when he returned home to find this remarkable addition to his family.

In due season he came back from Picton Island. A day or two later he came to see me and begged for a cake of soap; not the ordinary soap, but the magic soap of the color of dark glass and shaped like the egg of an upland goose. I did not understand what he was driving at, but he was very much in earnest. He told me that while he had been away his wife had borne a son as dark as was usual among the Ona at birth, but that by the time he set eyes on him, the tiny child's skin and hair had changed to a wonderful fairness. When questioned about this incredible transformation, his wife—supported in her story by two women who had attended her—attributed the miracle to a cake of magic soap that had been given to her by my sister, Alice. Some of the soap, she had gone on to say, had got into the baby's eyes, which had at once become as blue as the sky.

The proud father was so impressed by these wonders that he came seeking another cake of soap. Suspecting that he wanted to try its effects on himself and might be foolish enough to doubt his wife's story if the experiment failed, I hastened to tell him that the particular cake of soap given to his wife by my sister must have possessed some special virtue not to be found in any other tablet. He went away disappointed, but satisfied.

I suggested to Alice that we should take a photograph of the happy trio and send it to the manufacturers, in case they wished to use it as an unsolicited testimonial to the merits of their wonderful product. Alice, however, thought that it would not be quite the thing, so the photograph never went to Messrs. Pears.

Source: E. Lucas Bridges, *Uttermost Part,* 219–20.

Book 2
The Suspension of Disbelief

Nor do we fear that there is no home to which we can return.
We fell from it; but our home is your eternity and it does not fall
because we are away.

—St. Augustine

1

A New Angle

Launching a New Book

Nationalism is the "anomaly" which, Benedict Anderson claims, has consistently defeated Marxism, both in theory and in practice.[1] His *Imagined Communities* seeks, in a "Copernican spirit," to break from such "evolutionary/progressive" styles of thought.[2] As a structure of belonging, the nation's appeal cuts across modernity's ever-onward narrative of novelty, obsolescence, and change. People die for their nations, for nations, like older systems of belief and belonging, give meaning to death. This capacity to render death significant, this "strong affinity with religious imaginings," transcends that of any political ideology.[3] So Anderson launches us into the *Imagined Community*, following this structure of "horizontal comradeship," as it spreads out across the bounded spaces of the national realm.[4]

The paradoxical novelty of this theoretical departure lies in Anderson's insistence, "religious imaginings" notwithstanding, that the nation is a thoroughly modern institution. It is simply not possible, given the size of national populations, to know all of one's compatriots personally. To feel one with the national body, you must literally imagine the coexistence of masses of others who, though absent, live through the same experiences as you. Indeed, for all its seeming timelessness, nationalism is crucially dependent upon anonymity and absence. Such a state of parallel anonymity is only imaginable within the "homogenous empty time" of modern historical consciousness, a depersonalized and abstract temporality which exists over and above any individual.[5]

One can observe this horizontal timescape at work in the newspaper: its daily assertion of an abstract calendrical time connects the modern citizen, in his or her imaginings, with all other readers.[6] Such is the power of this communal anonymity that Hegel could even equate reading the paper with saying one's daily prayers.[7] With its fantastic fusion of the individual and the collective, this profanely illuminating image captures something of the national consciousness then dawning across Europe. The newspaper itself bears a "strong affinity with religious imaginings."

Anderson finds a similarly Hegelian presence in the nation's monumental forms: "No more arresting emblems of the modern culture of nationalism exist than cenotaphs and tombs of unknown soldiers."[8] Housing the spirit of an abstract social entity, such empty shrines evidence the decidedly archaic forms of belief and belonging structuring these national imaginings. Yet a startling modernity inheres to these tombs for the very anonymity they enshrine. As sites in which *any* self-sacrificing national can be evoked, they embrace a vision of radical equality and homogeneity. To identify with the unknown soldier is to imagine yourself the particular embodiment of a universal national spirit. It is, so to speak, *to step into a syllogism.*

Needless to say, this *Geist*-like logic—transcending the particular, rising to the universal—is pure fantasy. As Kant argued, well before Hegel, the syllogism cannot be founded on empirical fact. It can exist only as a figure of faith.[9] Philosophers have long rejected, and even ridiculed, it on these grounds. Bertrand Russell claimed that the only time he had ever encountered anyone actually thinking in a formal syllogism was in a letter from a German philosopher attempting to comprehend a mock-Hegelian commentary on *The Hunting of the Snark*.[10] Yet to find his syllogism, Russell needed hunt no further than the symbolic forms of the British national community. He could have stayed at home and addressed the newspapers, monuments, and even electoral systems all around him. The syllogism, and the imagined community it structures, may well be fictional. Yet when a group of believers unite in taking it for fact, they effectively realize it. Indeed, this unknown soldier fiction is so real that people do not simply believe in it—they die for it.

This fiction is so real that they die for it in Tierra del Fuego too. Caught in my own primitivist time capsule, I read the island, back in book 1, through the progressivist narrative of developmental history. Yet the imagined community swathes its horizontal way through these structures too. The trash of travel charts the various recapitulationist fantasies pegged to those evolutionary structures. Yet it has nothing to say about the fact that Tierra del Fuego is, and has been since the moment of colonization, split in two by the nations which uneasily divide it. Dispute over the Beagle Channel boundaries between Argentina and Chile led to near-wars in 1901–2, 1968, and then again most seriously in 1978, a few years after Chatwin's visit. The political scientist Michael Morris even argues—in direct contrast to my Marxist thesis—that "politics has been the driving force in the economic development of the far South."[11]

Indeed, it is simply not possible to pass off such forces as secondhand Western projections, like the magic soap and throwaway Coke bottles I addressed above. Quite to the contrary; Anderson argues that this syllogistic structure of horizontal allegiance derived its "modular" form from its initial appearance in the Americas.[12] From the early eighteenth century, the imagined community has always been there, orbiting outside of the evolutionary schemata that would forever map countries like Argentina and Chile as backward, imitative, and behind. In that book, written over a year before this writing, I attempted *an ethnohistory of the white colonial subject traveling through time to Tierra del Fuego.* My narrative crossed Chile and Argentina as indifferently as the trashy commodity humor I was tracing from Lucas Bridges into the present. Yet people have been prepared to die for these imagined communities—that fact cannot be so easily discarded.

This is why, in launching this second book, I want to mimic Anderson's "Copernican" departure. I shall break from the hierarchical imaginings of my earlier analysis, seeking to follow up that same ethnohistorical project and to accord it its truly national significance. For the subjects of the nationally contoured Tierra del Fuego travel through time as much as any recapitulative tourists. Yet to arrive at a "consciousness of connectedness" with their compatriots, these subjects move across "homogenous and empty" time, rather than up and/or down, its progressivist axis.[13] Each Argentine, as each Chilean, reads "unknown soldier" significance into the local streetscape, imagining the anonymous yet parallel lives which his or her unknown compatriots *simultaneously* experience. By reading across, rather than down, time I will seek to address the same project as previously—but from a new angle.

One year on, going back over through the same terrain, I will attempt to cut through the Northern Hemisphere's *denial of coevalness.* Trashing the trash of travel, I will try to comprehend the syllogistic system of horizontal imagining splaying out before me. Changing channels to observe this process, I shall focus on the *assertion of coevalness* inherent to the nation form.

No More Arresting Emblems Exist Than . . .

So, let's go stamp collecting! Don't turn off! There are worlds to be read in postage stamps. Stamps are as much, if not more, of a prerequisite for nationhood than any tired old monuments. "There must be *something*," as Kenneth W.

Anthony writes in *The Beginner's Guide to Stamp Collecting*, "about these small colored bits of paper."[14] Anthony is right—no more significant emblems of the modern culture of nationalism exist than postage stamps.

For him, this *something* is a function of the radically democratizing nature of the hobby, the way it cuts horizontal links across diverse sections of society. As in the following anecdote: "Some years ago," a certain "well-known architect" went, with colleagues, to inspect a large new house: "While they were examining the building, along came a fitter to connect a gas meter. To the surprise of the onlookers, the architect and the fitter greeted each other as old friends, as indeed they were. For both were keen members of their local philatelic society."[15] Could postage stamps offer the "consciousness of connectedness" of which Anderson speaks? Yet stamp collecting was not always so integral to the overcoming of class conflict. Right into the late nineteenth century, there had always been those who "were ready to pour scorn on the hobby, describing it as a pastime fit only for schoolboys."[16]

This all changed in 1893, when Prince George became an honorary vice president of the Philatelic Society of London. His stamp of royal approval seems, paradoxically, to affirm Anthony's postal reading of the history of modern democracy. It was, after all, the extraordinary nineteenth-century *embourgeoisement* of royalty which led Prince George all over Europe to adopt and affirm such a thoroughly middle-class hobby. This process was inseparable from the nationalization of royalty that Benedict Anderson describes through figures like Kaiser Wilhelm II. The radically leveling operation of nationalism served, according to Anderson, to bring the "dynastic realm" into line with the unknown soldier's coeval and anonymous imaginings. For in defining himself as "No.1 German," Wilhelm implicitly conceded "that *he was one among many of the same kind as himself,* that he had a representative function."[17]

Turning to the stamps themselves, it is in their representational function that they offer the most striking parallels with Anderson's nation form. In 1840 a complex and irrational British web of fixed routes and variegated postal rates was suddenly swept out of existence. In that year Sir Rowland Hill's reforms set in place a cheap, rationalized, and universally accessible postal service based on prepaid rates of uniform value. The outer manifestation of these reforms is of course the national stamp. Compare the nineteenth-century rise of the nation, as it cast off the "dynastic realm" and the "religious community," with all their dead-letter insistence upon the "non-arbitrariness of the sign."[18] Breaking from that complex and irrational web of allegiances, the nation came to promote syllogistically rational and universally accessible modes of representation. From universal suffrage to unknown soldier, it is only a small step to universal postage.

Partaking of the same transposable "modularity" as the nation, the stamp crossed the globe in decades.[19] This extraordinarily rapid diffusion is, for Anthony, analogous to the spread of rail, for "both the railways and cheap postage brought a greater degree of freedom and mobility to the man-in-the-street than he had ever known before."[20] Like the imagined community it wears on its sleeve, the stamp facilitates a freedom of horizontal communicability, irrespective of person or privilege. All of which leads Anthony to conclude, of Sir Rowland Hill, that "few individuals, probably, have added so much to the total of human happiness and prosperity."[21]

The Unknown Soldier Revisited

If my presentation of the above seems a bit tongue-in-cheek, it might suggest that not everybody licks the same stamp as Kenneth W. Anthony. Frantisek Langer does. He wrote *Ein Koffer aus Übersee*, a novel about the postal escapades of one Julio Popper. The novel begins in Prague, where a Czech philatelist is asking a favor of Popper, his desperado Romanian friend. Popper is on the point of fleeing Europe for a new life in Tierra del Fuego, and the stamp collector asks him, obviously enough, to send back some Fuegian stamps. A few such European novels have featured Popper and his *excentricidad philatelica*, "in spite," as the historian Boleslao Lewin writes, "of Europe's limited interest in Latin American affairs."[22] In Langer's version, the Romanian makes good in Tierra del Fuego, cranking up a return-to-sender narrative that ends with the surprised Prague philatelist receiving a postcard stamped "Colonia Popper."[23] Life is full of surprises.

My first experience of Popper—who was, after all, a real historical person—was just as novel. It requires a bit of prefacing. One day Dave and I took a walk along the Ushuaian foreshore. We passed the same Plaza de Mayo I described in book 1, laughed about the Philco Time Capsule, and then moved on down the foreshore, where more busts of San Martín and statues to the fallen dead lined up to meet us. The capital of Argentine Tierra del Fuego is littered with empty monuments like these.

"*Las Malvinas son Argentinas*" (the Falklands are Argentine) declaims one, a ten-meter-high, impossibly bloated, bronze map of the isles. Not that this symbolic blow to the national sovereignty was going to put Dave, an international finance student from Birmingham, now London-based, out of step. Fifteen years ago Dave might have died in that conflict. Now in Tierra del Fuego, with the enemy's monumental challenge looming over us, he seemed to find it all pretty funny. As if the insularities of national imagining could mean anything to a dropout bunch of round-the-world backpackers . . .

A few days later I bumped into the same character, puffing and now obviously put out. Dave had been running to make it to the Museo del Fin del Mundo
before closing time. He wanted to get his postcards stamped there, on this his
last night in Ushuaia. The museum doubles as a post office; it sells stamps and
even has a special postmark of its own. In fact, if you ask the curators, they'll actually stamp your passport with it. Dave was so put out because, as he told me
with a laugh, he'd only come to Tierra del Fuego "just to say I've been here," and
the passport stamp would have really topped it off. What?!? Carlos, a Sevillian
with me at the time, pulled out his passport and showed me. There it was, in
between a Chilean entry stamp and a Bolivian visa, a stamp with a picture of the
foreshore in front of us and a motto which read "Ushuaia, Argentina, the End
of the World."

The director of this tiny museum is a smart businessman. He knows just what
travelers are hunting for at the Uttermost Part of the Earth. Not only does the
museum stamp your postcards for you. Its central display cabinet highlights the
philatelic and numismatic excesses of Julio Popper, the Romanian dictator of
Tierra del Fuego. *Chile and Easter Island: A Travel Survival Kit* introduces Popper as follows: "For a few years the island even had a Romanian dictator, who
printed his own money and stamps, and maintained his own goldmines and a
private army until his death in 1893."[24] These stamps once created a storm in the
teapot of local politics. Looking over the shoulders of French and American tourists you can see the museum's rare exemplar. Serrated edges surround a border
labeled "TEN CENTS GOLD LOCAL." Inside the border is Popper's personal
hammer and sickle emblem, while a sash marked "TIERRA DEL FUEGO" runs
through the center of the design.[25]

The display panel takes up the story: Popper was a maverick Romanian adventurer who, in 1886, traveled to the virtually uncolonized northern beaches of
Tierra del Fuego and there found gold. Under the auspices of his newly adopted
Argentine nation, he set up an industrial gold-mining venture near present-day
Rio Grande. In splendid, windswept isolation, Popper proceeded to adopt all the
forces, forms, and appurtenances of a personalized nation-state up to and including the postage stamps. Not that Argentina seemed, at least at first, to mind. The
wielding of arms, the execution of summary justice, the Indian-killing, and all
the rest of the Romanian's stately activities went along unchecked, if not officially
endorsed. It was only when things reached this extreme—the printing of private
postage stamps—that Popper's fortunes suddenly threatened to come unstuck.

On July 3, 1891, a letter arrived in Buenos Aires for the director general of posts
and telegraphs, who found himself addressed in this lofty title by Ramon L.
Cortés, the local policeman and honorary head of the post office of San Sebas-

tian (population circa 12). In the letter the policeman claimed that Popper, though under Cortés's postal jurisdiction, had been affixing to his correspondence "a series of stamps which do not appear to me to be legal."[26] Sufficiently impressed by the gravity of these charges, the director general passed the matter on to the Ministry of the Interior. Tensions bubbled up as Popper proceeded to attack Cortés's own probity in the papers. The policeman then submitted a number of envelopes—with aforesaid stamps attached—to scrutiny, including one postmarked from "a fantastic region" called "Auricosta" (the Gold Coast).[27] The attorney general was called in, Popper redoubled his newspaper attacks, while Cortés responded furiously, publicly declaiming against the "monstrosity" of the Romanian's philatelic innovations.[28] The conflict was forgotten almost as soon as it had begun, though the lingering memory of it (or, rather, the resurrection of these ludicrous events in twentieth-century histories and museums)[29] has made Popper, alongside Lucas Bridges, one of the most famous of Fuegian colonists.

In fact, Popper's story runs right into the present, where it has acted to stir up a rather more potent brew of national tensions. A map Popper drew up in 1891 was to serve as a precedent for Argentine sovereignty claims against Chile, adding fuel to a dispute which has threatened to flare up throughout the twentieth century.[30] As you exit the Museo del Fin del Mundo and stare across the Beagle Channel, you see, some twenty kilometers away, the Chilean town of Puerto Williams. On the horizon you can just make out the anti-aircraft guns punctuating the Chilean foreshore and matching, installation for installation, the guns and monuments along the Argentine side. Way off to the left, at the very mouth of the channel, lie the impossibly tiny islands of Picton, Nueva, and Lennox. The significance of Popper's map lay in its early attribution of Picton and Nueva to Argentina.

Of course the conflict has nothing to do with these islets or even Tierra del Fuego itself. The point—and the only reason Popper's freakish testimony was at all invoked—is that the extrapolating line of longitude one draws south from Picton and Nueva serves, according to whether it is positioned above or below them, to advance vastly different national claims over resource rich Antarctica.[31] The triviality of the islands is hence inversely proportional to the significance Chile and Argentina have invested in them. Nations do, after all, go to war for little bits of rock and stone.

Alongside the Falklands/Malvinas potboiler, this simmering dispute has had huge effects on local settlement. In fact, Ushuaia's duty-free status is a direct result of Argentina's attempts to shore up local ties to the region. Such sovereign imperatives at times border on the surreal—to grasp hold of these tiny shards of sovereignty, Argentina has even gone so far as to promote the manufacture of television sets at the Uttermost Part of the Earth. Again, the point is that these nationalist absurdities cannot simply be laughed away. Even this freeze-frame image of the dispute suggests that the actions of these nation-states have, above and beyond all the claims of capital, directly contoured the terrain of contemporary Tierra del Fuego. To understand the forces driving Tierra del Fuego through time and into the present—for this is my project—I must take seriously the trash of the nation and all of the emotion invested in it. However fulsome the monuments, however tacky the sentiments, the continuing force of such national imaginings needs to impact upon my analysis.

Thinking the imagined community into Tierra del Fuego takes me straight back to the Plaza de Mayo, which Dave and I passed so offhandedly above. Having looped through Anderson's guide to the present, I should be ready to read something rather more serious into these stately monuments. Coming down from the high-flying enthusiasms of a Kenneth W. Anthony, having seen the sorts of things people die for, I should now be ready to ground my—

This is the point at which such researches threaten to come to ground—the very point at which they hit the shared present of national imagining. For how could anyone read "religious imaginings" into the off-white plaques and lifeless statues of this over-adorned and unloved Plaza de Mayo (one of Argentina's many)? Who but a traveler would even genuflect so far as to read the dirt-encrusted inscriptions? The placard of the time capsule, dedicated as recently as 1992, threatens to "*hermanarnos* [literally, to make us brothers and sisters with] those who succeed us in the passage of time." All members of the one national family. Yet the Argentines I asked were completely indifferent to these unknown monuments, not to mention the Philco Time Capsule alongside them and the summary list of governors, heroes, and other dead people memorialized in the names of the streets that lead up to this unloved Plaza de Mayo (not that anyone ever follows them there). Who would find their true selves in present-day surrounds like these?

Running into the present enshrined in this particular Plaza de Mayo is to run into an empty space. The plaza is a cenotaph in two senses, empty of both the living and the dead. For Anderson "no more arresting" figurations of nationalism exist than monumental spaces like these. He has etymology on his side—the word *monument* derives from the Latin *monere,* the basic meaning of which is "to put in mind," with further connotations of threat and coercion.[32] Yet what could be more arresting than the thought that such stately monuments, minding their own business, fail to arrest any imaginings at all? Indeed, even *known* soldiers fall prey to the anonymity of national imagining. Witness those endless miles of monumental dedications, informing nobody as usual that, in Robert

Musil's words, "from eighteen hundred and such and such to eighteen hundred and a little more the unforgettable So-and-so lived and created here."[33] The exemplarity of the unknown soldier monument may well reside in its monumental emptiness, a lifelessness it shares with so much other national iconography.

What do you do with Anderson's theories, the moment you characterize the modern culture of nationalism as *the tomb of the unknown monument?*

Launching a Series of Books

You realize that you are reading from the leaves of a very different book. Or, rather, that the same book is open to more than one reading. It would have to be for anyone to found a theory of the nation-state upon people's affective allegiance to places like the Plaza de Mayo (one of Argentina's many). To turn from the monument to the novel is to follow the lead of Anderson's own metaphors. He argues that the *Imagined Community* is as much a work of fiction as any nineteenth-century novel.[34] Opening out from the same imaginings as Hegel's newspaper, the novel presents its readership with a nationally bound socioscape marked by simultaneity and parallel anonymity. Reading such notions into the landscape, each individual national effectively writes his or her own novel.

I am going to dwell on this metaphor: the nation as a novel. Still tracking the forces driving Tierra del Fuego into the present, I shall read a few of these national novels to see where they take me beyond the tomb of the unknown monument. As Popper and his laughing onlookers make clear, such national spaces can easily take on a trashy and even absurd aspect. Considerations of genre might help explain how this best-seller form persists and even spreads in the face of such emptiness.

Nor is this the only insight to derive from importing a literary turn into this new book of mine. Literary analysis might help unfold that strange *pleasure of the text* which I feel as I now return, a year on, to write across these old travels. The fun of setting this narrative up—mimicking Anderson, Popper, Cortés, and company, parodying the national imaginings they stand for, playing around the Museum at the End of the World—reminds me of the pleasure of travel itself.

Notes

1. Anderson, *Imagined Communities*, 3.
2. Ibid., 4, 10.
3. Ibid., 10.
4. Ibid., 7.

5. Benjamin quoted in ibid., 24.

6. Ibid., 35.

7. Hegel paraphrased in ibid., 35.

8. Ibid., 10.

9. On Kant's critique, see Murrary, *Marx's Theory of Scientific Knowledge*, 33–34. While claiming that human intuition was incapable of grasping *all* the particulars necessary to arrive at a universal (for one must know all to be absolutely sure), Kant did accept that God might possess such understanding.

10. Attempting to read the comic issue of *Mind!* (a parody of the respectable philosophy journal *Mind*) in which the Hegelian commentary on *The Snark* appears, the German found himself puzzled by the mock advertisements surrounding it. He reasoned himself out of the difficulty as follows: "Everything in this magazine is a joke, the advertisements are in this magazine, therefore the advertisements must be jokes" (Russell quoted by Martin Gardner in Carroll, *The Annotated Snark,* 103). British humor defeats them every time.

11. Michael Morris, *Strait of Magellan,* 50.

12. Anderson, *Imagined Communities,* 113.

13. Ibid., 56.

14. Anthony, *Beginner's Guide,* 11.

15. Ibid., 125.

16. Ibid., 15.

17. Anderson, *Imagined Communities,* 85.

18. Ibid., 12, 19, 14.

19. Ibid., 113.

20. Anthony, *Beginner's Guide,* 55.

21. Ibid.

22. Lewin, *Quién Fue el Conquistador Patagónico,* 125.

23. As described in Lewin, "Atractivas Novelas Sobre Popper," 6–9.

24. Samagalski, *Chile and Easter Island,* 227.

25. The armchair ethnographer can view the reproductions in Lewin's canonical biography. The stamps are listed in many philatelic catalogues as well. Stanley Gibbons, as Lewin points out, with a certain irritation, mistakenly labels them Chilean (Lewin, *Quién Fue el Conquistador Patagónico,* 89).

26. Cortés quoted in Lewin, *Quién Fue el Conquistador Patagónico,* 125.

27. Ibid., 129.

28. Ibid.

29. Armando Braun Menéndez was a pioneer in this respect, not to mention an apologist for those earlier pioneers whose riches he inherited (see *Julio Popper*). His historiographic descendants have taken up similarly apologistic views, with the rare exception of Lewin, who resolutely refuses to glorify genocide in the name of the nation. See *Quién Fue el Conquistador Patagónico.*

30. See Belza, *En la Isla del Fuego,* 235; for more detail, see Mateo Martinic, *Historia de la Region Magallanica.*

31. For a brief account, see Pilkington, "Surface Tension," 25–27; for more extensive coverage, see Michael Morris, *Strait of Magellan.*

32. Hodge, "The Atlantis Project," 390.

33. Musil, *Posthumous Papers,* 61.

34. Anderson, *Imagined Communities,* 22–36.

2

Whose Imagined Community?

Book Review

Take José Joaquin Fernandez de Lizardi's *El Periquillo Sarniento,* the very first Latin American novel. Depicting the "movement of a solitary hero" through an endlessly "comparable" and coeval "world of plurals," this 1816 text shows "the 'national imagination' at work."[1] Anderson's gloss continues: "This picaresque *tour d'horison*—hospitals, prisons, remote villages, monasteries, Indians, Negroes—is nonetheless not a *tour du monde.* The horizon is clearly bounded: it is that of colonial Mexico. Nothing assures us of this sociological solidity more than the succession of plurals. For they conjure up a social space full of *comparable* prisons, none in itself of any importance, but all representative (in their simultaneous, separate existence) of the oppressiveness of *this* colony."[2]

The national inhabits a similarly fictional space in the *Imagined Community.* The national's "consciousness of connectedness" with Others is derived from the recognition that they, in their daily passage through "homogenous empty time," pass through *"comparable"* and coeval spaces.[3] Worldwide. Spreading from the eighteenth-century Americas over to Europe, this nation form then folds back down through the colonies to the late nineteenth century point at which it splits Tierra del Fuego in two. So the "world of plurals" Anderson diagnoses in the early Latin American novel passes into the very real "world of plurals" making up the book of nations today.[4]

The fiction invested in these far-flung places is not merely realized. It takes on sacred, indeed biblical, proportions—for the right to dwell on his metaphor, the unknown soldier is quite willing to die.[5] As the patron saint of Philippine nationalism *and* the foremost novelist of the islands, José Rizal seems an exemplary figure of this state of imagining. Anderson cites Rizal's nineteenth-century novel

Noli me Tangere to evidence the global diffusion of the nation's homogenous emp-ty time.[6] Compulsory reading in all Filipino schools, "the *Noli*" virtually defines the nation, while the image and name of its author hero is—as I know from my own travels there—affixed to practically every public space.

Rizal was first raised to this holy status by the American imperialists who sought, soon after invading the islands in 1898, to co-opt the figures of the national in-dependence movement. "His photographic likeness," writes Vicente L. Rafael, commenting on the effects of this canonization, "has adorned everything from stamps to currency notes, matchboxes to amulets, book covers to postcards."[7] It is this very banalization which leads Rafael to question Anderson's insistence on the "remarkable confidence of community in anonymity" which the *Noli* sup-posedly documents.[8] From representing a "solitary hero" in a novel nation Rizal has faded into unknown soldier anonymity for those who pass by—from Ma-nila's Rizal Park, through Rizal Avenue in Cebu, and down to the town of Rizal itself—the endless series of his homogenous and empty features.[9]

To read the nation-as-novel as it spreads out into such realms opens up the generic concerns I marked at the end of the previous chapter. How do I theorize the national forces driving Tierra del Fuego into the battle-scarred present, if their best-seller form seems so unloved and even absurd?

Turn to Arnoldo Canclini's *Julio Popper: Quijote del Oro Fueguino,* a book drip-ping with the comic absurdity of attempting to read the national's "world of plu-rals" unto the End of the World. Canclini wrote this biography of Popper in 1995 to celebrate the fact that Argentine Tierra del Fuego had finally received full provincial status. Hurray! "It has long been time," Canclini writes, hope-fully, "to stop treating him as some mere curiosity, one of those eccentricities that the human race occasionally produces."[10] If only the Romanian could fade into Rizal-like anonymity, if only Popper could be banal enough. Downplay-ing the stamps, the coins, the private army, the Indian-Killer photo, and all the other features that made his subject historical in the first place, Canclini attempts to memorialize the official provincialization of the End of the World through him. Stamps stamped out, coins uncoined, this homogenized Popper is to stand in for "those utterly unknown men who, seeking gold, or whatever other mat-ter . . . populated the zone and won it for civilization and the nation. One day the gold prospector will have a monument in Tierra del Fuego, just like the unknown soldier, to celebrate these civilian and nearly always foreign men who fought for our soil."[11]

So Popper, as unknown soldier, runs into the "man-in-the-street" whose new-found freedom and mobility—qua Kenneth W. Anthony's stamp-borne history of modernity—took him on the train down to Tierra del Fuego. As if a freak like

Popper could ever be man-in-the-street for any other than the one paltry street named after him in Rio Grande. Boleslao Lewin is displeased about this state of affairs. He wants Rio Grande itself to be named after Popper. If successful, Lewin's campaign could serve to realize the fictional "Colonia Popper" of Langer's *Ein Koffer aus Übersee.* For indeed, the historian and the novelist are reading their imaginings into the same book, the same mass-produced "world of plurals" placing a Mexican prison, a Filipino matchbox, and an Argentine street sign alongside each other in the one "homogenous and empty" bookcase.

If the nation-state is compulsory—though hardly compelling—reading across the globe, how am I to take its local representations at face value? Take the postcard James sent me in Ushuaia. James was a passport stamp collector. We had met years before in San Salvador. James boasted of having been to over one hundred countries. This card was postmarked Haiti. What can I make of this reading? How is any local "world of plurals" to be distinguished from the "world of plurals" marking James's passport, each page a leaf from the national novel, each different and all the same? Meanwhile ("one could argue that every essential modern conception is based on a conception of meanwhile"[12]), over in Calcutta, Partha Chatterjee is tearing into Anderson for his all-too-faithful reading of the "autobiography" of nations . . .[13]

"Whose Imagined Community?" asks Chatterjee, unfolding his research on nineteenth-century Bengali nationalism. The Bengalis certainly *took on* the modern forms of democratic governance and political economy. Such structures were viewed as the necessary and neutral "outer" shell of modern nationhood. In so doing these nationalists might seem to have acted like secondhand recipients of the West's homogenous and empty forms.[14] So runs the official "autobiography." Yet, Chatterjee counters, these Bengalis were far from *taken in* by the all-encompassing nation-state. There was also an "inner" realm of Bengali imaginings which served to encompass those social forms beyond the grasp of the colonist's universalizing institutions. For the Bengalis by no means placed faith and allegiance in the tomb of the unknown syllogism. On the contrary, they defined the spiritual substance of their communal identity against, and even beyond, the emptiness of the imagined community's modular forms.

Where will this reading take me?

Displacement

"The saddest exhibit" at the Museum of the Salesian Fathers in Punta Arenas is comprised of "two copy-book exercises and photos of the bright-looking boys who wrote them."[15] The Salesians taught these Indian children to write:

THE SAVIOUR WAS IN THIS PLACE AND I DID NOT KNOW IT
IN THE SWEAT OF THY BROW SHALT THOU EAT BREAD.[16]

"So," the traveler comments, "the Salesians had noted the significance of Gene-sis 3:19. The Golden Age ended when men stopped hunting, settled in houses and began the daily grind."[17]

In the Indians' place rose an "empire of *estancias,* coal-mines, freezers, depart-ment stores, merchant ships," property of José Menéndez and Moritz Braun, the greatest of the agricapitalists to descend on the island.[18] It was the sweat, mean-while, of immigrant laborers which brought cake to the tables of these plutocrats. Chatwin describes the anarchist uprising of 1921: corralled by the Argentine army at the Estancia la Anita, "the prize establishment of the Menéndez family," 120 Chilean workers were forced to dig the graves they now inhabit.[19] Chatwin wit-nessed the centennial of Menéndez's arrival in Punta Arenas. A band played in the central plaza, while women wearing "black dresses, pearls, furs and patent shoes" helped to unveil his memorial.[20] Meanwhile, "the crowd, which always turned out for a brass band, shambled round the ceremony with expressions of stone. Punta Arenas was a leftist town."[21]

From the 1870s to the 1970s, such moments slide across time and into each other throughout *In Patagonia.* "The story of the Anarchists," Chatwin writes at another point, "is the tail end of the same old quarrel: of Abel the wanderer, with Cain, the hoarder of property."[22] Chatwin's tale snakes connotatively through a landscape fixed into place by the descendants of Cain, that "hoarder of prop-erty": museums, mansions, prisons, graveyards . . . Continually tracing the evils of settlement, the traveler seems to live out his stance on this age-old quarrel. For Susannah Clapp, Chatwin's biographer, *In Patagonia* constitutes his "declaration of faith" in the wanderer's line.[23] It is hard, on the face of things, to disagree. For in all this voyaging Chatwin is following the example, and even the itinerary, of his Great-Uncle Charley. Never quite at home at home, Charley wandered back and forth from Punta Arenas at the turn of the century. Chatwin returns, in the 1970s, to observe the same paces as his footloose predecessor.

Yet the haphazard nature of this allegiance needs to be noted. How, after all, do you take Chatwin's wayside declarations seriously, given that "the object of this ridiculous journey" is none other than a nonexistent fragment of dinosaur skin?[24] *What,* as Chatwin would say, *am I doing here.* This phrase, "pronounced by Bruce with emphatic self-ridicule, and a stress on the 'am,'" is characteristi-cally Chatwinian.[25] Could this very self-distance manifest its author's faith in the wanderer's line?

I launched this new book with the aim of finding the national forces driving

Tierra del Fuego through time and into the present. To follow Chatwin's travels in this direction seems appropriate, given the space he devotes to surveying the marks and moments of human settlement, the stamp of Cain on the environment. It will, of course, take a little time to catch up with him, for Chatwin is indeed hard to pin down. Pinned to his own flight path, I want to ask Chatwin a question that was never meant to be answered: *What was he doing there?* (with a stress on the "doing").

Tour Guide

"Discover this city" runs the Desatur "City Tour" brochure, describing Punta Arenas, "the obliged stopping place for all the globe trotter and true adventurer [*sic*]."[26] The brochure is correct. Punta Arenas is an "obliged stopping place," as any backpacker will tell you. After all, it's the local Chilean capital. Once there, Desatur will take you, for U.S. $20, to all the "Museums of the City," as well as a whole range of "other interesting visits," including: "Monument to General Don Bernardo O'Higgins; Municipal theatre; Girl's High School where Gabriela Mistral, Nobel Literature Award, was principal; Municipal Cemetery; Monument to the Shepherd;" etc.[27] This list might well seem ludicrous and "all the globe trotter" might laugh at seeing themselves mangled through such broken English. Yet the fact is that *all the globe trotter* I met in the various hostels and hotels were following this very itinerary. What else could you do in Punta Arenas?

"What am I doing here," Tatiana was saying, and I was listening, in all my broken Spanish. Tatiana was born in Punta Arenas of Russian emigres and all she wanted was to travel, to visit Europe. Working at SERNATUR (the Servicio Nacional de Turismo), Tatiana had seen a world of foreign nationals pass through. He or she ambles into the office, asks for half-hearted directions to the "Museums of the City," makes one or two "other interesting visits," ticks this tedious town off, leaves it behind. Tatiana wanted to go to France, "simply to be there," she laughed, "to see the Eiffel Tower."

What would she do there? The tower, as Roland Barthes writes, "is *nothing,* it achieves a kind of zero degree of the monument; it participates in no rite, no cult, not even in Art."[28] Built on the same structural principle as the railway tracks then spreading out across Patagonia, the tower is "the first obligatory monument of all the sites visited by the foreigner or the provincial."[29] Yet why? "So paradoxical is the notion of an empty monument"—there is simply no reason to be there at all.[30]

Contrary to Barthes, I want to suggest that the tower, in its function as the "major sign of a people and a place," is a full participant in the modern culture of nationalism.[31] Isn't the "sign of a people and a place" always empty? As I began to argue in the previous chapter, such monuments, whether in Europe or its elsewheres, are endemic to the "homogenous and empty" culture of nationalism. Nor is there any European monopoly on this *writing degree zero,* as any "unknown shepherd" statue in Punta Arenas will attest.[32] I myself can make this testimony, for I visited the Eiffel Tower during a stopover on my "round-the-world" trip to Argentina and Chile.

In fact, continuing down through Patagonia, these empty sites serve as the "obliged stopping place[s]" connecting me and the mass of other travelers following the same itinerary. This is where you will find the unknown traveler, staring at a beachfront monument to "Barbarism and Civilization" in the Welsh colony of Puerto Madryn.[33] Chatwin cannot resist this overblown sight: "Soviet style" Tehuelche Indians depicted alongside sturdy "greybeards, young men with scythes, and big breasted girls with babies."[34] Yet, as the "major sign of a people and a place," such an unknown monument is by no means unique to Patagonia. The "world of plurals" is necessarily predicated, in each individual case, upon the residual presence of a "watered-down, non-serious, Sunday suit" set of such cultural markers: the shepherd, the Eiffel Tower, the Welsh beard, etc.[35] This, furthermore, is where you will hear the "universal language of travel" spoken.[36]

For if this locally grounded emptiness is a structural necessity of the national syllogism, the traveler seems obliged, with almost equal necessity, to take heed of its products. Chatwin pops up again, in a small Argentine town, now noticing a "bronze bust of General San Martín, the Liberator" (one of Argentina's many) in the central square.[37] *What is he doing here?* Waiting for his taxi, the traveler goes up to inspect the statue any Argentine knows to ignore. What is Chatwin doing but performing the task of national imagining in the citizen's stead?

"The 'external frontiers' of the state," writes Etienne Balibar, outlining this task, "have to become 'internal frontiers.' . . . External frontiers have to be imagined constantly as a projection and protection of an internal collective personality."[38] Surely it is the traveler who must, more than any national, constantly imagine this "internal collective personality." As a Parisian (though not as an intellectual) Barthes "alone can excuse himself" from the tower.[39] As a local, Tatiana, in the other hemisphere, alone can excuse herself from visiting all those "other interesting visits" of Punta Arenas (though she must give directions).[40] Chatwin, on the other hand, will visit the Salesian museum ("THE SAVIOUR WAS IN THIS PLACE . . .") and from there he will proceed back to the central plaza to observe the state commemoration of the Menéndez centennial. For it is the unknown traveler, passing through, who must constantly project an identity into the empty markers of the national domain.

At times this compulsion borders on the absurd. Following the line of Abel down to the museums and monuments of Punta Arenas, Chatwin makes sure to mark "the northern frontiers of an unusual kingdom which still maintains a court in exile in Paris."[41] Orélie-Antoine de Tounens "was thirty three (the age when geniuses die)" in 1859, the year he arrived in Chile and proclaimed his sovereignty over "the whole of South America from Latitude 42 to the Horn."[42] "Staggered by the magnitude of his act, the king retired to a boarding house in Valparaíso and busied himself with the Constitution, the Armed Forces, the steamship line to Bordeaux and the National Anthem (composed by a Sr Guillermo Frick of Valdivia)."[43]

The king's successor, "His Royal Highness Prince Philippe of Araucania and Patagonia," now "reigns modestly" from an office in the Faubourg Poissonière.[44] To get there, Chatwin had to pass "the Marxist daily *L'Humanité*" and "a cinema showing 'Pinocchio.'" Once there, the prince showed him "a court order allowing M. Philippe Boiry to use his royal title on a French passport," along with a "letter from the Consul of El Salvador in Houston recognizing him as head of a state in exile."[45] *What am I doing here,* Chatwin might ask, flipping back down to Patagonia to relate what happened when the king, back in 1860, finally left his boarding house to survey his immense domain. While hiring a servant for this purpose, Orélie-Antoine "made the common tourist's mistake of confusing fifteen for fifty pesos."[46] Swiftly descending into penury and insanity, the king spent the next twenty years fruitlessly attempting to return to his rightful realm.

He should have packed a guidebook. Chatwin, meanwhile, has wandered off across to Argentina and out of sight. In his wake, I invoke the theory of the nation again to think about the unknown traveler, constantly crossing the "external frontiers" of nations, as he or she zigzags back and forth from Argentina to Chile, tracing the national faultline down south to the End of the World. This *tour du monde* constantly turns into the national *tour d'horison* from which Anderson distinguishes it. Indeed, it may be this very shunting which compels one to read local difference along national lines. There must be something about the sideward gaze this practice produces. Witness the frequency with which travel guides are invoked to support attempts to read "a people and a place" into the streetscape. Benjamin, for instance, saw an 1852 Parisian travel guide as the "*locus classicus* for the representation of the arcades [*passagen*]."[47] Susan Buck-Morss and Margaret Cohen, following Benjamin there, both quote old travel guides to open their explications of his work on Paris, while Dean MacCannell sees Baedeker's turn-of-the-century Paris *Handbook for Travellers* as "still the best ethnography of modern cities so far available."[48] Flipping back to Ushuaia, the province's official tourist guidebook introduces its map of the city by exhorting us tourist/readers to avail ourselves of that wayward gaze: "We encourage you to discover an old Ushuaia with feature which may be easily unnoticed as they are concealed by modern life [*sic*]."[49]

Perhaps your sights, now reading novel significance into that streetscape, will alight upon Big Harbor Travel. "We will take you," the banner proclaims, in Spanish and English, "wherever your imagination suggests." A glance at the itineraries on offer reveals the preformed contours of such suggestions. All are arranged in national blocks: France, Germany, Brazil, Portugal, the United States. All visit the monumental markers of "a people and a place": the museums, the plazas, the public plaques. The independently minded might want to imagine their travels otherwise: they can flick through the guidebooks on offer, all of which are nationally defined and defining. The *Rough Guide to Chile* and the *Blue Guide: Argentina* set forth the various maps and itineraries through which the unknown traveler can read the nation into place. These traveler/tourist itineraries cross the globe and have an almost sacral force, as is apparent in MacCannell's ironic claim that in "'the Holy Land,' the tour has followed in the path of the religious pilgrimage and is replacing it."[50] This explains why the religion issue of Benetton's *Colors* magazine describes the *Travel Survival Kit: Israel* as the "traveller's bible."[51] What book could more faithfully observe the "religious imaginings" of the nation-state?

What book, if not the very book which I, still searching for Chatwin, have in my hands? To move from the monument to the book once more is to see *In Patagonia,* in the very wandering it documents, as an exemplary site for national imaginings (as exemplary as any "world of plurals" *Periquillo,* official-martyr *Noli,* or provincializing *Quijote del Oro*). Who better represents Anderson's "solitary hero" passing through a "sociological landscape" than the travel writer? What "citizen-tourist" could feel more driven to discover all those manifold places in which a society represents itself to itself?[52] Take the following approach to "the History of Buenos Aires," a tale which, in Chatwin's reading, "is written into its telephone directory. Pompey Romanov, Emilio Rommel, Crespina D.Z. de Rose, Ladislao Radziwil and Elizabeta Marta Callman de Rothschild—five names taken at random from among the R's—told a story of exile, disillusion and anxiety behind lace curtains."[53] So the travel writer underlines the extraordinary fate of the wanderer, cast out of Cain's domain and now forever *driven to read representations intended for the Other.* For if Chatwin's biblical mythology here finds itself in the most all-encompassing, all-inclusive, and absurdly anonymous of national novels—the telephone directory—is this not the ultimate example of what Anderson describes as the "'national imagination' at work"?

If anyone steps into the national syllogism, it is the traveler. This is where my book review takes me. Travel is nation fetishism.

Notes

1. Anderson, *Imagined Communities,* 30.
2. Ibid.
3. Ibid., 56, 25, 30.
4. Ibid., 30.
5. Ibid., 32.
6. Ibid., 26–28.
7. Rafael, "Nationalism," 610.
8. Anderson, *Imagined Communities,* 36. Rafael's article plays throughout on the contradiction between this community in anonymity "and the anonymity that persistently, even mechanically, haunts community" (611).
9. But see Ileto, "Orators and the Crowd," 93, for reference to that other Rizal, the Tagalog revolutionary martyr. Right up into the 1920s (twenty years after Rizal's actual death), insurrections against the new Filipino-American polity were led by peasants who claimed, "almost without exception," either to be Rizal or to be in some form of communion with him. Ileto's *Pasyon and Revolution* gives much insight into the philosophy of history structuring such subaltern "religious imaginings" so radically unlike the temporal framework Anderson reads into Rizal's writings. Rizal's final poem, "Mi Ultimo Adiós," is for Anderson an archetypal expression (alongside the *Noli*) of modern national sentiment (*Imagined Communities,* 142–43). Ileto writes, on the other hand, of those Rizalista sects which have read the poem as a prophecy of Rizal's second coming (an occurrence they seek, bending the fabric of time, to usher in through revolutionary activity; Ileto, *Pasyon,* 50 n. 51).
10. Canclini, *Julio Popper,* 181.
11. Ibid., 11.
12. Anderson, *Imagined Communities,* 24 n. 34.
13. Chatterjee, *The Nation and Its Fragments,* 6.
14. Ibid., 5–13.
15. Chatwin, *In Patagonia,* 136.
16. Ibid.
17. Ibid.
18. Ibid., 88.
19. Ibid., 99.
20. Ibid., 134.
21. Ibid.
22. Ibid., 116.
23. Clapp, *With Chatwin,* 25.
24. Chatwin, *In Patagonia,* 183.
25. So is the "bewilderingly unpunctuated" form in which it appears as the title of his *What Am I Doing Here.* See Clapp, *With Chatwin,* 175.

26. Desatur, *Punta Arenas City Tour.*

27. Ibid.

28. Barthes, "The Eiffel Tower," 7.

29. Ibid., 14.

30. Ibid.

31. Ibid., 3.

32. Ibid., 7.

33. Chatwin, *In Patagonia,* 24.

34. Ibid.

35. Gellner, *Nations and Nationalism,* 78.

36. Barthes, "The Eiffel Tower," 4, claiming that the tower "belongs to the universal language of travel."

37. Chatwin, *In Patagonia,* 12.

38. Balibar, "The Nation Form," 95 (Balibar is paraphrasing Fichte's *Reden an die Deutsche Nation* of 1808).

39. Barthes, "The Eiffel Tower," 4. MacCannell notes likewise that only the Parisian is excused from the obligatory requirement that "if one goes to Paris, one 'must see' Notre Dame, the Eiffel Tower, the Louvre . . . of course, the Mona Lisa" (*The Tourist,* 43). For MacCannell this "ritual attitude" justifies his analysis of tourism as a truth-seeking mode of "pilgrimage," the last refuge from an otherwise disenchanted, indeed palpably "spurious," modernity (43, 155). Untraveled informants tell him how they want "with all their hearts" to visit foreign sights like the tower (43). But how would MacCannell explain the half-hearted, but no less obligatory, pilgrimages traced in my archive?

40. Meaghan Morris suggests that the local's exemption from the pilgrimage—at least in Australia—may well be disappearing. Writing on Sydney Tower, and deliberately engaging with Barthes, she argues that there was something "symbolically inaugural" about the rhetoric through which this "'Eiffel Tower of the Southern Hemisphere'—'only higher'" was promoted to Sydney's inhabitants. Such promotions purported to turn locals into "'citizen-tourists'—becoming at one with 'foreign' tourists in our gaze at our own city, yet becoming at the same time the potential living *objects* of that self-same tourist gaze" ("Metamorphoses at Sydney Tower," 23, 21, 23). Again, even if locals visit the "'Eiffel Tower of the Southern Hemisphere'—'only higher,'" do they necessarily find themselves there?

41. Chatwin, *In Patagonia,* 18.

42. Ibid., 19.

43. Ibid., 21.

44. Ibid., 23.

45. Ibid., 18, 19.

46. Ibid., 21.

47. Benjamin cited in Buck-Morss, *Dialectics of Seeing,* 3.

48. Buck-Morss, *Dialectics of Seeing,* 3; Cohen, *Profane Illumination,* 1; MacCannell, *The Tourist,* 61.

49. Dirección Municipal de Turismo, *La Ciudad en el Fin del Mundo,* 11. The guidebook is sponsored by "American Express, the Official credit card of Ushuaia, Tierra del Fuego."

50. MacCannell, *The Tourist,* 43.

51. *Colors 8: Religion,* Sept. 1994, 118.

52. Anderson, *Imagined Communities,* 30.

53. Chatwin, *In Patagonia,* 7.

3

The Object of This Ridiculous Journey

Whose Rhetoric of Presence?

The end point of Bruce Chatwin's journey is an old colonial home at 182 Casilla Street, Punta Arenas. His travels to the End of the World take him, by the sort of uncanny inversion travelers so like to find in these parts, right back to the familial home, the residence of his Great-Uncle Charley. My return to the Museo del Fin del Mundo has taken me through a not dissimilar inversion. From investigating the nationalism besetting those at home in places like these, the "tourists' homing instinct" has led me to the national imaginings inspiring those who come to visit.[1] Taking Chatwin as an exemplary—unknown traveler—figure of these forces, I have read Benedict Anderson's book of nations right into his very travelogue. What better way to drive the traveler's nation fetish home?

But can this back flip escape the irony written into the line of Abel? Inasmuch as this maneuver keeps the structure of Anderson's theory intact, it leaves me open to the same critiques as him. "Whose Imagined Community?" asked Partha Chatterjee, describing those Bengali nationalists who pay *lip service* to the "outer" forms of the nation-state, yet locate their "inner" imaginings elsewhere.[2] To rend these outer and inner realms asunder is to pluck out the very heart of Anderson's work, for his unknown soldier ("no more arresting emblems exist . . .") represents the very spirit of their union.[3] Chatterjee's question applies equally to my argument, for the travels I have charted evidence a similar self-splitting. The traveler may visit and pay outer allegiance to the symbolic appurtenances of the nation-state. He may even end up at the domestic hearth at the End of the World. Yet for all this "outer" allegiance to the national pilgrimage, this exemplary figure is doing no more than *going through the motions*. He is not actually where he appears; his "inner" is elsewhere.

The traveler may be *doing* Chile and Argentina, passing through their respective museums, monuments, and manners, reading them to life—but this is not his object. Even after going inside and visiting Charley's house, Chatwin cannot rest. He may have found his home away from home, but he still has "one thing more to do in Patagonia."[4] He still needs to accomplish "the object of this ridiculous journey," that is, to find a mythical bit of Patagonian dinosaur skin.[5] Yet far from evidence of an all-driving "inner" faith, this object is a joke, another irony, just a stupid souvenir. So how can the traveler be said to subscribe to national imaginings if his mission is invested with such an in-deconstructable rhetoric of absence?

The host of other seekers whom Chatwin points to and parodies on his way down south seem to have forgotten this very *self-distance*. Take the burnt-out Haight-Ashbury hippie who takes a lift in the same truck as Chatwin. The hippie has lost his memory, his passport, and all the absent identity (a home away from his travels) they might register. All that survives in his obliterated mind is the mythical Patagonian treasure toward which he hitchhikes endlessly. Albert Konrad, an old friend of Charley, likewise loses his marbles and begins to mistake bare rocks for gold. Chatwin passes Albert's cabin en route to the Cueva del Milodón. Packed full of fool's gold, this worthless endeavor might well offer an analogy for the traveler's quest. Chatwin works it: "Now I too had gone mad," he writes, arriving at the cueva and finding nothing (but himself).[6] Yet he does not go mad, for he knows his own absence from the object—"in you more than you yourself"—which he seeks.[7] The traveler knows not to be taken in by his own stupid souvenir; his "inner" is elsewhere.

Which is why he would probably have enjoyed laughing at the North American tourist I saw in the Museo del Fin del Mundo. After inspecting Julio Popper's stamps in person, I wandered into the museum's souvenir shop. There I saw this visitor purchase, for 70 pesos (U.S. $70), a gold exemplar of one of Popper's famous self-made coins. Could this *yanqui* have "made the common tourist's mistake of confusing fifteen pesos for fifty" (as Chatwin writes of the king of Patagonia and Araucania)?[8] Perhaps. The traveler doesn't stop to ask, for the question of the tourist's investment is already decided in advance the moment he enters into the "universal language of travel."[9] A North American face, flattened into one-dimensional conversational currency, offers a perfect anecdotal moment. Imagine: "The *yanqui* tourist who buys souvenir coinage from the Romanian dictator of Tierra del Fuego." Tourists *are* taken in by their own stupid souvenirs, their "inner" is their "outer."

"We're just like sheep, aren't we?" said the package tourist I overheard in the Punta Arenas flight lounge on my way to Puerto Williams. Yes, you are, thought this author-traveler, storing the image up for repeated retellings. Such is the structure of the travel discourse which—cutting across the evolutionary schema of recapitulationist commodity humor—distinguishes travelers from tourists, their coeval cousins.

It is this distinction which problematizes any easy attempt to read national imaginings into the "all the globe trotter" travelogue.[10] The imagined community, for Anderson, links its subjects through a radically homogenizing "consciousness of connectedness."[11] They locate themselves within the syllogistic "socioscape" offered by forms like the museum, the novel, the tomb of the unknown soldier.[12] Travelers in Tierra del Fuego may seem, outwardly, to mirror and even outdo nationals in these pursuits. Yet in the process, they manifest a vocal *consciousness of disconnectedness* with those who follow the same flight path. As any traveler will tell you, the truth-seeking subject is a package tourist, a sheep with wings. It requires a tourist to be taken in by the object of something as absurd as a trip to the End of the World.

Such a finding, as I noted back in book 1, turns the very theory of travel on its head. John Frow, for instance, explains the dynamic growth of Third World tourism by way of the truth-seeking subject's belief in the "authenticity" he or she seeks.[13] In this he follows the thematic of Dean MacCannell's canonical *The Tourist,* which locates a "dialectic of authenticity at the heart" not simply of tourism but indeed of "the development of all modern social structure."[14] Mass-produced modernity, for MacCannell, is palpably "spurious"; authenticity must needs be sought elsewhere. Yet within the "semiotic structure" of tourism itself, Frow writes, expanding upon MacCannell, the "authenticity of the tourist object" is defined by the fact that it has not been created for tourism.[15] The dialectic hence necessitates that "every tourist," simply so as to pursue the authentic, "at some level denies belonging to the class of tourists."[16] The object of which Frow writes could be a place as much as a thing. Addressing souvenirs at one point, he quotes Victor Turner on "sympathetic magic" to argue that souvenirs are like "medieval relics."[17] Souvenirs are like relics, he claims, for the magic of such objects "works by establishing a metonymic relation with the moment of origin."[18] Is he talking about the furry (made-in-China) penguins you buy in Sergei's *drugstore* on Calle San Martin? For all the dialectical manuevers, Frow and MacCannell still leave us with the same fundamentally faithful subject.[19]

Whose Imagined Authenticity? Having one's passport stamped at the Museo del Fin del Mundo, hunting out a piece of dinosaur skin at the Cueva del Milodón, wearing "emphatic self-ridicule" on the sleeve of one's T-shirt . . .[20] Where is the "magic" medieval thinking running through all these assorted objects? Laughing at the Philco Time Capsule, looking at a few unknown shepherd statues (but what else is there to do?), proceeding to fill a book with anecdotes (and what are anecdotes but souvenirs?) . . . Where are the "religious imaginings" uniting all these *self-distant* projects?

Being There

It is the travelers, in this scenario, who misconstrue the rhetoric of the souvenir, that play of presence and absence which Susan Stewart describes as follows: "On the one hand, the object must be marked as exterior and foreign, on the other it must be marked as arising directly out of an immediate experience of its possess-or."[21] In this the souvenir is like the postcard, another technology which "represents distance appropriated" through the sender's metonymic relation to its distant origin.[22] Just as a postcard loses all meaning if you were not actually there in the place it represents, the souvenir insists on the traveler's *being there*—there at the very point of its purchase. You need to have been there, in your "outer" person, to conjure up the souvenir's sympathetic magic, a magic which operates irrespective of the conjurer's own "inner" state of mind. The "authenticity of the tourist object" is a function of one's "outer" actions. Once activated by your presence, that furry penguin proceeds to believe in the object of your travels for you.[23]

A simple experiment, conducted on a pair of unsuspecting Italian tourists, reveals the truth of these findings. I met the two in Punta Arenas, while waiting, amid aforesaid package tour sheep, to buy plane tickets for Puerto Williams, the truly southernmost town in the world. One was whining about the fare, the other giggling because they were going there "just to buy the T-shirt." Since they seemed to be in two minds about it all, I suggested that only one go to Williams. She could purchase two T-shirts and bring the extra one back for her friend. The fact that they then stopped talking to me underlines the *deictic* function Stewart sets forth—the point to the T-shirt relic is the traveler's presence in the place of its acquisition.

Whatever its ostensible object, whatever the "dialectic of authenticity" enlivening it, the traveler's compulsion simply to *be there* constitutes the presence that I must trace through Tierra del Fuego. However a Chatwin might ridicule the hollow magic of his object, the point is that he is there to pursue it and that it takes him on a trail which snakes through capital city, major monument, local museum, and all the other settled sites of the nation-state. The traveler's *consciousness of disconnectedness* toward all the coeval tourists following the same monument-run itinerary does nothing to alter the nation fetishism inherent to the itinerary. "We have spoken too much," as Pierre Bourdieu says in *Mapping Ideology*, "about consciousness, too much in terms of representation."[24] One will not find the unknown traveler in his or her self-distant representations. The "social world" which their actions map into place operates "in terms of practices."[25]

To analyze the nation in terms of practices, rather than consciousness, casts a paradoxical light on Chatterjee's argument. To think in this unimaginative fashion is to realize that his critique, for all its seemingly decisive "inner"/"outer" distinction, actually leaves the structure of Anderson's globalized nation form fundamentally intact. For Chatterjee shows that modular forms like the unknown soldier can be maintained and kept in place, even when emptied of all affective content. Even if no one breathes their "religious imaginings" into the stone-cold forms of the stately syllogism, such symbolic appurtenances will nonetheless hold their ground—worldwide. Not only will the unknown soldier's "outer" emptiness stay in place; it will even receive visits from the "outer" emptiness of the unknown traveler who, *going through the motions,* does just that.

So I flew into Chilean Puerto Williams to see Ushuaia splayed out, just twenty kilometers away, on the other side of the Beagle Channel. Remembering that shoreline now, with its massive and scarcely concealed anti-aircraft cannons, it is hard for me to ignore the dispute splitting the region's national imaginings in two. I realize that my current attempt to catch the unknown traveler in motion merely brushes the surface of that conflict's structural and/or affective causes. I doubt that you can explain such events through practices alone. A glance at the ever-present Chilean state emblem—*por la razón o la fuerza* (through reason or through force)—is enough to alert one to the nation-state's reliance upon consciousness and representation.[26] Yet *this* is not the traveler's flight path. He or she might send postcard analyses back from conflict zones like this; but the point is that such "distance appropriated" insights have power only because the traveler was there.[27] The point to *In Patagonia*—an extended series of postcards—is that Chatwin actually was in Patagonia.

As was the tourist I bumped into along the Puerto Williams foreshore. A peroxided art student, Ian had come to Williams "just to say that I've been there." He was starting his South American trip down there and had already planned to spend a month in each country on the continent. There was a strange formalism to this, he himself admitted, adding quite curiously, "I can't understand why I want to see all three Guianas, when I s'pose any three of the provinces of Brazil would be just as interesting." What Ian did understand, however, was that, however interesting Brazil might be, and however pointless his trajectory, he would indeed be visiting all three Guianas. That is what travelers do. Chatwin himself has an inkling of such unwritten itineraries. "We too," he suspects, like the penguins whose migrations he tracks down to Patagonia, could well "have journeys mapped out in our central nervous systems."[28]

This fuzzy idea runs my argument back into the line of the practice-based theory of social action which I mapped out in book 1. Separating consciousness from the biologized practices which supposedly drive it, Chatwin is only so far from the separation of consciousness and exchange which Sohn-Rethel diagnosed in the act of commodity exchange. In book 1 I answered his startling question— "Can there be an abstraction other than by thought?"—in the affirmative.[29] Here I want to claim that *there can even be itineraries outside of thought*.[30] From one end of the Mercator map projection to the other, travel practices contour around the sacred sites, civic centers, and holy boundaries of the nation-state. In following these "journeys mapped out" in his or her unknowing social practices, the traveler acts as *the nation personified* (in the sense that Marx describes the capitalist as "merely capital personified. His soul is the soul of capital, which has a vital impetus of its own").[31]

But suddenly I am brought back from reviewing these various nation-as-novels and into my own travels. *In Patagonia* itself drops from my hands, for the question for me is surely *What was I doing there?* (with a stress on the "doing").

I was laughing at Julio Popper, the Romanian dictator of Tierra del Fuego, unknown soldier to a later generation of passport stamp collectors. I was mimicking the prince of Patagonia and Araucania, as he flourishes a letter of recognition from the consul of El Salvador in Huston. The "social world" may work "in terms of practices," but it partakes of revealing representations too.[32] At such moments, the effective nation fetishism structuring the unknown traveler's practices bursts into parodic expression—only just as swiftly to be laughed at and projected back as the "religious imaginings" of the Other. Indeed, one can read only so much into these anecdotal inversions, more a "trick," as Benjamin says, "than a method."[33] However illuminating, such symptomatic moments are simply that, momentary glimpses of "journeys mapped out" elsewhere.

This is where my project ultimately leads me, beyond conscious representation, beyond the novel of nations I read with such pleasure. This very book drops from my hands, for all the fun I have had in setting it up: mimicking my tourist doubles, laughing about stamp collectors, paying lip-service to their national imaginings. Whatever the retrospective rhetoric, the point is that *I was there*. The traveler's nation fetish is personified in the flight paths which, regardless of the claims of "inner" consciousness, serve to map ideology into place. For that is where my travels saw me: paying visits to hollow tombs of unknown soldiers, being there, like the nation personified, inhabiting, in all my "outer" allegiance, an empty square in the capital of Argentine Tierra del Fuego.

Return to Sender?

Reining in a narrative from her subject's legendary flights of fantasy, Susannah Clapp, Bruce Chatwin's erstwhile editor, reads the traveler's traces into a "a clutch of the postcards" she received back in London: "the Museum of Modern Art, Hereford Cathedral Library, the New Moree Motel in New South Wales, the Musée de l'Annonciade in Saint-Tropez, the British Museum and elsewhere . . . [all of which reveal] . . . a taste for surprises, for stories and for a graceful line."[34] Chatwin was there, in all these places, representing "distance appropriated," standing in for what Anderson terms the "museumizing imagination" of the modern nation-state.[35] Here is the true "anomaly of nationalism": that the *nation personified* is figured in the one who ventures forth to observe it in others.[36] If anyone steps into the national syllogism, it is the traveler. Travel is nation fetishism.

So what? The traveler might visit the museum at the End of the World, have his or her passport stamped, and even send back a Chatwin-style *What am I doing here* postcard. Who cares? Coeval with all those other tourists following the same national itinerary, such a traveler might well be the true subject of Anderson's tomb of the unknown soldier. And? How does this self-domesticating trajectory serve to elucidate the national forces driving Tierra del Fuego through time and into the present? The letter—and for that matter the postcard—may indeed always arrive at its destination. But if travelers go abroad simply so as to send themselves back home, what does that matter?

Notes

1. Meaghan Morris, "At Henry Parkes Motel," 41.
2. Chatterjee, *Nation and Its Fragments,* 5–13.
3. Anderson, *Imagined Communities,* 10.
4. Chatwin, *In Patagonia,* 167.
5. Ibid., 182.
6. Ibid.
7. Lacan, *Four Fundamentals,* 263.
8. Chatwin, *In Patagonia,* 21.
9. Barthes, "The Eiffel Tower," 4.
10. Desatur, *Punta Arenas City Tour,* 1.
11. Anderson, *Imagined Communities,* 56.
12. Ibid., 32.
13. Frow, "Tourism," 146. However much I play with Frow's text, I find his argument convincing. His article is more than simply an attack upon the traveler's deluded "truth

claims." Frow discovers a dialectic of expansion within the very impossibility of ever attaining this "authenticity of the tourist object." Truth-seeking travelers must constantly search for the "un-touristed" object that will define them as not-tourist, simply so as to stay true to themselves. For "tourism destroys (in the very process by which it constructs)" this authenticity, requiring that the traveler move ever further and further afield in search of an impossible but propulsive selfhood (146). The neoimperial search for authenticity does indeed seem (the above criticisms aside) to characterize many Third World travel scenarios. Frederick Errington and Deborah Gewertz, for instance, describe a set of adventure travelers along the Sepik River in Papua New Guinea who proudly defined themselves as *not-tourist* by "their capacity to discriminate between the authentic and the inauthentic." The anthropologists cite an entry from the log book of a guest house in this increasingly enculturated region. Advising other travelers as to their prospective dealings with the locals, the entry suggests that those following should "be friendly and they will not treat you like a tourist. Explain difference between traveller and tourist. . . . Be respectful of haus tambarans and culture. Be a traveller not a tourist. It makes a big difference. . . . By the way, we had a fantastic time. Go for it, yea, to the max, far-fucking out!" (40). Such enthusiastic findings support Frow's model, which doubtless applies to many such extensions into peripheral regions. The package tourists whom Errington and Gewertz encounter on the same trip offer, on the other hand, a very different angle on the "semiotic structure" of their travels. Many of these informants seem not only aware of but even comfortable with the artificed (i.e., tourism-inspired) nature of the shows the locals put on for them. Here, at this other End of the World, it is the self-styled tourist who gives the lie to the truth-seeking subject. Doubtless such conscious "inauthenticity" is a necessary adjunct to the consolidation of tourist relations. For tourists do tread familiar pathways (another difficulty for Frow's argument), Tierra del Fuego among them. Lucas Bridges, incidentally, gives insights into the "authenticity of the tourist object" at the beginning of world tourism. He describes his first view of the scarcely believable *Hayn,* or initiation ritual, which had Selk'nam females suspend their disbelief in the males' impersonation of Fuegian spirits. This staginess led Bridges, at first, to believe that he was witnessing not a living ritual, but rather the "remains of a dying religion." He later complains about the touristization of these already fundamentally inauthentic and staged rituals. By the earlier part of this century, Bridges laments, "Indians were induced, for a few dollars, to enact some of their plays before scientific audiences" (*Uttermost Part,* 414, 428). Could Bridges be the prototype of Frow's truth-seeking travelers? If so, what of the resilient "falsity effect" I read into his self-representations in book 1?

14. MacCannell, *The Tourist,* 155.

15. Frow, "Tourism," 146.

16. Ibid.

17. Turner quoted in ibid., 145.

18. Ibid.

19. In fairness, MacCannell does mention two cases of tourists, in Tangier and in Las

Vegas, who were quite happy to dispense with the authentic search and simply laugh about the theater of it all (*The Tourist*, 104–5). He does not, however, explain how such experiences can be reconciled with his theory of the truth-seeking nature of tourism.

20. Clapp, *With Chatwin*, 25.

21. Stewart quoted in Frow, "Tourism," 145.

22. Stewart quoted in ibid.

23. Ibid.

24. Bourdieu, "Doxa and Common Life," 268.

25. Ibid.

26. There is something frightening in a critic's suggestion that this should be changed to "*Por la Fuerza de la Razón*" (through the force of reason); see Loveman, *Chile*, 7. Taussig has fleshed out this "something frightening" extensively in *The Magic of the State*, an (entranced) meditation on Benjamin's theory of the imbrication of violence and justice. His focus, in reading stately kitsch, on "artefactuality" of these "through the force of reason" representations runs parallel to the theories I have been advancing here (17). I nonetheless part with his superegoic (to put it roughly) focus. My unknown traveler cannot be seen as a mirror of the unknown soldier/citizen: law is a very different thing in each case. Nor do I fully accept Taussig's Bataillean reading of the "unknown soldier," when considered on its own terrain. See my "The Magic of the State," 193–207.

27. Susan Stewart quoted in Frow, "Tourism," 145.

28. Chatwin, *In Patagonia*, 83.

29. Sohn-Rethel, *Intellectual and Manual Labour*, 17.

30. Anderson's act-based theory of the "pilgrim functionary" has been a great influence upon my thinking here, however much our interpretations differ. He explains the "isomorphism" in Asia and Africa "between each nationalism's territorial stretch and that of the previous imperial administrative unit" by locating the imagined community's origins within the administrative journeys of colonial officials (*Imagined Communities*, 114). These pilgrimages were initially empty of the national "consciousness of connectedness" which locals ascending the educational and bureaucratic hierarchies would eventually read into them. As Anderson writes of early twentieth-century Indonesia: "The Rome of these pilgrimages was Batavia. . . . All these journeyings derived their 'sense' from the capital, in effect explaining why 'we' are 'here' together" (121–22). Here too *in the beginning was the deed.* Compare Hegel, on the "cunning of History": "human actions in history produce additional results, beyond their immediate purpose and attainment. . . . Something more is thereby accomplished which is latent in the action though not present in their consciousness and not included in their design" (*Reason in History*, 35). Yet however great an influence Anderson's "pilgrim functionary" has been upon my "unknown traveler," the "journeys mapped out" in my archive by no means necessarily lead to the *collective* conscious recuperation which both Anderson and Hegel discover—quite to the contrary. The "social world" which "works in terms of practices" does not need to be known as such—ever—to continue to work as such (Bourdieu, "Doxa and Common Life," 268).

31. Marx, *Capital,* 232.
32. Bourdieu, "Doxa and Common Life," 268.
33. Walter Benjamin, "Surrealism," in *Reflections,* 182.
34. Clapp, *With Chatwin,* 91.
35. Anderson, *Imagined Communities,* 178.
36. Ibid., 3.

4

And the Postage Stamp?

Stamp Collecting Revisited

The letter always reaches its destination and so does the postcard. But what of the postage stamp? The Museo del Fin del Mundo doubles as a post office. It even has its own postmark. There is something more to these stamps, the "ridiculous objects" I discarded above, as a mere symptom of the unknown traveler's nation fetishism. National imaginings, for the visitor to this museum, run right into the current postal service. "Obviously," as Kenneth W. Anthony reminds us, "there must be something about these small bits of colored paper."[1]

Indeed, if stamps are symptoms for the unknown traveler's wandering through Tierra del Fuego, they seem peculiarly apt ones. Witness the ghostly travelogue Benjamin conjures up from the page of his "Stamp Shop."[2] Like "Gulliver," he writes, "the child travels among the lands and peoples of his postage stamps."[3] Reading those national "visiting cards" again, and as if for the first time, Benjamin alights upon the philatelic image of Vasco da Gama, rounding Africa: "a travel brochure for the Cape of Good Hope."[4] A black swan tempts him toward another southern land, but the "postal parvenus" have him in hand, those "large, badly perforated, garish formats of Nicaragua or Colombia, which deck themselves out like banknotes."[5] Traversing the Southern Hemisphere from Africa to South America, this round-the-world reverie opens up a gallery of national imaginings. Here is Benjamin again, now musing over a postcard. With a picture on one side and a stamp on its obverse, the postcard reminds him of "a page by an old master that has different but equally precious drawings on both sides."[6]

Nor is Benjamin alone in tracing postal fantasy across the globe. In fact he could be reading the same postcard as Susannah Clapp; another of Chatwin's cards home featured reproductions of the work of Donald Evans. Chatwin devoted an essay (later published in *What Am I Doing Here*) to the thousands of miniature postage stamps which Evans painted in watercolor and displayed in actual stamp albums.[7] The artist invented forty-two imaginary communities for these stamps. "To my delight," writes Chatwin, "he also borrowed an image from me—the photo of a Timurid tower taken in an Afghan village on the Russian frontier."[8] Another stamp featured "a capital city called Vanupieds (Barefoot Vagabond) to describe his habit of roaming around the world. Many artists moan about being chained to their studios, but Donald Evans could set up in a railway waiting room. Perhaps the very portability of his work states his contempt for the arts and pretensions of settled civilization—the nomad's contempt for the pyramid."[9] Could postage stamps offer the nomad that "consciousness of connectedness" of which Anderson speaks?

In the foregoing narrative I dismissed the claims of conscious discourse, turning instead to answer Chatwin's *What am I doing here* question—although it was never meant to be answered. Showing how the traveler's deeds run along national lines, I argued that the line of Abel snakes right through that of Cain, the settler of these far-flung domains. Sending the traveler back to the home from which he started, such a conclusion might seem to bring my nationally run narrative to an end too. Indeed, the nationalism of my travels was already mapped out—regardless of what I now say in retrospect—into the footsteps that took me, in person, to Tierra del Fuego two years ago. In this state of stasis, I want now to reveal why such return-to-sender flight paths do matter.

My narrative at an end, I am going to concentrate on the postage stamps which have popped up at various moments through the last few chapters. This may seem a pointless sort of activity (people have always been "ready to pour scorn on the hobby").[10] How can stamp collecting have anything to do with travel? Obviously it doesn't, for all the prominence postage stamps have to the travel activities that pass through the Museo del Fin del Mundo. Yet for all the weakness of the philatelic links uniting Popper, Chatwin, Benjamin, and company, a focus upon the "semiotic structure" of these "small bits of colored paper" will nonetheless pay off. It will pay off because stamps are money. Elucidating how this is so will help illustrate why the "nomad's contempt for the pyramid" has such a "stagy quality" to it.[11]

Travel shall initially drop from the picture as I begin this illustration of the stamp form through a consideration of illustration itself. Correlating art form to stamp form, I shall try to situate the very being of the syllogism I have traced from Anderson up to this point. Precisely as an emblem, the stamp form is as much a syllogism as any unknown soldier. To set forth this numismatic/philatelic structure will, however, do more than just offer a weak link illustration of the traveler's nation fetishism. The new angle it offers on the nature of the imagined community itself will serve to display another side to the traveler's unthinking allegiance to the line of Cain. Therein I shall uncover what matters about the fact that travelers go abroad just to send themselves back home.

But to begin, I will take Kenneth W. Anthony's fantastically fetishistic advice. Forgetting about travel and all its ostensible objects, I am going to "Let the stamps tell the story!"[12]

What Is a Stamp?

Stamps are money. They bear their currency on their faces. Yet to illustrate their full value one needs to add that stamps are "old masters" as well.[13] Benjamin's postal reverie runs my analysis into the pages of Marc Shell's *Art and Money,* for, as Shell argues, art is money too.[14] Since the "art boom" eighties it has become increasingly difficult to claim, with Mallarmé, that the "two ways into which our needs divide" can indeed be divided into "aesthetics, on the one hand, and also political economy."[15] Shell claims—this is the novelty of the project he launches here—that it was never possible. He quotes the artist Daniel Spoerri: "In exchanging art for money, we exchange one abstraction for another."[16] One of Spoerri's works of art involved him signing a series of ten-deutsche-mark personal checks. Each was labeled a work of art and then sold for twenty marks. Such installations serve, for Shell, to elucidate the "architectonic principle" formally uniting art and money: just as each individual work incarnates the spirit of art, so does each individual coin embody the "abstraction" that is the spirit of exchange.[17] Art and money are in fact two sides of the same coin.

In fact, Christ is money too. As the particular incarnation of the universal divine spirit, the figure of "Jesus as god-man" is structured according to the same monetary allegory.[18] "That the Eucharist wafer," Shell writes, "is conceptually numismatic disturbed many Christian thinkers who . . . feared money as an architectonic principle competing with God."[19] In a cataloguing operation as relentless as Benetton's *Colors 9: Shopping* ("You are what you buy"), Shell rolls out a trajectory from the "god-man" through the icons seen to stand in for him and into the artworks of the present. For Shell's iconoclasm does not stop with Christ. In its opposition to commercial values, art has often been seen to constitute a privileged site for the modern sacred. Shell's argument flattens these two opposed sides into one sacrilegious surface, arguing instead that "artistic production," in its deep structure, has always already been "a form of commercial, even monetary allegory."[20]

Mallarmé's art/money divide runs through the social forms of modernity. For all the deeper structural coherence of terms like secular/sacred, factory/home, public/private, their apparent opposition is innate to the present. Tracing the historicity of such surface separations, Benjamin describes the nineteenth-century process by which "the private citizen enters the stage of history."[21] The stage is set within the home itself, as "living space becomes, for the first time, antithetical to the place of work."[22] The "true inmate" of this realm, according to Benjamin (who seems to have forgotten about women), is the collector: "To him falls the Sisyphean task of obliterating the commodity-like character of things through his ownership of them."[23] The impossibility of this task is apparent the moment one turns from high culture to more affordable domestic pursuits. Only the ultra-rich, Kenneth W. Anthony writes, can afford to collect "paintings by famous artists"—Donald Evans's highly sought canvases, perhaps?—"or old silver, or Chippendale furniture."[24] Stamps offer the "common man" his own private collection of "miniature works of art."[25] To him falls the Sisyphean task of assembling a stamp collection.

Unlike the artworks to which they are so analogous, stamps wear their currency on their sleeve.[26] By Shell's argument, this is no distinction. When Juan Davila paints a bar code onto the corner of his canvas, he allows—in postage stamp fashion—the commodity-like character of the artwork to surface.[27] Nor is the singularity claimed for the individual artwork sufficient to distinguish it from the mass-produced stamp. Each individual postage stamp is as unique as any one work of art, for both function as perfectly singular embodiments of a universalizing "abstraction" (on the one hand, the spirit of postage, on the other hand, the spirit of art). Both draw currency from the same "architectonic principle." So Shell takes issue with Benjamin's claim that in modernity the "mechanical reproduction of the work of art" acts to destroy the "aura" of the "original."[28] He would have done well, Shell remarks, to think more about coins. From the very first representations of "Jesus as God-man," the sacred *aura* of art has always already been illuminated by the mass-produced *aurum* (gold) upon which it is modeled.[29] Benjamin would have done well to think more about stamps, "miniature works of art" in monetary motion.

Can the same be said of political theorists? Three years after Sir Rowland Hill's invention of the postage stamp, the young Marx attacked the "transcendence and mystical dualism" crowning the Absolute Spirit of Hegel's syllogistic theory of the state.[30] The parallel with Anderson here is notable, for his unknown soldier—an eminently Hegelian creature—operates precisely as a conduit for the national's "religious imaginings."[31] Marx himself came to a similar conclusion in "On the Jewish Question": the modern state "fulfils the human basis of religion in a secular way."[32] The "mystical dualism," that is to say, of this supposed fusion of particular individual and universal spirit has an effective social power, precisely as a fantasy.

Yet already in that piece Marx was discounting the efficacy of such ideological devices; in the modern era, political power is itself "the serf" of "financial power."[33] Shell suggests one interpretation of this serfdom (for him a thoroughly Christian phenomenon)[34] in remarking that the Hegelian *Aufhebung* served to translate *sublatum*—the past passive participle of the Latin *tollere*—which included among its meanings "cancellation and cashing in."[35] By the time of *Das Kapital,* Marx had come to a similar viewpoint, realizing that the representational structure which valorizes diverse concrete labors as so many units of abstract labor time is syllogistic and fetishistic to the core. This, for Marx, is the truth of Hegel's imagined community. As Moishe Postone puts it, "the rational core of Hegel's dialectic is precisely its idealist character," a character it shares with Christ, commodity, coinage, and postage stamp.[36]

The neologism *Philatelie* was coined from the Greek *a-telia* (free from charge or tax).[37] Stamps exempt you from charges—once you have paid for them. They give money an alibi. And money gives the commodity an alibi, for the syllogistic figure Shell catalogues is ultimately *Art and Commodity,* not its secondary monetary form. Under capital, the "enigma of the fetishistic character of money" becomes "nothing more than the enigma of the fetishistic character of commodities," for under capital "the money form of an object is . . . simply the phenomenal form of the social relations which the object masks. In this sense every commodity might be regarded as a symbol, inasmuch as insofar as it has value, it is only a material wrapping for the human labor which has been expended in producing it."[38] The monetary form might well work its wonders in ancient Bethlehem, but the massive global diffusion of such syllogistic imaginings is rather a function of the spread of capital, a phenomenon predicated upon the rise of urban European "free labor" in the late Middle Ages.[39] So Marx traced the rise of a system of socially "objective domination" which operates "in such a way"— the production and exchange of commodities—"that individuals are now ruled by *abstractions,* whereas earlier they depended on one another."[40]

Benjamin's nostalgia for a lost "authenticity" may well be a collector's fantasy (cognate with the tourist fantasy Frow addresses). Yet, contra Shell, the trajectory Benjamin traces through the modern massification of commodified art forms is fundamentally correct. In fact this diffusion can be followed well beyond the current "dematerialization" of money (and, for that matter, postage stamps), for, again contra Shell, its motor is elsewhere.[41] Its motor lies in the contradictory dynamic of accumulation innate to the commodity itself, that "material wrapping for human labor." The contradiction inherent to the "Sisyphean" dynamic of a production process pegged to labor, yet reliant on continual technological advance, provides the propulsive force by which capital chases the bourgeoisie, syllogism in hand, "over the whole surface of the globe."[42]

Vanupieds

No wonder they try to escape. In the previous chapter I traced the Sisyphean process by which the unknown traveler attempts to move beyond the nation-state. This is not, however, the end of the matter. In fact, the traveler's difficulties begin at home. The rather surprising fact is that Bruce Chatwin was a collector of fine objects. He had even risen to a director's position at Sotheby's by the time he quit in 1966. "The collector dreams that he is not only in a distant or past world but also, at the same time, in a better one, in which although men are as unprovided with what they need as in the everyday world, things are free of the drudgery of being useful."[43] Such dreams seem to have run through Chatwin's biography. As did their concurrent and contradictory rejection. "And do we not all," he once asked, in a lecture entitled "The Morality of Things," "long to throw down our altars and rid ourselves of our possessions?"[44] Sick of the art world's "reliance on things," and compelled by his self-professed "horror of home," Chatwin decided, in the midsixties, to seek that "distant or past world" in travel instead.[45]

However half-hearted the resultant sojourn *In Patagonia,* these travels did indeed place their "solitary hero" in Patagonia—in the company of nomads like Donald Evans, who "could set up in a railway waiting room." Not that Evans's stamps could ever obliterate "the commodity like character of things," a Sisyphean task for the traveling artist as much as the homebound collector. Stamps, as I argued above, are phenomenal forms of objectified labor. They bear the imprint of a society whose forms of domination are objectively mediated through the commodification of labor. In this sense Anthony is correct in his estimation of these "small bits of colored paper," which he magnifies into "symbols of a social as well as an industrial revolution."[46] Indeed, stamps and trains have a strange— illustrative—affinity: "The railways and cheap postage brought a greater deal of freedom and mobility to the man-in-the-street than he had ever known before— and with these two commercial advantages the Victorians were ready to lead Britain into the forefront of world affairs."[47] Where does this "freedom and mobility" take him? "We trust," states the inscription on the Philco Time Capsule, "that the generations to come will preserve and guard this capsule, and take the measures necessary to ensure the success of its huge journey."

Of course these are merely illustrative connections. What of the "nomad's contempt for the pyramid"? What "commercial advantages" could arise from the unknown traveler's freedom from "the drudgery of being useful"? (This, I would suggest, is where one will find the fantasy of "authenticity" which Frow and MacCannell seek—in the traveler's own self-styled uselessness). "The Golden Age ended," writes the modern nomad, "when men stopped hunting, settled in houses and began the daily grind."[48] Inasmuch as a Chatwin attempts to recreate this Golden Age he strives to obliterate any connection between overseas travel and work. Theorists of the "post-industrial" activity of tourism tend to follow him.[49]

What of my own rhetoric: sending the traveler back home? Such narratives seem to illustrate what Meaghan Morris has described as "a masculinist tradition inscribing 'home' as the site both of frustrating containment (home as dull) and of truth to be rediscovered (home as real). The stifling home is the place from which the voyage begins and to which, in the end, it returns."[50] This home-away-from-home trope is endemic to a capital-driven "world of plurals" in which "living space" comes to appear so "antithetical to the place of work." Which is why turning, as Morris does, to consider the home-away-from-home as a site for work allows one to read this tradition from a very different angle.[51]

This is where the postage stamp will, in the following chapter, surface as an emblem for the *something* which serves to unite the various citizens of Vanupieds in a *consciousness of connectedness*.

Notes

1. Anthony, *Beginner's Guide*, 11.
2. Walter Benjamin, "Stamp Shop," in *One-Way Street*, 94.
3. Ibid.
4. Ibid.
5. Ibid., 93.
6. Ibid., 92.
7. Bruce Chatwin, "Donald Evans," in *What Am I Doing Here*, 263–68.
8. Ibid., 267.
9. Ibid.
10. Anthony, *Beginner's Guide*, 15.
11. The metropolitan nationalist's grief at the loss of empire always has a "stagy quality" to it; the racist distinctions integral to such phenomena are, according to Anderson, little akin to the spirit of the imagined community (*Imagined Community,* 111). Yes, for as Frantz Fanon pointed out, the globalization of capitalist relations of production makes the *direct* rule of domination unnecessary for those who remain ruling classes nonetheless. Why grieve for the loss of that "Manichean world" when it can be held in place simply through the "objective domination" of the commodity form (*Wretched of the Earth*, 31)?

12. Anthony, *Beginner's Guide,* 119.

13. Benjamin, *One-Way Street,* 92.

14. Shell, *Art and Money.*

15. Mallarmé quoted in ibid., 134.

16. Spoerri quoted in ibid., 85.

17. Ibid., 8.

18. Ibid., 7.

19. Ibid., 15.

20. Ibid., 58–60.

21. Walter Benjamin, "Paris," in *Reflections,* 154.

22. Ibid.

23. Ibid., 155.

24. Anthony, *Beginner's Guide,* 14.

25. Ibid., 11.

26. Anthony is, however, no miniature Mallarmé. In a chapter entitled "What's It Worth?" he claims that, provided "it is not taken to excess, I still consider that the financial aspect of stamp collecting gives the hobby a certain piquancy" (133). In correlating the stamp form to the money form (and pointing to that curious category of stamps featuring representations of currency), Shell would doubtless agree (*Art and Money,* 82). Revealingly, stamps lacking indexes of price and/or nationality are termed "mute" stamps (Anthony, *Beginner's Guide,* 71).

27. See Davila's *Frida,* 25.

28. Walter Benjamin, "The Work of Art in the Age of Mechanical Reproduction," in *Illuminations,* 212, 216, 214.

29. Shell, *Art and Money,* 155 n. 156. Benjamin glances at ancient coinage as one of the earliest modes of the "mechanical reproduction of the work of art." Such developments led "intermittently" through woodcuts, printing, and lithography and up to the camera ("The Work of Art" in *Illuminations,* 212–13).

30. Marx quoted in Murray, *Marx's Theory of Scientific Knowledge,* 31.

31. Anderson, *Imagined Communities,* 10.

32. Marx, "On the Jewish Question," 229.

33. Ibid., 245.

34. Shell rejects Marx's reading (conducted in "good Protestant fashion") of the "Jewish" essence of this phenomenon, seeing it instead as Christian to the core (*Art and Money,* 57). Murray's account of the "Theologics of Money and Capital" is interesting in this regard (see *Marx's Theory of Scientific Knowledge,* 191–94).

35. Shell, *Art and Money,* 128.

36. Postone, *Time, Labour, and Social Mediation,* 85. Gayatri Chakravorty Spivak, on the other hand, by reasserting Marx's articulation of the "textuality of the economic," serves to bring a not dissimilar argument into post-structuralist philosophy ("Speculations on Reading Marx," 42).

37. Anthony, *Beginner's Guide,* 135.

38. Marx, *Capital,* 69, 66.

39. Postone critiques Sohn-Rethel, similarly, for the latter's focus on the "the exchange abstraction" which unites both ancient and modern histories, as opposed to the totalizing abstraction of labor-time which comes to such prominence under capital (*Time, Labour, and Social Domination,* 156 n. 90). I agree with this critique. It does not, however, serve to alter any of Sohn-Rethel's (or Shell's) findings about the *second nature* of Bourgeois epistemology, so much as shift the base—from exchange to production—on which they are grounded.

40. Marx quoted in ibid., 125.

41. In an attempt to extend the Lukascian exploration of the cultural ramifications of the category of value, Fredric Jameson comments on that tired old "theme of the gold standard . . . which fatally suggests a solid and tangible kind of value as opposed to various forms of paper and plastic (or information on your computer)" ("Culture and Finance Capital," 257).

42. Postone, *Time, Labour, and Social Domination,* 298; Marx, *Communist Manifesto,* 36, 37.

43. Walter Benjamin, "Paris," in *Reflections,* 155.

44. Chatwin quoted in Clapp, *With Chatwin,* 132–33.

45. Chatwin quoted in ibid., 127, 55.

46. Anthony, *Beginner's Guide,* 55.

47. Ibid.

48. Chatwin, *In Patagonia,* 136.

49. See Meaghan Morris, "At Henry Parkes Motel," 9–12.

50. Ibid., 12.

51. Benjamin, "Paris," 154.

5

A Home away from Home

We, the Masters, Were Not Home

Chatwin *was* at home—often. Susannah Clapp describes the succession of houses in which the traveler wrote out his wanderings: his home in Gloucestershire, his various London flats, the home of a rich friend in Greece, a fort in Rajasthan . . . Traveling the world "with his huge amount of luggage," Chatwin made an odd sort of nomad.[1] As his editor for *In Patagonia,* Clapp has insight into precisely that person who was left "out of his books."[2] His first travels, one discovers, were actually business trips, "playing the pirate" for Sotheby's, his erstwhile employer.[3] Chatwin decorated his successive homes with objects collected in the process. No wonder his friends—and Clapp was one—found his frequent "denunciations of acquisitiveness" so amusing.[4]

Not that she wishes to exploit the "benign contradiction" which Chatwin personified.[5] There is a certain homage in the very irony through which Clapp domesticates her subject's pretensions; in finding the nomad at home, she partakes of the same anecdotal "difference-in-similarity, and similarity-in-difference" which pervades his texts.[6] Yet the domestic interior Clapp furnishes does not end here, on the contradictory figure of the nomadic collector of *objets d'art.* To follow such illustrative contradictions out beyond the anecdotal and personable and into the social domain to which such figures are ineluctably linked is to uncover just why travel is ever pegged to home.

The fact is that, however adventurous, *the traveler is always in someone else's home.* Much of *The Songlines,* for instance, was written in Rajasthan, in the fort where Chatwin and his wife, Elizabeth, were hosted by a local landowner. "Food arrives," wrote Chatwin, "three times a day, on solid mahogany trays, carried by a procession of astonishingly beautiful girls and their mothers."[7] This postcard image is far from particular to Chatwin's own travels. Compare the service in "the formerly royal city of Udaipur," where Madhur Jaffrey finds her recipe for "The Lake Palace Hotel's aubergine."[8] Prior to setting out the ingredients, Jaffrey mentions that the palace has now been "converted, as most Indian palaces seem fated to be, into a spectacular hotel."[9] Food, feudal relations, hotels, and tourism: opening these anecdotal scenarios further will allow me to unfold the texture of the strange fate Jaffrey mentions. (And the postage stamp? The unknown object of these travels will here reveal itself).

Home Economics

I want to argue that there is a particular form of gendered exploitation written into the malign contradictions of the Third World travels for which Chatwin has become so emblematic. "When people go on holiday," Cynthia Enloe explains, "they expect to be freed from humdrum domestic tasks. To be a tourist means to have someone else make your bed."[10] Theorists of tourism rarely consider this in their analysis of such supposedly "post-industrial" behaviors; "domestic labor," as Meaghan Morris writes, "is simply subsumed, by implication, in the shift from 'work' to 'leisure.'"[11] Seeking to unravel the gendered "voyage/*domus*" opposition, Morris points, in passing, to tourism's role in the increasingly globalized "homework economy."[12] To follow this lead will require further unraveling, for the homework economy works precisely through its seeming subsumption within the domain of "leisure."

In societies based on wage labor, the worker's remuneration tends to the level of subsistence, the amount "socially necessary" to ensure his (*sic*) "daily reappearance at the factory gates."[13] This "iron law of wages" forms the cornerstone of Marx's theory of value. In adopting this law, Marx glanced only in passing at the variable social factors which go into the definition of subsistence. He concentrated on the factory floor itself to highlight the alienating logic by which the surplus produced beyond such subsistence accrues to the capitalist.[14] That this factory model of social organization has not pervaded social life in totality, whether in the core or at the periphery, is evidence of a blindness in Marx's assumptions. It is clear that types of nonwaged work have always been integral to capitalism, housework being a prime example.[15] Yet however outside Marx's reckonings, housework, inasmuch as it "decreases the share of subsistence borne by capital," has been of direct assistance to capital.[16] The male worker can be paid less if his reproduction as a worker is reliant upon the broad social assumption that "he 'naturally' enjoys the labor that is located in the leisure sphere, outside the boundaries of capitalist production, as part of his self-realization."[17] The "living space," which in the nineteenth century becomes, as Benjamin says, so "antithetical to the place of work" is nonetheless integral to it.

Hence Joan Smith, Immanuel Wallerstein, and Hans-Dieter Evers suggest that patriarchy, far from simply an illiberal throwback, is "an entirely modern affair and is one of the fundamental political components of the modern world economy."[18] This is equally true for much of the work for which women do receive wages. Women's work provides the overwhelming share of the world's "cheap labor"—"labor made cheap," as Enloe prefers to call it.[19] This is particularly true of the countries the unknown traveler passes through on the way down south to the End of the World. In many such communities, the subsistence wage necessary for the reproduction of a female worker is seen as less than that necessary for a male worker, on the understanding that "her wages are merely supplemental; that the real wage . . . is being earned by the adult man of the family."[20] A similar situation pertains when tasks like "sewing, food preparation, housekeeping or physical nurturing" are seen as somehow natural to women.[21] Such activities, often performed in the woman's own home, are readily viewed as an extension of her unwaged domestic work. As such, the proportion of the labor product which accrues to the female worker, as the amount "socially necessary" to enable her subsistence, is, *by definition,* made lower than the proportion accorded the male worker.

Unlike housework, such labor is subject to the law of value, inasmuch as the woman worker sells her labor power as a "free laborer." Like housework, *labor made cheap* illustrates how patriarchal structures outside the law of value per se can nonetheless be called upon to benefit the maintenance and the expansion of a system of accumulation based upon value. Capital, yet again, has a vested interest in keeping women in "their" place—like hotels, "homes away from home" for so many postindustrial tourists. Hotels are run on "humdrum domestic tasks" like making beds.[22] Indeed, the labor-intensive industry of "leisure" tourism is entirely reliant upon the gendering of the tasks integral to it: "cleaning, washing, cooking, serving."[23] When relegated to women these jobs can be made to appear so much a part of the hotel's homely atmosphere.[24] A travel writer might even notice such "astonishingly beautiful" women, though usually the fact that they are serving him dissolves into the tourist brochure aesthetics of her smile. Yet from tower to hotel room, from hotel to *hospedaje,* gendered labor relations form the exploitative underside to the traveler's masculine transcendence through motion.

Chatwin's personal contradictions suddenly take on an emblematic function when read in these terms. There is a definite parallel between his occupations and those of Benjamin's collector who, bringing his treasures home from abroad, attempts to "obliterate the commodity like character of things."[25] Such a fantasy—

a domestic space beyond the rigors of the commodity-driven and alienating workplace—can be achieved only by ignoring women's domestic labor, the endless "drudgery" required to make the collector feel at home. The unknown traveler abroad is trotting out a similar fantasy, industrializing it even, in the myriad hotel rooms, homes away from home, through which he or she runs. To obliterate the "commodity like character of things" is even more of an impossibility for the traveler, for travel is run precisely upon the commodification of domestic "drudgery"—*women's labor made cheap*. Here my illustrative postage stamp re-enters the picture and takes on concrete form. This is the ultimate object of these travels: the objectification of labor into commodity form.

This contradictory combination of travel and commerce extends beyond the personal confusion of home and abroad which Clapp reads in Chatwin's postcards. It extends into the patriarchal fabric of contemporary global capitalism, for travel is big business: in 1991, it accounted for 7 percent of all world exports.[26] The word *export* perhaps makes clear just how industrial a process this is, for all the rhetoric which female faces lend to the pursuit of leisure. The "invisible factories" of women attendant upon such a process constitute the "homework economy" to which Morris refers.[27] Such small-sounding ventures are integral to the "global restructuring" which leads contemporary capitalist magnates—Benetton is a prime example—to subcontract to informal factories and home-based workers.[28] Accompanied by labor deregulation at the official level, these processes have led to "an increasing feminization of labor" worldwide.[29] Indeed, there is nothing backward about these patriarchal strategies. By helping to counteract the declining rates of profit which Marx predicted would beset the increasingly technologized factories, the "homework economy" helps maintain the "sustained process of accumulation" innate to capital.[30]

Whatever his or her "contempt for the pyramid," the unknown traveler "roaming around the world" has an invisible hand in these processes.[31] The "very portability" of such work—the commodification of *women's labor made cheap*—ensures that its fundamentally industrial nature will not be recognized.[32] Of course the traveler is simply exchanging commodities (services for cash) at the going price, the surplus of which runs elsewhere. As an agent, however, of these moves of capital, he or she is integral to the "invisible factory." Travel helps forge the chains which tie this "export" industry into the global economy of homes away from home. Hotel, *hospedaje*, guest house: this is where you will find the unknown traveler, relaxing from the "humdrum domestic tasks" of others. Travel serves to secure the "relentless expansion of commodity relations" outside the seeming domain of capital.[33] For this is where you will find the commodity form too. If anyone steps into *that* syllogism, it is the traveler. Travel is commodity fetishism.

Doppelgänger

At this juncture—Vanupieds, according to my travel guide—a whole series of contradictory doubles reveal their underlying coherence: factory and home, citizen and nomad, capitalist and traveler, even postage stamp and domestic labor. As a site for the exchange of commodified labor, travel links the fantastic commodity logic I articulated through the stamp form with the gendered labor relations integral to tourism. Passing through myriad homes-away-from-home on the way down to the pyramid at the End of the World, the unknown traveler helps settle capital's mode of "objective domination" into place. Such a subject— a citizen of Vanupieds to be sure—is necessarily doubled and split, for the flight path he or she serves "has a vital impulse of its own."[34]

This is why the traveler's *consciousness of disconnectedness* is so illusory. Far from eternal enemies, Cain and Abel are actually traveling on the same train, "at the forefront of world affairs."[35] It was not, after all, the landlocked hoarding of property so much as the international movement of capital which led to the colonization of Tierra del Fuego. "At a luncheon in Rio Gallegos," writes Chatwin in his graphic account of the massacre of Patagonian anarchists in 1921, "the local president of the Argentine Patriotic League spoke of 'the sweet emotion of those moments.'"[36] Most of those present were English colonists who had traveled across the world to reach Tierra del Fuego, a fact Chatwin highlights ironically, without allowing it to upset his Cain and Abel opposition of travel and settlement, nomadism and domestication. Such cozy anecdotes are innate to the "semiotic structure" of tourism, which constantly casts up doubles who serve to voice the traveler's own *itineraries outside of thought.* For to follow this contradiction out beyond the anecdotal is to see that there is no necessary opposition between travel and settlement. "Colonization," Meaghan Morris writes, "may be precisely a mode of movement (as occupation) that transgresses limits and borders."[37] Colonization may be a traveler's occupation.

It may even be a leisurely one. "That tourism is not discussed as seriously by conventional political commentators as oil or weaponry" says a lot, in Enloe's view, "about the ideological construction of 'seriousness.'"[38] Witness Chatwin, arriving in Tierra del Fuego, forgetting the king of Patagonia and Araucania to turn, now deadly serious, to an account of the genocide. "The Ona's [Selk'nam's] sheep rustling threatened the companies' dividends (in Buenos Aires the explorer Julio Popper spoke of their 'alarming communist tendencies') and the accepted solution was to round them up and civilize them in the Mission—where they died of infected clothing and the despair of captivity."[39] Chatwin passes on to detail that other solution: the mass shootings, the accusations of cannibalism, the pound paid for each severed Indian ear. The one ironic-tragic reference Popper receives in Chatwin's text rings strangely to anyone familiar with the ironic-comic status the Romanian has since attained in the region's museums and travel guides. Chatwin was clearly ignorant of the ludicrous side of Popper's story. Had Popper's stamps then been on display, the "ideological construction of seriousness" might have left Chatwin a little confused by this *first time as farce* confusion of Cain and Abel in the self-same individual.

Though doubtless he would have eventually found himself at the Museo del Fin del Mundo anyway. After all, it is hard to imagine a better way to occupy one's traveling than by writing "*What am I doing here*" on the back of a postcard from the End of the World. In the process he might have laughed at some of the tourists you see there, living out "ridiculous objects" like visits to Julio Popper's museumized stamp collection. Such a projective structure reiterates the symptomatic utterances I charted, for all their trashiness, throughout book 1. Lucas Bridges's magic soap anecdote plays on a similar displacement, to read his fetish, down time, into the eyes of the Other. Laughing, on the other hand, at a coeval North American tourist affords the traveler a cross time revelation of a similar set of disowned allegiances. Such projective structures have persisted through this retrospective narrative of mine too. Inasmuch as I evince a *consciousness of disconnectedness* with Chatwin's Cain and Abel illusions, I strive to obliterate the fact that I, in Tierra del Fuego, was *going through the same motions* as him.

Yet "there must be *something*" about these conscious discourses.[40] In Tierra del Fuego, I couldn't resist telling my fellow travelers about the *yanqui* tourist. "The American tourist who buys a Julio Popper coin at the End of the World!" The traveler holds the tourist to his fetish. I couldn't resist pressing his face against the coin, sparking off another anecdote, imprinting his features onto the "ridiculous object" we both sought. That was my face.

On the Wing . . .

But it was *not* my face too. The point of self-absence to which I shall finally— going home—address myself is the commodity form. Subsuming such disparate figures within the one syllogistic form, it is the fetish of commodities which has ultimately structured the various objects of these travels in Tierra del Fuego.

Here I disagree with Meaghan Morris, who rejects the syllogism as a logical impossibility, and indeed as an imperial mode of analysis too. Morris critiques those theorists who, "constructing guides to the Present, or theories of the tourist's homing instinct," invoke figures like Chatwin to universalize the particular practice such figures are seen to exemplify.[41] "There are," as she puts it, "no exemplary users" of any given space: "the operative *simultaneity* of programs and proximities [crossing any given space] makes the effort to take any one as exemplary . . . only one of the more aggressively territorial programs competing to found its place."[42] Much as I agree with this formulation, I think Morris fails to recognize that such a program is precisely that of capital. Through the mediation of individual social agents, capital, as *capital personified,* acts to impose its exemplary representation of labor: each "concrete labor" in all its particularity, taken as an "expression" of so much "identical human labor" in all its universalizing homogeneity.

That is a syllogism—or at least an attempt to impose one—and it is not "only one of" but *the* most "aggressively territorial" representation of the present. Moving from one commodity-run practice to another, travel enacts the logic of "settled civilization"—inasmuch as it is the logic of capital—at every step. It is this which brings Julio Popper himself—the freak of Fuegian philately, a singular figure if ever there was one—into the fold of exemplary travelers. Popper's postage stamps bespeak the syllogistic mode of representation concurrently advancing upon Tierra del Fuego. So Popper achieved "solidarities" with the other colonial magnates, all of them citizens of Vanupieds. All were united by the "unknown soldier" commodity form.

By the same token, I disagree with Anderson's assertion that "in world historical terms the Bourgeoisie were the first classes to achieve solidarities on an essentially imagined basis."[43] The bourgeoisie achieved their solidarities on an essentially commodified basis. In fact it has been argued that nations are the result of this process, that the demands of the industrial division of labor necessitated the grouping of bounded cultural entities within which "free labor" could move interchangeably.[44] Balibar counters that it "is quite impossible to 'deduce' the nation form from capitalist relations of production," and in many ways I agree.[45] Yet this is not my flight path. Insofar as I have followed the unknown traveler through these nationally contoured domains, I claim that the capital—Vanupieds—of these travels *is* capital.

Whose Imagined Community? Like money, the postage stamp is "simply the phenomenal form of the social relations which the object masks."[46] As such this object enshrines, like a tomb, the same commensurable store of "dead labor" as any other commodity.[47] Any other can identify with and be exchanged for the stamp, for all partake of the parallel anonymity integral to the "religious imaginings" of capital. The suspension of disbelief holds these unknown syllogisms in circulation, uniting them, through our very actions, in their international migrations through homogenous and empty time.

Indeed, it is not simply that "individuals," under the fetishistic structures of capital, "are ruled by abstractions."[48] When Commodity A (stamps or tourist services "or what not") finds its value and measure of equivalence in Commodity B, "an abstraction outside of thought" is fetishistically enacted. Through the imaginings locked within the individuals' unthinking actions, "the things (commodities) believe in their place, instead of the subjects."[49] It is "precisely in this absurd form" that postage stamps can be said to possess among themselves a "consciousness of connectedness."

When the sheep had wings—doubtless they still do—this was the *something* by which they flew.

Notes

1. Clapp, *With Chatwin,* 203.
2. Ibid., 1.
3. Ibid., 108.
4. Ibid., 132.
5. Ibid., 132–33.
6. Ibid., 97.
7. Chatwin quoted in ibid., 158–59.
8. Jaffrey, *Indian Cookery,* 77.
9. Ibid.
10. Enloe, *Bananas, Beaches, and Bases,* 33.
11. Meaghan Morris, "At Henry Parkes Motel," 46 n. 22.
12. Richard Gordon quoted in ibid., 33.
13. Michael Burawoy quoted in Smith, "Non-Wage Labor," 64.
14. Marx, *Capital,* 158–59; compare 230–312 on the struggle over the work day. As Marx shows, this struggle did not concern the principle of subsistence wages but rather the amount of time one could be forced to work for them (i.e., the extent of the surplus product accruing to the capitalist).
15. See also Ernesto Laclau's work on the potential imbrication of precapitalist and capitalist modes of production, a condition he diagnosed as a fundamental accompaniment to capital's advance into the periphery ("Feudalism and Capitalism in Latin America," 37).
16. Smith, "Non-Wage Labor," 74. As Joan Smith, Immanuel Wallerstein, and Hans-Dieter Evers comment in their joint introduction to *Households and the World-Economy,* "one of the contradictions of capitalism is that the optimal functioning of the law of value seems to require that it *not* be universally applied" (10–11).
17. Schiel, "Development and Underdevelopment," 127.
18. Smith, Wallerstein, and Evers, "Introduction," 13.
19. Enloe, "Silicon Tricks," 13.
20. Ibid.

21. Ibid.

22. Enloe, *Bananas, Beaches, and Bases,* 34.

23. Ibid.

24. Ibid.

25. Walter Benjamin, "Paris," in *Reflections,* 155.

26. David Harrison, "International Tourism," 4.

27. I take the phrase *invisible factories* from Mies, *Laceworkers of Narsapur.*

28. See Ward, "Introduction and Overview," 1–22; on Benetton's "Post-Fordist economic policies," see Giroux, "Consuming Social Change," 17.

29. Pettman, *Worlding Women,* 163.

30. Laclau, "Feudalism and Capitalism," 38.

31. Bruce Chatwin, "Donald Evans," in *What Am I Doing Here,* 267.

32. Ibid.

33. Frow, "Tourism," 151.

34. Marx, *Capital,* 232.

35. Anthony, *Beginner's Guide,* 55.

36. Chatwin, *In Patagonia,* 101.

37. Meaghan Morris, "At Henry Parkes Motel," 43.

38. Enloe, *Bananas, Bases, and Beaches,* 40.

39. Chatwin, *In Patagonia,* 111.

40. Anthony, *Beginner's Guide,* 11.

41. Meaghan Morris, "At Henry Parkes Motel," 37.

42. Ibid., 41.

43. Anderson, *Imagined Communities,* 77.

44. See Gellner, *Nations and Nationalism,* 49, who adds of this "drive towards new [social] units constructed on the principles corresponding to the new division of labour," that "those who are its historic agents known not what they do, but that is another matter."

45. Balibar, "The Nation Form," 89.

46. Marx, *Capital,* 66.

47. Ibid., 319.

48. Marx quoted in Postone, *Time, Labour, and Social Mediation,* 125.

49. Zizek, "How Did Marx Invent the Symptom?" 34.

Bibliography

Adams, Parveen, with Michel Onfray, Francois Serge, Alucquére-Rosanne Stone, and Sarah Wilson. *Orlan: Çeci est Mon Corps, Çeci est Mon Logiciel.* London: Black Dog, 1996.

Adorno, Theodor W., and Max Horkheimer. *Dialectic of Enlightenment.* London: Verso, 1972.

Althusser, Louis. "Ideology and Ideological State Apparatuses (Notes towards an Investigation)." In *Mapping Ideology,* ed. Slavoj Zizek. London: Verso, 1994. 100–141.

Anderson, Benedict. *Imagined Communities: Reflections on the Origin and Spread of Nationalism.* 2d ed. London: Verso, 1991.

Anthony, Kenneth W. *Beginner's Guide to Stamp Collecting.* London: Sphere Books, 1971.

Arens, William. *The Man-Eating Myth: Anthropology and Anthropophagy.* New York: Oxford University Press, 1979.

Assoun, Paul-Laurent. *El Fetichismo.* Buenos Aires: Ediciones Nueva Visión, 1994.

Augustine, St. *Confessions.* London: Penguin, 1961.

Balibar, Etienne. "The Nation Form: History and Ideology." In *Nation, Class, Ambiguous Identities,* ed. Etienne Balibar and Immanuel Wallerstein. London: Verso, 1991. 86–106.

———. *The Philosophy of Marx.* London: Verso, 1995.

Barthes, Roland. "The Death of the Author." In *Image-Music-Text.* London: Fontana Press, 1977. 142–48.

———. "The Eiffel Tower." In *The Eiffel Tower and Other Mythologies.* New York: Noonday Press, 1979. 3–17.

Bastian, Adolf. "The Waning of Primitive Societies." In *Adolf Bastian and the Psychic Unity of Mankind: The Foundations of Anthropology in Nineteenth Century Germany* by Klaus-Peter Koepping. St. Lucia, Australia: University of Queensland Press, 1983. 215–19.

Baudrillard, Jean. *The Ecstasy of Communication.* New York: Semiotext(e), 1987.

———. "Fetishism and Ideology: The Semiological Reduction." In *For a Critique of the Political Economy of the Sign.* St Louis: Telos Press, 1981. 83–97.

Belza, Juan Esteban. *En la Isla del Fuego.* Vol. 1, *Encuentros.* Buenos Aires: Instituto de Investigaciones Históricas Tierra del Fuego, 1974.

Benjamin, Walter, *Illuminations.* London: Fontana, 1973.

————. "Konvolut N [Theoretics of Knowledge; Theory of Progress]." *Philosophical Forum* 15.1–2 (Fall–Winter 1983–84): 1–39.

————. *One-Way Street and Other Writings.* London: New Left Books, 1979.

————. *Reflections, Essays, Aphorisms, and Autobiographical Writings.* Ed. Peter Demetz. New York: Schocken Books, 1978.

Boon, James. *Other Tribes, Other Scribes: Symbolic Anthropology in the Comparative Study of Cultures, Histories, Religions, and Texts.* New York: Cambridge University Press, 1982.

Borrero, José María. *La Patagonia Tragica: Asesinatos, Pirateria, y Esclavitud.* 2d ed. Buenos Aires: Zagier and Urruty, 1989.

Bourdieu, Pierre. "Doxa and Common Life: An Interview by Terry Eagleton." In *Mapping Ideology,* ed. Slavoj Zizek. London: Verso, 1994. 265–77.

Bowie, Malcolm. "Psychoanalysis and the Future of Theory." In *Psychoanalysis and the Future of Theory.* Oxford: Basil Blackwell, 1993. 11–45.

Braun Menéndez, Armando. *Julio Popper: El Dictador Fueguino.* Buenos Aires: Editorial Lito, 1937.

Breton, André. *What Is Surrealism: Selected Writings of André Breton.* Ed. Franklin Rosemont. New York: Pathfinder Press, 1978.

Bridges, E. Lucas. *Uttermost Part of the Earth: Indians of Tierra del Fuego.* New York: Dover, 1988.

Bridges, Reverend Thomas. *Yámana-English Dictionary.* Ed. Ferdinand Hestermann and Martin Gusinde. Buenos Aires: Zagier and Urruty, 1987.

Bryson, Bill. *Neither Here nor There.* London: Picador, 1996.

Buck-Morss, Susan. "Aesthetics and Anaesthetics: Walter Benjamin's Artwork Essay Reconsidered." *October* 62 (Fall 1992): 3–41.

————. "The City as Dreamworld and Catastrophe." *October* 73 (Summer 1995): 3–26.

————. *The Dialectics of Seeing: Walter Benjamin and the Arcades Project.* Cambridge, Mass.: MIT Press, 1991.

Caillois, Roger. "Mimicry and Legendary Psychasthenia." In *October: The First Decade, 1976–1986,* ed. Annette Michelson, Rosalind Krauss, Douglas Crimp, and Joan Copjec. Cambridge, Mass.: MIT Press, 1987. 59–74.

Canclini, Arnoldo. *Julio Popper: Quijote del Oro Fueguino.* Buenos Aires: Editores Emecé, 1993.

Carrick, Jill Maree. "The Surrealist Image in Postmodern and Visual Culture." M.A. thesis, University of Melbourne, 1990.

Carroll, Lewis. *The Annotated Snark: The Full Text of Lewis Carroll's Great Nonsense Epic, The Hunting of the Snark.* Ed. Martin Gardner. London: Penguin, 1962.

Chakrabarty, Dipesh. "Marx after Marxism: History, Subalternity, and Difference." *Positions: East Asia Cultures Critique* 2.2 (Fall 1994): 446–63.

————. "Postcoloniality and the Artifice of History: Who Speaks for 'Indian' Pasts?" *Representations* 37 (Winter 1992): 1–26.

Chapman, Anne. *Drama and Power in a Hunting Society: The Selk'nam of Tierra del Fuego.* Cambridge: Cambridge University Press, 1982.

Chatterjee, Partha. *The Nation and Its Fragments: Colonial and Postcolonial Histories.* New Jersey: Princeton University Press, 1993.

Chatwin, Bruce, *In Patagonia.* London: Picador, 1977.

————. *The Songlines.* London: Picador, 1988.

————. *What Am I Doing Here.* London: Johnathan Cape, 1989.

Chow, Rey. "Postmodern Automatons." In *Feminists Theorize the Political,* ed. Judith Butler and Joan W. Scott. New York: Routledge, 1992. 101–17.

Clapp, Susannah. *With Chatwin.* London: Jonathan Cape, 1997.

Clifford, James. "On Ethnographic Allegory." In *Writing Culture: The Poetics and Politics of Ethnography,* ed. James Clifford and George Marcus. Berkeley: University of California Press, 1986. 98–121.

————. *The Predicament of Culture: Twentieth-Century Ethnography, Literature, and Art.* Cambridge, Mass.: Harvard University Press, 1988.

Cohen, Margaret. *Profane Illumination: Walter Benjamin and the Paris of Surrealist Revolution.* Berkeley: University of California Press, 1995.

Cook, James. *The Voyage of the Resolution and the Adventure, 1772–75.* Vol. 2 of *The Journals of Captain James Cook and His Voyages of Discovery.* Ed. J. C. Beaglehole. Cambridge: Cambridge University Press, 1961.

Coombe, Rosemary. "Embodied Trademarks: Mimesis and Alterity on American Commercial Frontiers." *Cultural Anthropology* 11.2 (1996): 202–24.

Copjec, Joan. *Read My Desire: Lacan against the Historicists.* Cambridge, Mass.: MIT Press, 1994.

Crick, Malcolm. "Tourists, Locals, and Anthropologists: Quizzical Reflections on 'Otherness' in Tourist Encounters and Tourist Research." *Australian Cultural History* 10.10 (1991): 6–18.

Darwin, Charles. *Charles Darwin's Diary of the Voyage of the H.M.S. Beagle.* Ed. Nora Barlow. Cambridge: Cambridge University Press, 1933.

————. *The Origin of the Species and The Descent of Man.* New York: Random House, 1871.

————. *The Voyage of the Beagle.* Ed. Milicent E. Selsam. Kingswood: World's Work, 1913.

Davila, Juan. *Frida.* In *Transcontinental: Nine Latin American Artists,* ed. Guy Brett. London: Verso, 1990. 25.

Desatur. *Punta Arenas City Tour/Reccorido por Punta Arenas.* Punta Arenas, Chile: Desatur, n.d.

Dimond, Peter, dir. *New Guinea Patrol.* Commonwealth Film Unit for the Department of Territories, 1958.

Dirección Municipal de Turismo. *La Ciudad en el Fin del Mundo/The City at the End of the World, Ushuaia.* Ushuaia: Dirección Municipal de Turismo, n.d.

Dittborn, Eugenio. *Airmail Painting No.49 Jemmy Button*. In *Transcontinental: Nine Latin American Artists,* ed. Guy Brett. London: Verso, 1990. 76.

———. "Correcaminos—Roadrunner." In *Transcontinental: Nine Latin American Artists,* ed. Guy Brett. London: Verso, 1990. 72–73.

Dolar, Mladen. "'I Shall Be with You on Your Wedding Night': Lacan and the Uncanny." *October* 58 (Fall 1992): 5–23.

Durán, Fernando. *La Historia de la Sociedad Explotadora de Tierra del Fuego*. 2d ed. Valparaiso: Sociedad Explotadora, 1951.

Durkheim, Emile. *The Elementary Forms of the Religious Life*. New York: Macmillan, 1965.

Edwards, Peter. *The Story of the Voyage*. Cambridge: Cambridge University Press, 1994.

Enloe, Cynthia. *Bananas, Beaches, and Bases: Making Feminist Sense of International Politics*. Berkeley: University of California Press, 1990.

———. "Silicon Tricks and the Two Dollar Woman." *New Internationalist* 227 (Jan. 1992): 12–14.

Errington, Frederick, and Deborah Gewertz. "Tourism and Anthropology in a Post-Modern World." *Oceania* 60.1 (1989): 37–54.

Escobar, Arturo. *Encountering Development: The Making and Unmaking of the Third World*. Princeton: Princeton University Press, 1995.

Escudero, Juan. "The Logic of Biosphere, the Logic of Capitalism: Nutrition in Latin America." *Review* 14 (Winter 1991): 1–25.

Fabian, Johannes. *Time and the Other: How Anthropology Makes Its Object*. New York: Columbia University Press, 1983.

Fanon, Frantz. *The Wretched of the Earth*. London: Penguin, 1967.

Forster, Johann Reinhold. *Observations Made during a Voyage round the World*. Ed. Nicholas Thomas, Harriet Guest, and Michael Dettelbach. Honolulu: University of Hawai'i Press, 1996.

Foucault, Michel. *The Archaeology of Knowledge and the Discourse on Language*. New York: Pantheon Books, 1972.

———. *The History of Sexuality*. Vol. 1, *An Introduction*. London: Penguin, 1978.

———. *Language, Counter-Memory, Practice*. Ed. Donald Bouchard. Ithaca: Cornell University Press, 1977.

———. *The Order of Things: An Archaeology of the Human Sciences*. New York: Random House, 1970.

———. "Politics and the Study of Discourse." In *The Foucault Effect: Studies in Governmentality*. Ed. Graham Burchell, Colin Gordon, and Peter Miller. London: Harvester Wheatsheaf, 1991. 53–72.

———. "Truth and Power." In *The Foucault Reader: An Introduction to Foucault's Thought*. Ed. Paul Rabinow. London: Penguin, 1984. 51–75.

Frazer, James. "Introduction: Baldwin Spencer as Anthropologist." In *Spencer's Last Journey: Being the Journal of an Expedition to Tierra del Fuego by the Late Sir Baldwin Spencer, with a Memoir*. Ed. R. R. Marrett and T. K. Penniman. Oxford: Clarendon Press, 1931. 1–12.

Freud, Sigmund. *The Interpretation of Dreams*. London: Allen and Unwin, 1954.

———. *Jokes and Their Relation to the Unconscious*. London: Penguin, 1976.

———. *The Standard Edition of the Complete Psychological Works of Sigmund Freud*. Ed. James Strachey. 24 vols. London: Hogarth Press and the Institute of Psychoanalysis, 1960–74.

———. *Totem and Taboo: Some Points of Agreement between the Mental Lives of Savages and Neurotics*. In *The Origins of Religion*. London: Penguin, 1985. 43–224.

Frow, John. "Tourism and the Semiotics of Nostalgia." *October* 57 (Summer 1991): 123–51.

Galbraith, John Kenneth. *A History of Economics: The Past as the Present*. London: Hamish Hamilton, 1987.

Gellner, Ernest. *Nations and Nationalism*. Oxford: Basil Blackwell, 1983.

Gerth, H. H., and C. Wright Mills. "Introduction." In *From Max Weber: Essays in Sociology*, ed. H. H. Gerth and C. Wright Mills. New York: Oxford University Press, 1946.

Giroux, Henry A. "Consuming Social Change: The 'United Colors of Benetton.'" *Cultural Critique* 26 (Winter 1993–94): 5–31.

Gould, Stephen Jay. *The Mismeasure of Man*. London: Penguin, 1981.

Greenblatt, Stephen. *Marvellous Possessions: The Wonder of the New World*. Chicago: University of Chicago Press, 1991.

Greene, John C. "Darwin as a Social Evolutionist." In *Science, Ideology, and World View: Essays in the History of Evolutionary Ideas*. Berkeley: University of California Press, 1981. 95–128.

Gusinde, Martin. *Los Indios de Tierra del Fuego: Resultado de mis Cuatro Expediciones en los Años 1918 hasta 1924, organizadas bajo los auspicios del Ministerio de Instrucción Publica de Chile*. 3 vols. Buenos Aires: Centro Argentino de Etnología Americana, 1982.

Haggard, Rider. *King Solomon's Mines*. London: Penguin Popular Classics, 1994.

Harrison, David. "International Tourism and the Less Developed Countries: The Background." In *Tourism and the Less Developed Countries*, ed. David Harrison. Belhaven: Sussex, 1992. 1–13.

Harrison, Paul. *Inside the Third World: The Anatomy of Poverty*. 2d ed. New York: Penguin, 1981.

Hegel, Georg W. F. *Phenomenology of Spirit*. Oxford: Oxford University Press, 1977.

———. *Reason in History: A General Introduction to the Philosophy of History*. Indianapolis: Bobbs-Merrill, 1953.

Hodge, Bob. "The Atlantis Project: Necrophilia and Touristic Truth." *Meanjin* 49.3 (1990): 389–401.

Huyssen, Andreas. "Foreword: The Return of Diogenes as Postmodern Intellectual." In *Critique of Cynical Reason* by Peter Sloterdijk. Minneapolis: University of Minesota Press, 1987. ix–xxxix.

Ileto, Reynaldo. "Orators and the Crowd." In *Reappraising an Empire: New Perspectives on Philippine-American History*, ed. Peter Stanley. Cambridge, Mass.: Harvard University Press, 1984. 85–113.

————. *Pasyon and Revolution: Popular Movements in the Philippines, 1840–1910.* Manila: Ateneo de Manila University Press, 1979.

Iyer, Pico. *Falling off the Map: Some Lonely Places of the World.* London: Jonathan Cape, 1993.

Jaffrey, Madhur. *Indian Cookery.* 2d ed. London: BBC Enterprises, 1989.

Jameson, Fredric. "Culture and Finance Capital." *Critical Inquiry* 24 (Autumn 1997): 246–65.

Jay, Martin. *Downcast Eyes: The Denigration of Vision in Twentieth Century French Thought.* Berkeley: University of California Press, 1994.

Johnson, Randal. "Tupy or Not Tupy: Cannibalism and Nationalism in Contemporary Brazilian Literature and Culture." In *On Modern Latin American Fiction,* ed. John King. New York: Noonday Press, 1987. 41–60.

Kay, Ronald. *El Espacio de Aca, Señales para una Mirada Americana: A Propósito de la Pintura y la Gráfica de Eugenio Dittborn.* Santiago, Chile: Editores Asociados, 1980.

Lacan, Jacques. *The Four Fundamentals of Psychoanalysis.* London: Penguin, 1979.

————. *The Seminar of Jacques Lacan.* Book 7, *The Ethics of Psychoanalysis.* London: Routledge, 1992.

Laclau, Ernesto. "Feudalism and Capitalism in Latin America." In *Politics and Ideology in Marxist Theory.* London: Verso, 1977. 15–49.

Lefort, Claude. "Marx: From One Vision of History to Another." In *The Political Forms of Modern Society: Bureaucracy, Democracy, Totalitarianism.* Ed. John B. Thompson. London: Polity Press, 1986. 139–80.

Lévi-Strauss, Claude. *Tristes Tropiques.* London: Penguin, 1976.

Lewin, Boleslao. "Atractivas Novelas Sobre Popper." *Karukina,* 21–22 Oct. 1977, 6–9.

————. *Popper, un Conquistador Patagónico: Sus Hazañas, sus Escritos.* Buenos Aires: Editorial Candelabro, 1967.

————. *Quién Fue el Conquistador Patagónico Julio Popper.* Enlgd. vers. of *Popper, un Conquistador Patagónico.* Buenos Aires: Editorial Plus Ultra, 1975.

Lindstrom, Lamont. *Cargo Cult: Strange Stories of Desire from Melanesia and Beyond.* Honolulu: University of Hawai'i Press, 1993.

Lothrop, Samuel K. *The Indians of Tierra del Fuego.* New York: Heye Foundation, 1928.

Loveman, Brian. *Chile: The Legacy of Hispanic Capitalism.* 2d ed. New York: Oxford University Press, 1988.

Lukács, Georg. "Reification and the Consciousness of the Proletariat." In *History and Class Consciousness: Studies in Marxist Dialectics.* Cambridge, Mass.: MIT Press, 1971. 83–222.

MacCannell, Dean. *The Tourist: A New Theory of the Leisure Class.* London: Macmillan, 1976.

MacDonald, A. M., ed. *Chambers Etymological English Dictionary.* Edinburgh: W. W. Chambers, 1961.

Magee, Paul. "Changing Channels." *LIKE* 5 (Summer–Autumn 1997–98): 29–31.

———. "A Gleam of Magic in the Eyes of the Other at the Uttermost Part of the Earth." *Journal for the Psychoanalysis of Culture and Society* 3.2 (Fall 1998): 99–107.

———. "The Magic of the State." Rev. of Michael Taussig's *The Magic of the State. UTS Review* 3.2 (Nov. 1997): 193–207.

———. "With Chatwin." *Arena Magazine,* Aug.–Sept. 1997, 53–55.

Marcus, Julie. "The Journey out to the Centre: The Cultural Appropriation of Ayers Rock." In *Aboriginal Culture Today,* ed. Anna Rutherford. Sydney: Dangaroo Press, 1988. 254–74.

Marx, Karl. *Capital: A Critique of Political Economy.* Vol. 1. London: Dent, 1974.

———. *The Communist Manifesto.* In *Karl Marx on Colonialism and Modernization: His Despatches and Other Writings on China, India, Mexico, the Middle East, and North Africa.* Ed. Shlomo Avineri. New York: Anchor Books, 1969. 35–37.

———. *Contribution to the Critique of Political Economy.* Chicago: Charles Kerr, 1904.

———. "On the Jewish Question." In *Writings of the Young Marx on Philosophy and Society.* Ed. Loyd D. Easton and Kurt H. Guddat. New York: Anchor, 1967. 216–47.

———. *Selected Works.* Vol. 2. Ed. Vladimir Adoratsky. Moscow: Marx-Engels-Lenin Institute; London: Lawrence and Wishart, 1942.

Mateo Martinich, Beros. *Historia de la Region Magallanica.* Vol. 1. Punta Arenas, Chile: Universidad de Magallanes, 1992.

———. *Noguiera, el Pionero.* Punta Arenas, Chile: Ediciones de la Universidad de Magallanes, 1986.

McClosky, Donald. *The Rhetoric of Economics.* Madison: University of Wisconsin Press, 1985.

Mehlman, Jeffrey. *Walter Benjamin for Children: An Essay on His Radio Years.* Chicago: University of Chicago Press, 1993.

Merrett, R. R. "Memoir." In *Spencer's Last Journey: Being the Journal of an Expedition to Tierra del Fuego by the Late Sir Baldwin Spencer, with a Memoir.* Ed. R. R. Marrett and T. K. Penniman. Oxford: Clarendon Press, 1931. 14–45.

Michaels, Eric. *The Aboriginal Invention of Television in Central Australia.* Canberra: Australian Institute of Aboriginal Studies, 1986.

———. "Para-ethnography." In *Bad Aboriginal Art: Tradition, Media, and Technological Horizons.* London: Allen and Unwin, 1994. 165–76.

Mies, Maria. *The Laceworkers of Narsapur: Indian Housewives Produce for the World Market.* London: Zed Press, 1982.

Miller, Jacques-Alain. "Extimité." In *Lacanian Theory of Discourse: Subject, Structure, Society,* ed. Mark Bracher, Marshal W. Alcorn Jr., Ronald J. Carthell, and Françoise Massardier-Kenney. New York: New York University Press, 1994. 74–87.

Morris, Meaghan. "At Henry Parkes Motel." *Cultural Studies* 2.2 (1988): 1–47.

———. "Metamorphoses at Sydney Tower." *Australian Cultural History* 10.10 (1991): 19–31.

Morris, Michael. *The Strait of Magellan.* Dordrecht: Martinus Nijhoff, 1989.

Murray, Patrick. *Marx's Theory of Scientific Knowledge.* Atlantic Highlands, N.J.: Humanities Press International, 1988.

Musil, Robert. *Posthumous Papers of a Living Author.* Hygiene, Colo.: Eridanos Press, 1987.

Naipaul, V. S. *The Return of Eva Peron.* London: Penguin, 1981.

Nandy, Ashis. *The Intimate Enemy: Loss and Recovery of Self under Colonialism.* New York: Oxford University Press, 1983.

Neumann, Klaus. "Finding an Appropriate Beginning for a History of the Tolai Colonial Past: Or, Starting from Trash." *Canberra Anthropology* 15.1 (1992): 1–19.

Pagden, Anthony. *European Encounters with the New World: From Renaissance to Romanticism.* New Haven: Yale University Press, 1993.

Pearson, Michael. "Travellers, Journeys, Tourists: The Meanings of Journeys." *Australian Cultural History* 10.10 (1991): 125–33.

Perich, Jose S. *Extinción Indigena en la Patagonia.* Punta Arenas, Chile: Impressos Horizonte, 1995.

Pettman, Jan Jindy. *Worlding Women: A Feminist International Politics.* London: Allen and Unwin, 1996.

Pilkington, John. "Surface Tension." *Geographical Magazine,* June 1991, 25–27.

Popper, Julio. "Tierra del Fuego." In *Quién Fue el Conquistador Patagónico Julio Popper* by Boleslao Lewin. Buenos Aires: Editorial Plus Ultra, 1975. 435–48.

Postone, Moishe. *Time, Labour, and Social Mediation: A Reinterpretation of Marx's Critical Theory.* Cambridge: Cambridge University Press, 1993.

Prosser de Goodall, Rae Natalie. *Tierra del Fuego, Argentina.* Buenos Aires: Ediciones Shanamaiim, 1975.

Quesada, Alberto, and Juan Kuniger, dirs. *Yaktemi, Mi Tierra.* 1995.

Rafael, Vicente L. "Nationalism, Imagery, and the Filipino Intelligentsia in the Nineteenth Century." *Critical Inquiry* 16 (Spring 1990): 591–611.

Rathje, William, and Cullen Murphy. *Rubbish! The Archaeology of Garbage.* New York: HarperPerennial, 1992.

Rosemont, Franklin. "André Breton and the First Principles of Surrealism." In *What Is Surrealism: Selected Writings of André Breton,* ed. Franklin Rosemont. New York: Pathfinder Press, 1978. 1–140.

Ruiz, Raul, dir. *Het dak van de Walvis.* Film International, 1981.

Samagalski, Alan. *Chile and Easter Island: A Travel Survival Kit.* Melbourne: Lonely Planet, 1987.

Schiel, Tilman. "Development and Underdevelopment of Household Based Production in Europe." In *Households and the World-Economy,* ed. Joan Smith, Immanuel Wallerstein, and Hans-Dieter Evers. Beverly Hills, Calif.: Sage Publications, 1984. 101–30.

Searle, John. "What Is a Speech Act?" In *Language and Social Context,* ed. Pier Paolo Giglioli. New York: Pelican, 1972. 136–53.

Shell, Marc. *Art and Money.* Chicago: University of Chicago Press, 1995.

Shelley, Percy Bysshe. *A Defence of Poetry.* In *A Defence of Poetry and The Four Ages of Poetry,* ed. John E. Jordan. Indianapolis: Bobbs-Merrill, 1965. 25–80.

Sischy, Ingrid. "Advertising Taboos: Talking with Luciano Benetton and Oliviero Toscani." *Interview,* Apr. 1992, 68–71.

Sloterdijk, Peter. *Critique of Cynical Reason.* Minneapolis: University of Minesota Press, 1987.

Smith, Joan. "Non-Wage Labor and Subsistence." In *Households and the World-Economy,* ed. Joan Smith, Immanuel Wallerstein, and Hans-Dieter Evers. Beverly Hills, Calif.: Sage Publications, 1984. 64–89.

Smith, Joan, Immanuel Wallerstein, and Hans-Dieter Evers. "Introduction." In *Households and the World-Economy,* ed. Joan Smith, Immanuel Wallerstein, and Hans-Dieter Evers. Beverly Hills, Calif.: Sage Publications, 1984. 7–13.

Sohn-Rethel, Alfred. *Intellectual and Manual Labour: A Critique of Epistemology.* London: Macmillan, 1978.

Spencer, Sir Baldwin. *Spencer's Last Journey: Being the Journal of an Expedition to Tierra del Fuego by the Late Sir Baldwin Spencer, with a Memoir.* Ed. R. R. Marrett and T. K. Penniman. Oxford: Clarendon Press, 1931.

———. *Wanderings in Wild Australia.* London: Macmillan, 1928.

Spivak, Gayarty Chakravorty. "Can the Subaltern Speak?" In *Marxism and the Interpretation of Culture,* ed. Cary Nelson and Lawrence Grossberg. Urbana: University of Illinois Press, 1988. 271–313.

———. "Speculations on Reading Marx: After Reading Derrida." In *Post-Structuralism and the Question of History,* ed. Derek Attridge, Geoffrey Bennington, and Robert Young. Cambridge: Cambridge University Press, 1987. 30–62.

Stratton, Jon. *Writing Sites: A Genealogy of the Postmodern World.* Hertfordshire, England: Harvester-Wheatsheaf, 1990.

Taussig, Michael. *The Devil and Commodity Fetishism in South America.* Chapel Hill: University of North Carolina Press, 1980.

———. *The Magic of the State.* New York: Routledge, 1997.

———. *Mimesis and Alterity: A Particular History of the Senses.* New York: Routledge, 1993.

———. "On Desecration." Paper presented at the conference "Desecration and Mimesis," Australian National University, Canberra, July 1, 1996.

———. *Shamanism, Colonialism, and the Wild Man: A Study in Terror and Healing.* Chicago: University of Chicago Press, 1987.

———. "State Fetishism." In *The Nervous System.* New York: Routledge, 1992. 111–39.

Taylor, Julie. "The Outlaw State and the Lone Rangers." In *Perilous States: Conversations on Culture, Politics, and Nation,* ed. George Marcus. Chicago: University of Chicago Press, 1993. 283–303.

Toscani, Oliver, ed. *What Does Aids Have to Do with Sweaters? A Hundred Love-Hate Letters on Benetton Advertising.* Rome: Arnoldo Mondadori, 1993.

Turner, Victor. "Pilgrimages as Social Processes." In *Dramas, Fields, Metaphors.* Ithaca: Cornell University Press, 1974. 166–231.

Uys, Jamie, dir. *The Gods Must Be Crazy.* Twentieth Century-Fox, 1987.

Vinikas, Vincent. *Soft Soap, Hard Sell: American Hygiene in an Age of Advertisment*. Ames: Iowa State University Press, 1992.

Ward, Kathryn. "Introduction and Overview." In *Women Workers and Global Restructuring*, ed. Kathryn Ward. Ithaca: ILR Press, 1990. 1–22.

Williamson, Judith. *Decoding Advertisements: Ideology and Meaning in Advertising*. London: Marion Boyars, 1978.

Wolseley, John. *Patagonia to Tasmania, Origin Movement Species: Tracing the Southern Continents*. Melbourne: Queen Victoria Museum and Art Gallery and the University of Melbourne Museum of Art, 1996.

Zizek, Slavoj. "How Did Marx Invent the Symptom?" In *The Sublime Object of Ideology*. London: Verso, 1989. 11–53.

———. "How the Non-Duped Err." In *Looking Awry: An Introduction to Jacques Lacan through Popular Culture*. Cambridge, Mass.: MIT Press, 1991. 69–86.

———. *Tarrying with the Negative: Kant, Hegel, and the Critique of Ideology*. Durham: Duke University Press, 1993.

Index

Adorno, Theodor W.: and Max Horkheimer, 69–73, 91, 104–5

Advertising: and primitivism, 21–22, 24, 39–40, 46–48, 58n.5; as unbelievable, 22, 24–28, 29n.22, 53, 58–59n.7. *See also Objet trouvé;* Pears' soap; "Popular" culture; "White man's magic"

Althusser, Louis, 43n.46, 54, 76

Anderson, Benedict: critiqued, 129–30, 136n.8, 139, 143, 147n.30, 164; Hegelian leanings of, 117–18, 147n.30, 152; *Imagined Communities,* 117–21, 124–25, 128–30, 136nn.8 and 9, 139, 141, 145, 147n.30, 150, 155n.11, 164; on nations as novels, 125, 128–29, 135; on travelers, 128, 134, 147n.30

Anecdotes. *See* Jokes; "White man's magic"

Anthony, Kenneth W.: on progress, 120–21, 124, 129, 154; on stamp collecting, 119–21, 152, 149, 156n.26

Argentina: as backward/modern, 93–95, 97–98n.60, 119; Falkland Islands, 121, 123; nationalism in, 32–33, 118–25, 129–30; Patagonia, 34, 133–34. *See also* Tierra del Fuego; Ushuaia

Art: Bruce Chatwin on, 149–50, 154, 158; Marc Shell on, 151–54, 156nn.26, 29, and 34; and money, 151–54, 156n.29; stamps as, 120–21, 150, 152. *See also* Benjamin, Walter

Australia: inhabitants of, 37, 103; travel in, 5–6, 101–2, 149

Balibar, Etienne, 133, 164

Barthes, Roland, 9–10, 132–33, 137

Baudrillard, Jean, 29n.16, 55, 58, 104, 107n.15

Beecher, Henry Ward, 46, 58–59n.7

Belza, Juan Esteban, 59n13, 72–73

Benetton: advertising of, 10–12, 17n.34, 46; *Colors* magazine, 11–12, 17n.41, 55, 74, 151; production process of, 10–11, 54, 161

Benjamin, Walter: on childhood, 88, 91–92; on collective dreams, 38–40, 53–54, 61n.46; on the collector, 152, 154, 160–61; on commodity culture, 60–61n.34, 61n.45, 94, 152, 154; critiqued, 39, 152–53; on the home, 106, 152, 159–60; on *objet trouvé,* 37–40, 144; *Passagen-Werk,* 16, 32, 34, 38–40, 53, 134–35; "Stamp Shop," 149, 151; on structure, 92, 103; "Theses on the Philosophy of History," 18n.55, 33–34; "This Space for Rent," 26–28, 39

Boon, James, 81, 87

Borrero, José María, 71, 78–79n.16

Bourdieu, Pierre, 142–43, 147n.30

Breton, André, 20, 86

Bridges, Lucas: childhood of, 40, 45, 77, 89–90; as colonial capitalist, 40–41, 54, 71–73; desire to find fetish, 51–52, 63–66, 74–77, 83, 89–90; on Fuegian Indians, 41, 52, 145–46n.13; humanity of, 40–41, 72–73; *Uttermost Part of the Earth,* 21–22, 40–41, 45–46, 50–52, 63–67, 75–77, 83–96, 104–5, 113–14, 145–46n.13

Bridges, Thomas, 10, 40, 89–90; the *Yámana-English Dictionary,* 10, 17n.28, 21

Buck-Morss, Susan, 88–92, 134

Caillois, Roger, 76, 95

Cain and Abel, 131–35, 139, 150–51, 162–63

Canclini, Arnoldo, 129
Capital. *See* Labor relations; Marx, Karl;
    Neoimperialism; Value
Chakrabarty, Dipesh, 55, 59–60n.23
Chatterjee, Partha, 130, 139, 143
Chatwin, Bruce: on art, 149–50, 154, 158;
    childhood dreams of, 8, 93; and dinosaur
    skin, 7–8, 82, 131, 140–41; as exemplary
    traveler, 139, 163–64; going through the mo-
    tions, 7–10, 81–82, 133–35, 139–40, 143–44;
    and Great-Uncle Charley, 7–8, 82, 90, 131,
    139–40; and home, 139–40, 154–55, 158–61;
    In Patagonia, 7–10, 13, 15, 21, 81–82, 93, 101,
    130–35, 139–40, 143–45, 154, 158, 162–63; on
    Lucas Bridges, 82, 93; as primitivist, 21, 35;
    as recapitulationist, 35, 81–82, 93, 154; *Song-
    lines*, 101, 158; as unbeliever, 8–10, 13, 82,
    131, 135; *What Am I Doing Here*, 9, 131, 134,
    136n.25, 150, 163
Childhood: and Bruce Chatwin, 8, 93; dreams
    of, 88–94; and Lucas Bridges, 40, 45, 77,
    89–90; revisited, 7, 8, 81–82, 149; toys of,
    88, 91–92. *See also* Naïve, the; Primitivism;
    Recapitulationism
Chile, 118–19, 122–24, 134, 147n.26. *See also*
    Tierra del Fuego
Chow, Rey, 84–85, 94
Clapp, Susannah, 136n.25, 145, 149–50, 158, 161
Clifford, James, 4, 18n.50
Cohen, Margaret, 134
Commodity. *See* Fetish of Commodities
Consciousness: Alfred Sohn-Rethel on, 49–50,
    53, 144; "of connectedness," 119–20, 141,
    147n.30, 150, 165; critique of "reflexive
    awareness," 74–77, 83, 95–96, 103–5; of dis-
    connectedness, 141–42, 162–63; as illusory,
    10, 53–56, 90–92, 102–5, 139–45, 162–63; as
    separate from fetish, 49–50, 53–56, 65–66,
    102, 162–65; Slavoj Zizek on, 10, 50, 52–53,
    55–57, 104; versus being there, 142–44,
    147n.30, 154, 163. *See also* Cynicism; Irony;
    Mastery; Taussig, Michael; Uncanny, the
Colonialism: and Fuegian genocide, 9–10, 40–
    41, 45, 69–73, 122, 162–63; and Lucas
    Bridges, 40–41, 54, 71–73; and neoimperial-
    ism, 10–11, 155, 155n.11, 159–64; and Thomas
    Bridges, 10, 17n.28, 21, 40, 89–90; in Tierra
    del Fuego, 32–35, 40–41, 45, 69–73, 122–23;
    and trajectory of production, 34, 60–
    61n.41, 153–54, 159–61, 163–65. *See also* Tem-
    porality

Coombe, Rosemary, 21
Cortés, Ramon, 70, 122–23, 125
Cynicism: in modernity, 26–28, 56, 58–59n.7,
    77, 141; Peter Sloterdijk on, 10, 13, 56; post-
    1960s, 10–13, 26–28, 56, 88–92; Slavoj Zizek
    on, 10, 50, 52–53, 55–57, 104. *See also* Benet-
    ton; Consciousness; Irony; Temporality

Dalí, Salvador, 4, 22, 28
Darwin, Charles: on Fuegian primitivity, 20,
    71, 79–80n.33; as social Darwinist, 28n.6,
    42–43n.25, 79–80n.33
Davila, Juan, 152
De Brosses, Charles, 55, 58
Derrida, Jacques, 101
Dittborn, Eugenio, 101–2
Dolar, Mladen, 106

Enloe, Cynthia, 5, 159, 162
Errington, Frederick, 145–46n.13
Escobar, Arturo, 93
Evans, Donald, 149–50, 152, 154
Evers, Hans-Dieter, 160, 165n.16
Evolution: Charles Darwin on, 20, 28n.6, 42–
    43n.25, 71, 79–80n.33; Johannes Fabian on,
    35–37, 93. *See also* Primitivism; Recapitula-
    tionism; Temporality

Fabian, Johannes, 35–37, 93
Fanon, Frantz, 155n.11
Fetishism: of feet, 11, 55; history of concept, 55,
    58; native "canned fetish," 56–58, 63–66; of
    stamps, 151, 156n.26. *See also* "White man's
    magic"
Fetish of commodities: as absurd, 40, 49, 165;
    in bourgeois epistemology, 50, 54–56, 152–
    53; defined, 48–50, 153–54, 164–65; and
    God, 49–50, 67, 151–53, 156n.34, 164; and
    other methods of production, 47–48, 59–
    60n.23, 165n.15; Slavoj Zizek on, 10, 50, 52–
    53, 55–57, 104; Walter Benjamin on, 60–
    61n.34, 61n.45, 94, 152, 154. *See also* Marx,
    Karl; *Objet trouvé*; Sohn-Rethel, Alfred;
    Taussig, Michael; Value
Fitzroy, Captain James, 48, 102
Flaherty, Robert J., 52
Ford, Henry, 35
Foucault, Michel: as archaeologist, 25–26,
    30n.30, 100, 105; critiqued, 6–7, 25–26,
    100–101, 105; *The History of Sexuality*, 25,
    100–101; in Tierra del Fuego, 4–7, 100–101;

and the "truth effect," 6, 16nn.13 and 14, 25–26, 92, 100–101

Frazer, Sir James, 37, 93

Frow, John, 141, 145–46n.13, 153, 155

Freud, Sigmund: on dreams, 39, 105; *Jokes and Their Relation to the Unconscious,* 64, 83–87, 91, 93; as recapitulationist, 20, 84–87; *Totem and Taboo,* 20, 36; on the uncanny, 103, 106

Fuegian Indians: abducted, 71, 102, 162; genocide of, 9–10, 40–41, 45, 69–73, 122, 162–63; Lucas Bridges on, 41, 52, 145–46n.13; and mimicry, 52, 75–77; nomenclature of, 28n.8; "stagy" culture of, 58n.4, 145–46n.13; as "world's most primitive inhabitants," 20–21, 36–37. *See also* Catwin, Bruce; "White man's magic"

Galbraith, John Kenneth, 40

Garbage, 14–16, 34–35, 39–40, 43n.43. *See also* Objet trouvé; Travel

Gellner, Ernst, 166n.44

Gender: and home, 152, 155, 158–61; and labor, 155, 159–62; and travel, 155, 159–60. *See also* Women

Genocide: Bruce Chatwin's description of, 9–10, 162–63; history of, 9–10, 69–73, 122; Lucas Bridges on, 40–41, 45; rhetoric of, 69–73, 126n.29, 162

Gewertz, Deborah, 145–46n.13

Globalization: Benetton and, 10–11, 54, 161; and production, 34, 60–61n.41, 153–54, 159–61, 163–65. *See also* Neoimperialism

God: of commodity exchange, 49–50, 67, 151–53, 156n.34, 164; of the nation, 117–18, 128–29, 136n.9; the "traveler's bible," 7–8, 16n.19, 135; of walkers, 9, 16n.20, 130–31, 135, 155. *See also* Fetish of commodities; Pilgrimage

Guidebooks, 7–8, 134–35

Hegel, Georg W. F.: Marxist leanings of, 56, 60n.34, 147n.30, 152–53; on representation, 55, 117–18, 125, 152–53

Hill, Rowland, 120–21, 152

Home: the Other's, 11–13, 23–24, 158–61; as site for work, 155, 159–62; the traveler at, 101–3, 139–40, 154–55, 158; women at, 152, 155, 158–61

Horkheimer, Max: and Theodor W. Adorno, 69–73, 91, 104–5

Indio blanco: and boomerang lessons, 68, 74; and the English, 89, 93; Lucas Bridges as, 40–41, 65–67, 75–77, 89–96; and other colonists, 59n.13, 78n.11. *See also* Chatwin, Bruce

Insanity, 22, 107n.15, 140

Irony: in anecdotes, 65, 163; and deixis, 142–43, 145; as ideology, 7, 10–13, 163; and self-distance, 7–10, 74–77, 80–82, 140–44; in travel discourse, 4–7, 81–82, 99, 139–44, 146–47n.19. *See also* Consciousness; Cynicism

Jameson, Fredric, 157n.41

Jokes: the naïve as, 11–13, 23, 67–68, 86–87, 140–41; not taken seriously, 65–69, 75–76; pushed too far, 23, 41, 72–74, 80n.41, 142; Sigmund Freud's theory of, 64, 84–87, 91, 93; the "sudden laugh from nowhere," 66–67, 83–87, 93–94; taken seriously, 14, 46–47, 163. *See also* "White man's magic"

Kant, Immanuel, 54, 105, 118, 126n.9

Labor relations: and anarchists, 131, 162; feminization of, 155, 159–61; neoimperial, 10–11, 155, 159–61, 163–64, 165nn.15 and 16

Lacan, Jacques: on displacements, 42n.8, 56, 105; on *extimité,* 103, 140; on "real fools," 56, 102

Langer, Frantisek, 121, 130

Laughter. *See* Jokes

Lévi-Stauss, Claude, 14–15, 18n.50

Lewin, Boleslao, 121, 126n.25, 129–30

Logic: commodity syllogism, 153–54, 161, 163–64; as critical tool, 87–88, 95, 101, 163–64; and "man-in-the-street," 121, 129–30; national syllogism, 118–21, 128–30, 133–35, 141, 143, 152; postal syllogism, 120–21, 150–54, 164

Lothrop, Samuel, 21, 37, 51–52

MacCannell, Dean, 134–35, 137n.39, 141, 146–47n.18, 155

Magritte, René, 26

Mallarmé, Stephen, 151–52

Marcus, Julie, 5–6

Marx, Karl, 61n.45, 152–53, 159, 161; *Capital,* 40, 42n.16, 47–50, 60n.34, 71, 144, 153, 165n.14; *The Communist Manifesto,* 34–35, 154; *The Eighteenth Brumaire of Louis Napo-*

leon, 54, 73; *On the Jewish Question*, 152–53; as recapitulationist, 35, 42n.16

Marxism, 35, 40, 92, 106, 156n.36

Mastery: made uncanny, 95–96, 101; as misrecognition, 66–67, 82–88, 92–96; and violence, 101, 143, 147n.26. *See also* Consciousness

McClosky, Donald, 14

Menéndez, José, 70–73, 79n.21, 131, 133

Michaels, Eric, 10

Mimicry: and Fuegian Indians, 52, 75–77; ideational mimetics, 66–67, 83–87; of Yekaifwaianjiz, 76, 83, 85, 105

Money: and art, 151–54, 156n.29; and commodity, 153–54, 157n.41; and stamps, 149–54, 162

Monuments: Benedict Anderson on, 125, 128–29, 135; the Eiffel Tower, 132–33, 137nn.39 and 40; function of, 118, 124, 132–33, 143; as hollow, 32–33, 121, 124–25, 132–33, 137nn.39 and 40; identifying with, 118, 137n.40, 144; Michael Taussig on, 33, 147n.26; Philco Time Capsule, 32–35, 39, 57, 121, 124, 141, 154; to San Martín, 121, 133; tomb of the unknown, 124–25, 129

Morris, Meaghan, 137n.40, 159, 161–64

Morris, Michael, 119

Museums, 132–34, 145; Museo del Fin del Mundo, 122–25, 139–41, 149–50, 163; Salesian, 130–31, 133

Musil, Robert, 33, 124–25

Naïve, the: believe for us, 12–13, 19, 81–82, 103–5, 144; dream for us, 39, 89–92; laughing at, 11–13, 23, 67–68, 86–87, 140–41; Sigmund Freud on, 86–87, 91

Nationalism: American origins of, 119, 128; anonymity of, 117–18, 129–30, 136n.8, 143–44; Benedict Anderson on, 125, 128–29, 135; defeats Marxism, 117–19, 124, 164, 166n.44; disinterest in, 32–33, 121, 124, 129, 133; inner and outer, 130, 133, 139–40, 143–44; laughing at, 32–33, 125, 132–35; and national novel, 121, 125, 128–35, 144; produces garbage, 121, 124, 129–30, 132–33, 147n.26; as religion, 117–18, 128–29, 135, 136n.9, 143; in Tierra del Fuego, 118–19, 143; and travel, 133–35, 142–45

Neoimperialism: of contemporary tourism, 5, 16n.5, 145–46n.13, 154–55, 160–65; feminization of labor under, 155, 159–62; labor rela-

tions under, 10–11, 155, 155n.11, 159–64; travel and, 5, 16n.5, 145–46n.13, 154–55, 160–65. *See also* Value

Objet Trouvé: as method, 38–41, 77; obsolescent, 27–28, 53; Third World variant of, 38–39, 52–53; as trick, 37–39, 48, 66–67, 144

Pears' soap: in advertising, 46–47, 58n.5, 58–59n.7; anecdote of, 21–22, 24, 27, 45–47, 90, 113–14

Philco Time Capsule: described, 32–35, 121, 154; significance of, 33–35, 39, 57, 154; as trash, 32–35, 121, 124, 141

Pilgrimage: as national itinerary, 132–35, 137n.39; outside thought, 142–44, 147n.30, 162–63; Victor Turner on, 5–6, 141

Popper, Julio: coins of, 122, 129, 163; as dictator, 122, 140, 144; and *excentricidad philatelica*, 73, 121–23, 129, 140, 163; as freak, 123, 129–30, 144, 164; photo of, 69–73, 78–79nn.16 and 17, 80n.38, 129; as representative colonist, 72–73, 129–30, 162, 164

"Popular" culture, 22–28, 102–5; Jean Baudrillard on, 29n.16, 55, 58, 104, 107n.15. *See also* Advertising

Postage: and art, 101–2, 149–54; postcards, 142–43, 145, 149–50; return-to-sender motif, 101–2, 121, 150. *See also* Stamps

Postone, Moishe, 60–61n.41, 62n.52, 153, 157n.39

Poststructuralism: falsity effect, 92, 100–101, 103, 145–46n.13; irrelevance of "truth effect," 4–13, 81–82, 87, 139–45; postulate of truth-seeking subject, 5–7, 100–101, 141–42; a priori ideology, 53–58, 62nn.52 and 54, 104. *See also* Consciousness; Cynicism; Irony; Mastery

Primitivism: and advertising, 21–22, 24, 39–40, 46–48, 58n.5; of commodity culture, 21–22, 32–35, 57, 89–90; as infantilization, 36, 52–53, 84–88, 93; and "linguistic immediacy," 20–22, 28–29n.9; and mimicry, 66–67, 83–87, 75–77, 105; "world's most primitive inhabitants," 52, 59n.13, 67. *See also Indio blanco;* Naïve, the; Recapitulationism; Temporality

Progress: and cynicism, 26–28, 56, 58–59n.7, 77, 141; and progressivist framework, 15, 35–39, 60–61n.41, 86–87, 92–96; as spread of postage stamps, 119–21, 152, 149, 156n.26; as spread of railways, 121, 132, 154–55, 162; and trajectory of production, 34, 60–61n.41, 153–54, 159–61, 163–65

Projection: genocide as, 69–73, 126n.29, 162; jokes as, 64, 84–87, 91, 93; and recapitulationism, 84–87, 93. *See also* Adorno, Theodor W.

Quesada, Alberto, 23

Rafael, Vicente, 129

Recapitulationism: and Bruce Chatwin, 35, 81–82, 93, 154; in jokes, 84–87, 93; and Karl Marx, 35, 42n.16; pushed too far, 86–88, 92–96; as scientific discourse, 15, 35–37; and Sigmund Freud, 20, 84–87; in surrealism, 18n.50, 20, 86; as travel, 15, 35–37, 82, 154. *See also* Primitivism

Representation: Benedict Anderson on, 125, 128–29, 134, 135, 147n.30; Georg W. F. Hegel on, 55, 117–18, 125, 152–53; and stamps, 120, 149–55, 164; *See also* Cynicism; Irony; Logic; Translation

Rizal, José, 128–29, 136n.9

Ruiz, Raul, 3–4

Russell, Bertrand, 118, 126n.10

Salvage ethnography, 14–16, 22, 34–35, 39–40, 41, 64–65, 100, 102; Sir Baldwin Spencer and, 15–16, 37, 93, 101; and travel, 7, 73, 99, 122, 130, 141–42, 144, 163

Self-reflexivity. *See* Consciousness

Sheep, 70; tourists as, 19, 22, 25, 104, 140–41; when the sheep had wings, 3–4, 165

Shell, Marc, 151–54, 156nn.26, 29, and 34

Sloterdijk, Peter, 10, 13, 56

Smith, Joan, 160, 165n.16

Sohn-Rethel, Alfred: on bourgeois epistemology, 54–55, 62n.54, 106, 157n.39; on consciousness during exchange, 49–50, 53, 144; critiqued, 62n.52, 157n.39

Souvenirs. *See* Travel

Spencer, Sir Baldwin, 15–16, 37, 93, 101

Spivak, Gayatri Chakravorty, 156n.36

Spoerri, Daniel, 151

Stamps: collectors of, 120–21, 150, 152; as money, 149–54, 162; as national icons, 119–23, 126n.25, 149–50; representational function of, 120, 149–55, 164

Stewart, Susan, 142

Surrealism: banalization of, 20, 22, 26–28, 37; and garbage, 14–15, 37–39; Michael Taussig on, 38–39, 48; national, 32–34, 123–24; and *objet trouvé*, 27–28, 38–41, 48, 52–53, 66–67, 77, 144; "psychic automatism," 20, 26–28; "true face" of, 32, 40, 95; Walter Benjamin on, 37–40, 144

Syllogism. *See* Logic

Taussig, Michael: on commodity time, 35, 57; *The Devil and Commodity Fetishism in South America*, 47–48, 59n.11; on method, 47–48, 59n.11, 66, 77; *Mimesis and Alterity*, 52–53, 66, 69, 74–77, 83, 104–5; on monuments, 33, 147n.26; on *objet trouvé*, 38–39, 48

Temporality: allochronism, 35–37, 93–95; commodity-time, 35, 37; and cynicism, 10–13, 26–28, 56, 58–59n.7, 77, 88–92, 141; as "homogenous, empty," 15, 54, 117–19, 128–29; progressivist framework of, 15, 35–39, 60–61n.41, 86–87, 92–96; rationalization/routinization of, 26–28, 51, 60n.34; time of the nation, 117–21, 128, 163; and trajectory of production, 34, 60–61n.41, 153–54, 159–61, 163–65. *See also* Anderson, Benedict; Benjamin, Walter; Primitivism; Tenses

Tenses: ambivalent present, 39, 41, 63–66, 73–77; future perfect, 32–34, 41n.2, 42n.8, 50, 77; one-dimensional past, 39, 41, 46, 64–65; primitive present, 32–33, 38, 52–53, 57, 88

Tierra del Fuego: Beagle Channel dispute in, 118–19, 123–24, 143; colonization of, 32–35, 40–41, 45, 69–73, 122–23; in fantasy, 3–4, 39, 81; industry in, 5, 23, 81; naming of, 81; nationalism in, 118–19, 143; Puerto Williams, 7, 123, 143; Punta Arenas, 19, 28, 130–33. *See also* Fuegian Indians; Popper; Ushuaia

Tomb of the unknown: monument, 124–25, 129; shepherd, 132–33, 141–42; soldier, 118–20, 124–25, 139, 141, 143; syllogism, 130, 164; traveler, 133–35, 139, 143, 147n.30, 161

Tounens, Orélie-Antoine de (king of Araucania and Patagonia), 134, 140, 144, 162

Tourists: distinguished from travelers, 134, 140–44, 145–46n.13; laughing at, 19, 22–23, 105, 140, 163. *See also* Travel

Translation: "broken English," 99, 103, 106–7n.3; in colonial contact, 40, 51–52, 64, 75–76, 86–90. *See also* Jokes; "White man's magic"

Travel: gendering of, 155, 159–60; as nation fetishism, 133–35, 142–45; and neoimperialism, 5, 16n.5, 145–46n.13, 154–55, 160–65; as recapitulationism, 35–36, 81–82, 154; semiotic structure of, 141, 162; souvenirs ("trash") of, 7, 73, 99, 122, 130, 140–42, 144, 163; theories of, 4–7, 141, 145–46n.13; and tourists, 19, 22–23, 105, 134, 140–44, 145–46n.13
Turner, Victor, 5–6, 141

Uncanny, the, 84, 95, 103–5, 106, 107n.12
Ushuaia: Disco Dalí, 4, 22; documentaries about, 23, 99; duty-free status of, 23, 123–24; as the "End of the World," 7, 122; and mundanity, 23–24, 134–35; Museo del Fin del Mundo, 122–25, 139–41, 149–50, 163; Philco Time Capsule, 32–35, 39, 57, 121, 124, 141, 154; Plaza de Mayo, 32, 121, 124–25, 144

Value: as central category of capital, 153, 157n.41; defined, 48–50, 60–61n.41, 159–60; the "iron law of wages," 159–60, 165n.14; Moishe Postone on, 60–61n.41, 62n.52, 153, 157n.39; and nonwage labor, 159–61, 165nn.15 and 16; and surplus, 71, 159; and trajectory of production, 34, 60–61n.41, 153–54, 159–61, 163–65; use-value, 55, 59–60n.23. *See also* Fetish of commodities; Marx, Karl
Vanupieds, 150, 155, 162, 164

Wallerstein, Immanuel, 160, 165n.16
"White man's magic": anecdotes about, 13, 18n.50, 59n.13, 65, 89–90; campfires to oil rigs, 81, 96n.2; Coke bottle, 12, 15, 46, 67; linked to fetishism of commodities, 47–58; "magic lantern," 50–53, 64, 86–88, 94–95, 103; in native hands, 38–39, 47–58; Pears' soap, 21–22, 24, 27, 45–47, 90, 113–14; Philco Time Capsule, 33–35, 39, 57, 154; on rebound, 50–52, 63–68, 74–78
Williamson, Judith, 24–25, 27
Women: and commodity culture, 84, 94; at home, 152, 155, 158–61; under neoimperialism, 155, 159–62; and travel, 155, 159–60; and work, 155, 159–62

Zizek, Slavoj, 10, 50, 52–53, 55–57, 104

Paul Magee is a writer. He holds degrees in history from the University of Melbourne and diplomas in language and literature from the Institut Immeni Pushkina, Moscow, and the Escuela Salvador Miranda, San Salvador. He has published academic work on Filipino liberation theology, the poetry of Octavio Paz, Marxist theory, and psychoanalytic logic. He is currently working on an opera libretto and has just finished "A Book That Opens," a collection of prose that turns into poetry.

Typeset in 10.5/13 Adobe Garamond
with Veljovic display
Designed by Dennis Roberts
Composed by Jim Proefrock
at the University of Illinois Press
Manufactured by Thomson-Shore, Inc.

University of Illinois Press
1325 South Oak Street
Champaign, IL 61820-6903
www.press.uillinois.edu